HOMEMAKERS' GUIDE
to
FOODS FOR PLEASURE AND HEALTH
and
HANDBOOK FOR HYGIENIC LIVING

First printing, July 1976

Library of Congress Catalog Card Number: 76-17403
ISBN 0-914532-12-X

Printed in the United States of America

Natural Hygiene Press,
A division of
The American Natural Hygiene Society
1920 W. IRVING PARK RD.   CHICAGO, ILL. 60613

HOMEMAKERS' GUIDE
to
FOODS FOR PLEASURE AND HEALTH
and
HANDBOOK FOR HYGIENIC LIVING

For the Homemaker:
>   Hygienic (Vegetarian) Menus
>   Food Preparation
>   Recipes
>   Marketing Tips
>   Storing Food
>   Entertaining
>   Eating Out
>   Traveling

A Bird's-Eye View of Natural Hygiene

Some Things You Want to Know
and
Don't Know Whom to Ask

By HANNAH ALLEN
>   Author of:
>   DIAGNOSIS CANCER
>   THE HAPPY TRUTH ABOUT PROTEIN
>   DON'T GET STUCK!
>   YOUR FIRST FAST—WHAT TO EXPECT
>   THE INSIDE STORY or HOW TO COPE
>   WITH DIGESTIVE PROBLEMS
>   ORGANIC GARDENING IN FLORIDA

Published by
Natural Hygiene Press, Inc.   1975

DEDICATION

To my dear husband,
my biggest fan and severest critic,
whose steadfast help and encouragement
made all things possible.
To Ruth Vaughn Phillips
for the excellent cover
design and art.

FOODS FOR PLEASURE AND HEALTH
CONTENTS

ACKNOWLEDGMENTS

My sincere appreciation to our good friends, Dr. and Mrs. John M. Brosious, of St. Petersburg, Florida, whose encouragement, inspiration and advice helped immeasurably in the writing of this book.

Many thanks to Peter N. Reuter, of Clearwater, Florida, whose zeal and Herculean efforts for Natural Hygiene triggered my long delayed intention to write this book.

A special thank you to Larry Newton, of Montreal, Canada, whose suggestion and urging several years ago provided the original incentive for this book, which has been dormant all this time, and has finally reached fruition.

How can I ever forget R. J. Cheatham and his Shangri-La Natural Hygiene Institute, where I fasted in 1967? Thank you, R. J., for teaching me about Natural Hygiene, for supervising my fast and recovery, and for helping me over the rough spots.

I must also express my heartfelt appreciation to all the professional hygienists—may their tribe increase! They have been the bulwark of the Hygienic movement, with their selfless devotion to the betterment of mankind, their availability for consultation, and their excellent courses of instruction at the Annual Natural Hygiene Health Conferences.

And my love and thanks to my husband, Lou, for his collaboration and assistance in preparing the manuscript.

Desiderata

GO PLACIDLY AMID the noise & haste, & remember
what peace there may be in silence. As far as possible without
surrender be on good terms with all persons. Speak your truth
quietly & clearly; and listen to others, even the dull & ignorant;
they too have their story. Avoid loud & aggressive persons,
they are vexations to the spirit. If you compare yourself with
others, you may become vain & bitter; for always there will be
greater & lesser persons than yourself. Enjoy your achievements
as well as your plans. Keep interested in your own career,
however humble; it is a real possession in the changing fortunes
of time. Exercise caution in your business affairs; for the world
is full of trickery. But let this not blind you to what virtue there
is; many persons strive for high ideals; and everywhere life is full
of heroism. Be yourself. Especially, do not feign affection.
Neither be cynical about love; for in the face of all aridity &
disenchantment it is perennial as the grass. Take kindly the
counsel of the years, gracefully surrendering the things of youth.
Nurture strength of spirit to shield you in sudden misfortune.
But do not distress yourself with imaginings. Many fears are
born of fatigue & loneliness. Beyond a wholesome discipline, be
gentle with yourself. You are a child of the universe, no less
than the trees & the stars; you have a right to be here. And
whether or not it is clear to you, no doubt the universe is un-
folding as it should. Therefore be at peace with God,
whatever you conceive Him to be, and whatever your labors &
aspirations, in the noisy confusion of life keep peace with your
soul. With all its sham, drudgery & broken dreams, it is
still a beautiful world. Be careful. Strive to be happy.

FOUND IN OLD SAINT PAUL'S EPISCOPAL CHURCH, BALTIMORE; DATED 1692

Desiderata: "Something desired as essential."

INTRODUCTION

Fiddlesticks! No one ever reads an introduction!

(Upon being asked how he managed to be so effective with his backwoods congregation, the parson explained:
"First I tells 'em what I'm gonna tell 'em, then I tells 'em, then I tells 'em what I tole 'em!")

I'm going to skip the first (the introduction) and the last (the summary) and just try to tell it like it is.

Do I have your attention?

I. The Promise of This Book

HERE IT IS!! In response to a need and an increasing demand, here is the encyclopedic book of everything you want to know about food and don't know whom to ask. Questions *are* being asked all over the United States and Canada, and elsewhere, and here are many of the answers.

Here are the menus and recipes which can be so helpful in making the changeover to the Hygienic diet (with the resultant improvement in your health), and which so many people have been demanding. Here are practical ideas for day-to-day meal planning, a variety of palatable, tempting combinations for family and friends, and satisfying, feasible, economical suggestions for dining out and traveling.

Here is the information to allay the doubts and fears of beginners in Natural Hygiene, and to help solve the problems which may beset Hygienists along the road to a better life.

Here is detailed information for people who are bewildered by an approach so different from everything they have been taught. Here is a reference work, specifying and clarifying the many aspects of these differences.

Here is documentation of the many facets of our discussions of a more rational approach to attaining and retaining optimal health.

Here is the sorely needed information about Hygienic First Aid for Accident and Health emergencies.

Here are just a few of the thousands of case histories which prove the efficacy of the Hygienic system.

Here is an all-in-one basic book, suitable also for use in study groups. Untold numbers of people have been seeking a book such as this. Now it is available—with the fervent hope that it will bring the reader a happier, healthier life.

II. The Promise of Natural Hygiene

What greater delights does life have to offer to a healthy hungry person than the inviting appearance, subtle fragrance and delicious savor of a luscious meal?

And what greater satisfaction can be realized than the attainment of a discriminating palate which enhances the enjoyment of the very foods which help to preserve good health and prolong life?

This is the promise of Natural Hygiene, along with the security of Health Independence (living without drugs and medics).

The choice is yours—through the food you eat and the way you live. If you didn't choose moderation and obedience to Natural Laws in your twenties, the second best time is right now.

The study of Natural Hygiene will convince you that Hygienic living will make it possible for you to achieve your greatest potential good health and longevity, and to die when your biological clock runs down, instead of from degeneration produced by failing to cooperate with Nature.

The use of drugs and surgery ignores the cause and treats the effects. Drugs suppress the symptoms, lower the fever, stop the pain, and you pay the price later on for interfering with the wisdom of the organism: chronic disease evolves—cancer, heart disease, hardening of the arteries, stroke, arthritis, and other degenerative diseases.

Surgery and post-surgical care involve mutilating,

shocking and poisoning the body. Very rarely does the body require surgical interference.

Natural Hygiene, on the other hand, may rescue you from potential or actual drug addiction, free you from dependence on physicians and checkups, and show you how to avoid the surgeon's knife. Isn't it time to end the physician—drug, hospital—surgery syndrome?

You will learn that there are very few pathological conditions which cannot be helped by Natural Hygiene; that in many desperate situations, if there is any hope, it is through Natural Hygiene; that any reversible condition, and many pronounced irreversible, may be conquered; that it is possible to turn back the clock and add years to your life.

Since I discovered the Hygienic system eight years ago, I have seen, and heard about, so many astounding recoveries (including my own) that there can be no doubt of its efficacy. Indeed, at the Natural Hygiene seminars and conferences, such stories are commonplace.

One of our Florida friends who adopted Natural Hygiene three years ago has been successful in correcting a descended testicle and a hernia by proper exercise and support, and a raw food diet. He has also had a dramatic improvement in his eyes and memory, and has corrected his hypoglycemia (low-blood sugar), as well as a heart murmur.

Another Florida friend who has had gouty arthritis, and has been on the drug Benamid, orally and by injection, for thirty years, has had an almost unbelievable remission of his symptoms, simply by the improvement of his diet along Hygienic lines, for a period of three or four months. He has not had a Benamid tablet or injection for the past four months. Formerly, if he omitted the oral Benamid for even one day, his hands would swell, as well as his feet and legs up to his hips, and he would require an emergency injection of the Benamid.

I will never forget our Indianapolis friend, a man of

around thirty-eight years of age, who developed a large tumor on his left kidney, visible on the outside of his body. Instead of submitting to the recommended excision of the kidney, he elected to go to a Hygienic fasting retreat in Florida for a 30 day fast, and came back minus the tumor. That was our introduction to Natural Hygiene.

Another of our Indianapolis friends, who had been extremely obese most of his life (nicknamed "Lard") and had crippling rheumatoid arthritis, and some additional crippling from a bad fall from a loft, went to the Health School at San Antonio, Texas, fasted 27 days, and has lived hygienically since then (for the past ten years or so). He is now about 63 years old, lean, muscular, tanned, and in vigorous, vibrant health. He gives rather spectacular exercise demonstrations, including shoulder stands and head stands.

Underlying all these recoveries is one simple foundation: the fact that every living organism has, as part of its very existence, a vital capacity for recuperation, through which its wastes are eliminated, its injuries repaired and its impairments healed; and if human beings live in accordance with Natural Law, they can remain in good health all their lives, or evolve good health, in all remedial cases, if they are sick.

For 3,000 years, the medical system has been searching for cures, and medicating man. Especially in the last half century, scientists have been frantically trying to discover some panacea to outwit Nature and cure diseases caused by wrong habits of living.

Individual fortunes have been dissipated in the vain search for cures for terminal illnesses, and fortunes of tremendous magnitude have been acquired by the armies of chemical industries, and the purveyors of these cures.

Senator Edward Kennedy, on the January 10, 1975 television presentation of CBS Reports (entitled "Rx: Take with Caution") said that, according to the report of a Senate Sub-Committee, adverse drug reactions cause approximately 120,000 deaths annually, and cost the public an estimated two billion dollars, that 80% of these adverse drug reactions can be anticipated and prevented, and that these risks are inexcusable.

Dan Rather, reporter on the same program, said that drugs which are supposed to keep people healthy are instead causing serious problems, and leaving the public in a state of bewilderment, which might not be so bad if it also marks the beginning of awareness.

For those seeking weight reduction, Natural Hygiene is the closest thing to a panacea that can be found. Through Hygienic living, you can accomplish your objective of weight reduction, and, at the same time, relieve your body of its accumulated toxic load, and experience a remarkable improvement in your health and well-being.

Learn about Natural Hygiene. When you realize the inevitable consequences of the violation of Natural Laws, and become aware of the experiences of thousands of grateful, rejuvenated Hygienists, you will know that the only approach to the preservation of good health is to remove the causes of disease.

III. What is Natural Hygiene?

Natural Hygiene is at once the last frontier of suffering mankind, and the revival of man's primeval way of life. It incorporates all that is beneficial in Nature and attempts to use it intelligently to supply our physiological and biological needs for perfect health.

The basic principle of Natural Hygiene is that good health is normal and natural, and that we can achieve and maintain it by eliminating the causes of ill health; and by supplying the body with its natural requirements, determined by a study of anatomy and physiology (the parts of the body and their functions). Natural Hygiene makes understandable the causes of disease, so that they may be avoided; and provides the knowledge of how to overcome existing disease.

The emphasis is on Natural Living and Proper Nutrition for the maintenance of good health, and Rest and Fasting for its restoration. A diet based on foods from the plant kingdom is an important component of the Hygienic system, but even if you are not prepared to accept a meatless diet, exposure to and study of Natural Hygiene may still result in significant improvements in your diet and health, to the extent that you refrain from overeating, practice food combining, and increase your consumption of raw foods, along with the elimination of toxic substances, such as drugs, tobacco and alcohol, and the avoidance of divitalized foods.

The hit-or-miss, Russian roulette diet, common today, is often the key that unlocks for you a Pandora's box of discomfort, suffering and disease.

The modern Hygienic movement was started in 1831 by Sylvester Graham, who found drugging and the treatment of established disease to be a wrong approach. Read about Dr. Jennings, Dr. Trall, Dr. Tilden and many others who followed Graham's lead, in "The Greatest Health Discovery—Natural Hygiene and Its Evolution, Past, Present and Future". These intrepid pioneers unveiled the mystery surrounding disease, exposed the evils of the drugging practice, restored health to thousands of people, and initiated the struggle to gain acceptance for principles based on Natural law.

Dr. Herbert M. Shelton, Ph. D., has been the foremost leader in the modern evolution of Natural Hygiene. He established a Health School near San Antonio, Texas, where thousands of people have recovered their health through fasting. He is the prolific author of numerous volumes on correct living for the prevention of disease and the regaining of health. He is also the publisher and editor of the Hygienic Review, an informative journal on health and disease for the lay person.

Man builds his own disease—or good health. Common sense care of one's body in accordance with unchanging Natural Laws is all that is necessary, "not some peculiar kind of food or vitamin preparation nor a disagreeable asceticism or fanaticism" as aptly phrased by Dr. William L. Esser, D.C., N.D., Florida Professional Hygienist.

The Law of Homeostasis is an absolute, irrefutable, dependable law of Nature: "If you give living things (your body, or plants in your garden) the right conditions, they will automatically proceed in the direction of health. Give them the wrong conditions and you will produce disease, as the cells instinctively try to defend themselves." (See ADDENDUM for "Laws of Human Life".)

Disease is an abnormal condition which results from violating the laws of Nature and every disease is evidence that the body is attempting to purify, cleanse and repair itself, in response to conditions that require a defensive action on the part of the organism. Healing is a function of life itself and cannot be forced from outside the body.

I quote Dr. Alec Burton, D.O., D.C., N.D., Professional Hygienist in Australia: "Hygiene in its proper role of education should teach us to respect our limitations and learn our needs, so that we can adequately supply them." If you live within your personal limitations and according to the laws of Nature, you will attain the highest degree of health possible for you.

It is true that we do not all have the same start: the first important factor in attaining optimal health is the selection of the right parents! (I didn't!) But more fortunate individuals from good stock will still eventually pay the price for the violation of Natural Law. While your ancestry determines your greatest potential good health and longevity Hygienic living will make it possible to achieve them and to die when your biological clock runs down, instead of from degeneration produced by failing to cooperate with Nature.

The limitations are not in Hygiene, but in your own body, which is governed by three influences:

1. Heredity (as indicated above)
2. Nutrition
3. Environmental Factors

These three together determine your constitution and your inherent strengths and weaknesses. If these weaknesses have produced pathological conditions that restrict the degree to which nutrition can influence some parts of your body, professional evaluation of the pathology may be necessary to determine adaptations of the Hygienic diet to your needs. It must be recognized that the body has the same needs in ill health as in good health, but in accordance with its reduced capacity and limitations.

The Hygienic diet consists of fruit, nuts and seeds, and green leafy vegetables, eaten raw. The source of all foods in the Hygienic diet should be the plant kingdom; if foods of animal origin are occasionally used (such as unsalted butter or unprocessed cheese) it is considered a compromise. (See Chapter VII—The Hygienic Diet)

Proper combining of food is emphasized (See Chapter X—Food Combining), as well as no between meal snacking, no more than two or three meals a day, and no beverages except pure water, used only when thirsty and not with meals. (See Chapter VII, Part 9—Water)

Flesh food is not recommended, as this is not the natural food of man. It is highly putrefactive. (See Chapter VII, Section 4, Meat)

No drugs or treatments should be used in dealing with illness. Drugs mask the condition of the patient, and after twenty-four hours of drugging, no physician can determine the patient's true state. Many drugs and treatments cause irreparable damage to the organism. (See Chapter VI—The Medicine Show)

Instead, bed rest and fasting (total abstinence from all food, except water) are recommended. Healing is a normal activity of the body, which proceeds constantly in relation to the need and the amount of energy available. Much energy is used in physical activity, but the amount used in digesting, absorbing and assimilating food is tremendous. Bed rest and fasting allow the body to use its energy to repair tissue, restore function and "clean house". It is interesting to note that animals in the wild state, and many domestic animals, abstain from food when sick or injured. (See Chapter IV and read "Fasting Can Save Your Life" by Dr. Herbert M. Shelton.)

For maximum benefits from a fast, it must be a time of complete rest:
1. Mental
2. Emotional
3. Physical
4. Sensory (Eyes and Ears)
5. Physiological (Organs and Systems continue at a reduced rate, with the exception of the Elimination System, which is greatly accelerated at this time)

In the treatment of established disease, and for prolonged fasting, it is advisable to seek the help and advice of a Professional Hygienist. (See List of Professional Hygienists in Addendum.)

I quote from "Getting the Most Out of Hygiene" by Dr. Herbert M. Shelton, "The application of Hygiene to the *preservation* of *good health* is simplicity itself and any individual of average intelligence can understand it and apply it to his individual life or the life of the family.

"As applied to the many varied conditions of *impaired health,* greater knowledge and skill are required for careful adjustment of the elements of health to the current needs and capacities of the enfeebled organism."

A Hygienic program also includes:
1. Regular vigorous physical activity in fresh air, in-

volving all parts of the body, strenuous enough to keep the pulse elevated to around 150 for at least 20 minutes and causing heavy breathing, at least 5 times weekly, with no more than one day's break in the continuity (if your age and physical condition will allow).

Regular exercise is absolutely essential to healthy life and for the restoration of health (muscles atrophy when not used). Learn what you can do, according to your own needs and capacities—and do it regularly.

Calisthenics, bicycling, jogging, brisk walking (and dancing, if not in smoke-filled rooms) are all excellent forms of exercise. Weight training for strength and body development can be adapted and programmed for almost all ages and physical conditions, and will bring about a significant improvement in health. The type of exercise must be chosen according to the results desired and the strength and condition of the individual. Exhausting or imprudent exercise can do much more harm than under-exercising or no exercise.

Exercise improves the tone and quality of every tissue of the body. It accelerates the processes of assimilation and excretion, and the improved metabolism can bring about a dramatic change in the entire organism. Exercise will influence all parts of the body and you can increase by as much as 20% the amount of oxygen transported from the lungs to the blood. Exercise improves the bone structure and you are less liable to have breaks.

Ten minutes of vigorous exercise triggers an increase in the production of the body's own cortisone by the adrenal glands. (Use of the drug cortisone damages the adrenals so they atrophy and do not function—adrenals also produce adrenalin.) "Exercise can have an important bearing on anemia"— Dr. Burton, July, 1973.

Don't breathe through your mouth or take forced

deep breathing exercises (hyperventilation)—this disturbs the acid-alkaline balance and may cause dizziness and tetany (muscle cramps). If we exercise vigorously, we will breathe deeply.

Don't eat before or during activity—wait 2½ hours after eating for vigorous exercise—early morning before eating is the best exercise time, though some people prefer bedtime.

Exercise performed primarily for health is "Hygienic exercise"—"Corrective" and "Remedial" exercise may be used in the correction of specific problems. (See "Exercise" by Dr. Herbert M. Shelton.)

Develop and practice correct, erect posture, whether seated, standing, or walking. A cramped position inhibits proper breathing and causes vital organs to suffer.

Special exercises for the eyes are also useful for the improvement of vision through the principles of relaxation. See "The Bates Method" by Dr. William H. Bates and "Help Yourself to Better Sight" by Margaret Darst Corbett.

2. Adequate rest and sleep—Relax before bedtime and stay in bed 8 to 10 hours at night during the hours of darkness (darkness is necessary for life—the cells of the body are active when it is light), and get some additional rest during the day (in a darkened room, if possible)—two hours or one hour or one-half hour, or even ten minutes. Rest when tired. I frequently remember an admonition in a lecture given by Cyl Margulies at one of the Hygienic Health Conferences, in which she gave this sage advice: "Never be tired!"

3. Fresh air by day and by night—Try to sleep, work, exercise, eat and *live* where the purest possible air is available, and don't pollute your own air with such products as deodorant sprays or insecticides, or by permitting smoking in your home or office. To the extent possible, avoid breathing dusty or pol-

luted air, especially when exercising: don't dance in smoke-filled rooms, or walk or jog on streets carrying heavy traffic. Try to avoid breathing very cold air. Some of these things are difficult to avoid if you live in a city, as does most of our population.

Carbon monoxide from automobiles is very damaging to our bodies, as it has a greater affinity with the hemoglobin of the blood than does oxygen.

As air passes over mountains, trees and great bodies of water, it is purified.

4. Regular sun baths and air baths—sun baths over all or most of your body, a minimum of 3 or 4 times weekly for a minimum of 20 minutes—maximum 7 times weekly for one hour. In the winter, use the noonday sun; in the summer, it is best to sun yourself when it is cooler, in the early morning or evening. Don't use sunglasses—the eyes are portals which receive beneficial effects from the sun's rays. If you wear prescription eyeglasses, remove them at least part of the time when you are out-of-doors. Get some sun on the closed eyelids, and avoid looking directly into the sun when your eyes are open. (Some of the sun's rays will penetrate through light, porous clothing.)

Take air baths daily—a good time is during your morning exercise, or a nude siesta in the heat of the afternoon. A daytime air bath is best, when the skin may also be exposed to natural light. If this is not possible, take your air bath in the morning, or even in the evening, if no other time is available. Don't get chilled. During the Winter season in Northern climates, expose your nude body for your air bath in a warm room, in which the air is reasonably fresh. (Not as good as windows wide open, but better than no exposure to the air.)

It is of the utmost importance to expose the skin to sunlight and air—the sun bath and air bath are more important than the water bath.

Dr. Shelton says on Page 485 of Volume III of

the Hygienic System: "Sunlight is vitally important in the nutritive processes of both plant and animal life, an accessory nutritive factor . . . somewhat like that of the vitamins."

Sunshine is the source of all energy and of life and health. Sunshine on the skin is necessary for an adequate supply of Vitamin D in the body, because it enables the skin to synthesize Vitamin D from dehydro-cholesterol in the skin. Adequate exposure to sunlight will rectify the calcium-phosphorus balance.

Dr. Shelton states (Page 539 of Volume III, Hygienic System): "Air playing over the body may increase metabolism 50% in ten minutes. Thyroid extract, medicine's only claimed stimulant of metabolism, is said to require a year to accomplish the same thing."

People who live in Florida, at sea level, where there is an abundance of sunshine and warm weather, experience improved health.

5. Personal Control:
   a. Self-discipline and the cultivation of emotional stability, not by suppressing your emotions and turning them inward, but through greater understanding of yourself and those around you. Think and disseminate happy, pleasant thoughts; combat destructive negative emotions (fear, grief, anger, envy, self-pity, excessive sensitivity, quarreling, vengefulness) by vigorous physical activity; restore stability by periods of solitude, or in communion with Nature, or through music.
   b. Fortitude and self-reliance: Develop perseverance, versatility, the ability to be equal to any difficulty, and to "roll with the punches".
   c. Beauty and order in your surroundings.
   d. Organization of your time to avoid last minute stresses.
6. Meaningful relationships with other people: Affectionate, reciprocal interchange by word, touch and

deed; considerate and thoughtful actions; concern for the happiness and welfare of others, and generous giving of yourself to that end.

Dr. Hans Selye in "Stress Without Distress" recommends "altruistic egotism", a form of cooperation that appears everywhere in Nature: deliberately helping others in order to gain their goodwill and trust for your own good. This hoard of goodwill gives you a sense of security and self-esteem to cushion you against the hurts and frustrations no human can avoid. *Earn* your neighbor's love. (Dr. Selye has doctorates in medicine, science and philosophy.)

7. Some rewarding activity: Work that brings satisfaction and fulfillment refreshes the body and spirit.

It is only "work" if you'd rather be doing something else. Don't stay "trapped" in a job that represents "slavery". If "emancipation" must be postponed, find an avocation you enjoy.

Dr. Hans Selye in Modern Maturity, (December-January, 1974–75): "Complete freedom from stress is death. Don't try to avoid stress—it's the very salt and spice of life. But do learn to master and to use it. People (especially older people) must find work that is compatible with their capacities physically and mentally—*and where they can win*. This is simply a code of behavior based on the laws of Nature. Some of us are turtles and some of us are racehorses. Force a turtle to run like a racehorse and you'll kill him. Force a racehorse to stand in his stall all day and you'll kill him too. . . .

"Forced retirement of a person who is full of life and full of things to do is like shutting off all the valves on a steam kettle which then only blows up. . . .

"Find the occupation that is pleasant for you and at which you are good. For a longer, healthier and more rewarding life, adjust yourself to Nature, and live in harmony with your surroundings. The individual, here, is his own best doctor. Find your own stress level, the one that is proper for you."

8. Knowledge: A healthy curiosity will lead to the acquisition of a store of knowledge, which is the stepping stone to awareness and understanding. Learn by seeing when you look, listening when you hear.

9. Recreation: Regular "escape" from routine into a world of relaxation and enjoyment, which you anticipate with pleasure, and which refreshes, stimulates and re-creates your enthusiasm for life.

10. Moderation (avoidance of excesses) in all activities and functions, including the sexual activity. Dr. William L. Esser at the 1966 Natural Hygiene Health Conference, said: "The normal human form is beautiful indeed and the powerful attraction which brings the male and female together is one of the greatest of human experiences. Natural Hygiene urges that it be kept fresh and new, rather than allowed to become sordid and perverse. Let sex serve to ennoble the human spirit rather than degrade it." (By inconsiderate practices, excesses or promiscuity) "Normal sex life will last far beyond the limitations usually set by the conventional mode of living, if good healthful practices are established. Many couples who have remained childless for years, yet earnestly desired children, have frequently found themselves capable of producing fine, healthy offspring after being introduced to the principles of Natural Hygiene." (See Pages 163–167, "The Greatest Health Discovery," Natural Hygiene Press)

Additional Recommendations for Hygienic Living:

A Hygienist does not smoke nor use alcoholic beverages, of course. Nor does he use vitamin pills or food supplements. (See Chapter VII, Section 7)

A Hygienist does not take hot or cold baths, because

their debilitating or stimulating effects deplete the nerve energy. Bathe for cleanliness only, using no soap, or a mild soap without detergents or perfumes. No deodorants are needed—your Hygienic diet does not produce foul odors.

The body should be maintained at a comfortable temperature at all times, and no constricting clothing should be worn. In this connection, I was interested to see an article in the St. Petersburg *Evening Independent* on April 1, 1974, by E. L. Cole, M.D., headed "Snug Clothing Affects Organs". He writes about a report in the Journal of the American Medical Association, concerning a study by Howard W. Gabriel III, Ph.D., in which Dr. Gabriel found that heat associated activities such as hot baths, tight fitting underclothing and dark tight fitting pants could cause oligospermia (deficiency of semen) in the male. Dr. Cole also said that both male and female frequently develop an itching, rash and/or fungus infection called monilia in the genital area, and that the remedy is looser, lighter colored and cooler clothing.

In public, wear as little clothing as good taste, temperature and the law allows; sleep and rest nude, using sufficient covering, and a bed warmer, if necessary, to prevent chilling.

Go barefoot whenever you can; or wear thongs, sandals or comfortable low-heeled shoes, ventilated, if possible.

Wash the hair in plain warm water as often as necessary to keep it clean, scrubbing the hair and scalp briskly with the fingers and hands, and rinse with cool water. If you do use shampoo, use the mild, non-detergent varieties. Dry quickly with towels, air and/or sun. If you must use a hair dryer, use one that blows, not a cap. Don't brush the hair while wet—it stretches and damages the hair. After the hair is dry, brush with a natural bristle brush. This gets all the dirt out, after it is loosened by the plain water scrubbing.

Don't use hair sprays—they are extremely toxic when

inhaled. People who work in beauty parlors can get aplastic anemia from such pollution of the air. Don't use bleaches and dyes. Use hair dressings sparingly or not at all.

It is not necessary to use tooth pastes or powders. Efficient brushing of all surfaces and over the gum line (with a soft tooth brush that will not damage the gums) after meals, will accomplish the removal of food residues to keep at a minimum the formation of tartar or plaque (caused mostly by cooked foods). Plaque is the hard substance the dentist scrapes off when you have your annual or semiannual dental prophylaxis or cleaning. The use of dental floss at least once daily is advisable, as plaque may form if food deposits remain on and between the teeth more than 24 hours. The most important tooth brushing time is after the last meal of the day (or the last snack!). The Hygienic diet, with its preponderance of raw foods, provides necessary chewing exercise and helps to clean the teeth.

In "Dictionary of Man's Foods", Dr. William L. Esser states: "When oranges or other citrus fruit form a regular part of the diet, it is a good practice to rinse the mouth following a meal, as citric acid is inclined to cause erosion of the dental enamel."

Conventional diets and excessive plaque deposits may lead to pathological conditions of the mouth and gums, frequently resulting in radical oral surgery and wholesale or premature extractions of sound teeth.

Hygienists rarely get headaches or colds; most go on for years without these problems, or any concern about constipation. Best of all, should the Hygienist have any rare indisposition, he knows exactly what to do and where to go: he stops eating and goes to bed.

A Hygienist will not usually need to concerned about weight control, as Hygienic living and eating will usually normalize the weight. If there are weight problems related to digestion or assimilation or nervous or emotional problems, one should consult a Professional Hygienist, as a fast may be indicated. People who are grossly obese will usually be advised to fast, and to maintain the full Hygienic regimen after the fast, because they will have a special problem.

The fat cells of the body increase in number as you gain weight, but when you lose weight, the fat cells *do not decrease in number*—they simply grow smaller. Therefore, if you have ever been obese, with the inevitable multiplication of the number of fat cells, you will have a constant struggle against obesity thereafter, because of the impossibility of reduction in the number of fat cells.

CANCER

The Hygienic body of knowledge reveals that cancer is not a "mystery" affliction whose cause is unknown, or a plague or visitation on certain unfortunate individuals. Instead, we find that the pattern of the development of cancer can be traced through the seven stages of Toxemia (the primary cause of all disease), and is reversible in all but the 7th stage. (Read "Toxemia Explained" by Dr. J. H. Tilden, M.D.)

The *First Stage* is *Enervation* and is relatively nontoxic. This is the phase when we may be over-eating, eating wrong foods or combinations of foods (or getting insufficient rest, fresh air or sunshine, or exercise; or depriving our bodies of some needed vital factor), so that excretion is inhibited and we have used up more energy than we can replace.

If this first phase is allowed to continue too long, we come to the *Second and Third Stages: Toxicosis* and *Irritation*. If not corrected by a change in living habits, this leads to the fourth, fifth and sixth stages. The *Fourth Stage—Inflammation* (Vicarious Elimination) is set up when the digestive and urinary systems are not carrying off the toxins rapidly enough.

The *Fifth Stage* is *Ulceration*.

The *Sixth Stage—Fibrosis* is when the cells undergo

changes, are unable to replace themselves, and are replaced by scar tissue.

In these latter stages, a prolonged fast, followed by Hygienic living, may still save the patient. But if these changes are not made, the *Seventh Stage,* or *Irreversible Cancer,* dooms the patient, because the cells become so deranged in their functional power that they cannot survive. (Natural Hygiene can help Irreversible Cancer patients to prolong their lives and die peaceably and in comfort.)

According to modern medical science, action must wait upon diagnosis or the discovery of focal infection or pathological change. Meanwhile, nothing is done to correct the *causes* of the presenting symptoms in the early stages, and degeneration continues. (See my booklet, "Diagnosis Cancer!")

IV. It's The Least I Can Do
(After My 29 Day Fast)

I first learned about Natural Hygiene about eight years ago. I had dumped the drugs and outgrown the medics some ten years before, and mistakenly substituted the so-called natural supplement school of thought. Giving up the junk foods and the drugs did have some positive results, but after several years of that new program (which included the regular and generous use of supplements and flesh foods), some new nasty symptoms developed, including mucous membrane inflammation and skin rashes in and around the mouth and nose; uterine tenderness, swelling and pain; recurrent visual distortions; and various digestive malfunctions.

These are all symptoms of an overburdened and clogged elimination system, plus possible liver damage, due to the body's abortive attempts to dispose of the toxins from the excessive and putrefactive proteins and concentrates, and the fermentations from wrong combinations of foods.

When I finally discovered Natural Hygiene around the Fall of 1966, I knew I was at last on the right track. A friend, a man of about 45, had a large tumor on his left kidney (the large mass being visible on the outside of his body) and had been told it was necessary to remove the kidney. Instead, he opted to enter a Hygienic Resort in Florida and fasted for 30 days. At the end of the 30 days, the mass had diminished from the size of a fist to the size of a grape, and, after returning home and continuing on a Hygienic regime, it disappeared altogether. He returned to his astounded physicians and surgeons for examination, and they could find no sign of the tumor. (I have since learned that this case history is but one of thousand of similar experiences, and, at Hygienic seminars and conferences, such stories are commonplace.)

Shortly thereafter, early in 1967, I took a prolonged fast of 29 days instead of surgery, for a digestive malfunction.

When I visit my misguided friends at their hospital bedsides, and see their pathetic suffering, with tubes in their noses, mouths, arms and torsos, with their glazed, drugged eyes, and rambling, incoherent attempts at conversation, it wrings my heart and my mind, as I recall my quiet, restful time of fasting, when my eyes were bright, my mind keen and clear, and each day brought me closer to my goal.

Anyone who has experienced a prolonged fast can never be persuaded to turn away from Natural Hygiene —Nature at work in your own body is a wondrous revelation.

I learned that when we go without food, no matter what the reason, even for prolonged periods of abstinence, for 30, 60 or even 90 days in some obese individuals, the functioning tissues are still receiving nuturiment. Surpluses of stored materials in the body are used for this purpose, and the fast does not suspend metabolism, but rather increases its efficiency. The vital tissues are nourished first from the food reserves; and then the fat, various deposits and abnormal growths (such as most tumors and adhesions) are broken down, absorbed and eliminated through a process called autolysis. The essential organs and tissues of the body remain intact, and no cells are lost. Every cell that was there before the fast has been replaced by a smaller, younger and more vital cell. This is the reverse of normal replacement cells, which gradually age.

At all times (whether we are fasting or feasting), all of the parts and functions of the body work in unison, with but one purpose, the preservation of the organism, despite anything we may do to thwart it. During a fast, the thwarting has ceased and been replaced by cooperation with Nature, and healing and rebuilding takes place in all areas, so that when we emerge from the prolonged fast we perhaps undertook because of a circulatory problem, we find we have lost our digestive and arthritic problems as well.

Throughout my fast, it was obvious that all of the processes of my body were continuing at a reduced rate, with the exception of the organs of elimination, which were greatly accelerated at this time. I felt I had a box seat at an absorbing drama, of which I was the star.

After breaking my fast and a period of building some weight and strength, I returned to home and work, revitalized, happy and relatively symptom-free. The nastiest problems were completely absent, other problems were improving more and more and on the way out, and, best of all, I had not submitted to the only alternative, hospitalization and surgery, and—I still have all my "spare parts". (I did not agree with the surgeons that I could spare them.)

Since my fast in 1967, I have lived Hygienically, my diet has been 75% to 85% raw food, mostly organically grown. I exercise daily (calisthenics and/or walking/ jogging; dancing and gardening). I take my sun baths four to seven times weekly and air baths daily. I try to get sufficient sleep and rest and to cultivate emotional poise, and am improving in these areas. I am engaged in many rewarding activities; in fact, here too I must discipline myself, as I sometimes find myself doing too much, for I love life and the hours and days are so full. Robert Louis Stevenson's "Happy Thought": "The world is so full of a number of things, I'm sure we should all be as happy as kings", emphasizes how much life has to offer.

During my working years, I took my lunch to a nearby park. I removed as much clothing as possible, depending on the season, to expose my body to sunlight and air. Even in the Winter, I at least removed my hose, so my legs could absorb some sunlight and air. I used my lunch hour to best advantage by allocating the first 15 minutes to walking and running, the next 30 minutes to eating, and the last 15 minutes to resting. When other people took coffee breaks, I took "rest breaks" or "walk breaks". Some days I skipped lunch, and utilized the whole hour for exercise and rest.

I learned long ago to guard against preoccupation with any one facet of life, be it health, religion, family, or any other involvement.

The development of versatility and self-reliance, a well-rounded personality and a lively interest in all phases of life around us, will not only improve our health and enjoyment of life, but will be a form of insurance. A narrow life can be destructive, a broad life offers many alternatives in times of stress.

Diversification and variety in your interests and activities may actually be rejuvenating, as indicated by Sir Winston Churchill, in his book, "Painting as a Pastime". He wrote: "Change is the master key. A man can wear out a particular part of his mind by continually using it and tiring it, just as he can wear out the elbows of a coat. One cannot mend the frayed elbows of a coat by rubbing the sleeves or shoulders, but the tired parts of the mind can be rested and strengthened by using the other parts."

Both my husband and I take frequent 36 hour fasts for rest and rejuvenation, whenever we feel they are indicated.

I have made a study of Natural Hygiene by avid reading and multiple contacts, have attended many Natural Hygiene seminars and courses, and have also continued to study other schools of thought in health and nutrition, for comparisons and whatever else I might glean.

I have learned that there are very few pathological conditions which cannot be helped by Natural Hygiene; that in many desperate situations, if there is any hope it is through Natural Hygiene; that any reversible condition and many pronounced irreversible may be conquered; that it is possible to turn back the clock and add years to your life. The best thing you can save for your old age is yourself. It happened to me and it can happen to you.

I had the opportunity and privilege of conducting a series of five sessions on Natural Hygiene at a nearby high school, Clearwater Central Catholic High School, at the request of the principal, and the response of the young people (to what was to them a totally new concept), was amazing and heartening, for they, of course, hold the keys to the future.

I have done everything I could in two cities to create and perpetuate functioning Natural Hygiene Chapters, where the meetings could provide study courses, and could be used as a clearing house and information center for questions and problems. I will continue to acquire and disseminate Natural Hygiene information, and help whenever possible.

It's the least I can do after what Natural Hygiene has done for me.

V. Emergencies
(Applying Hygienic Principles)

It is important to know what to do in an emergency. It may be even more important to know what not to do.

Don't panic. Think. The basic needs of life will always apply. Fresh air, warmth, rest and sleep, no poisons (drugs). Take whatever immediate action is necessary (as outlined below) and phone a Professional Hygienist for advice (even Long Distance). A calm reassuring attitude (without manifestation of panic, worry or stress) of the person caring for the victim, will be an important factor in providing the proper environment for recovery.

1. (A) *Heart Attack* (Coronary Occlusion or Myocardial Infarction: OR Obstructed Blood Vessel)

   (B) *Stroke* (Cerebral Hemorrhage: Ruptured Blood Vessel With Destruction of Brain Tissue)

   Action: (a) Recumbent position (head should be somewhat elevated— don't move.) (Remove restrictive clothing)

   (b) Fresh Air

   (c) Warmth

   (d) Fast

   (e) Artificial Respiration (Mouth-to-Mouth Resuscitation) and fairly vigorous cardiac massage may be necessary if heart appears to have stopped.

   Nothing else worth while can be done.

The body repairs itself. Drugs will
only cause additional problems.

2. *Accidents*—(A) *Fractures and Dislocations*

Don't move an accident victim (except to save
his life) especially if there is a fracture or dislocation. A broken bone can wait for professional help.
Get an Osteopath or Orthopedist. Keep injured
member immobile. If in shock or unconscious or
in a faint, don't try to revive the patient. If in
horizontal position, he will revive spontaneously.

When I fell and broke my arm in the Fall of
1972 in a city in Indiana, I was taken to a hospital.
I accepted a general anaesthetic for setting the
broken bone, and one talwin injection on each of
the first two days. Thereafter, I refused all drugs
during my week's stay. I refused all food for 24
hours, thereafter accepted tiny fruit and vegetable
meals, supplemented by nuts brought to me from
the outside. The first few nights I slept little, but
was allowed to walk in the corridors as much as I
wished, to relieve the pain and discomfort. The
healing was rapid. When I left the hospital, I felt
fine and ravenously hungry.

(B) *Hemorrhages and Transfusions*

For hemorrhage, a dry cloth cover over the surface will help to make a larger surface area to aid
in clotting; the blood should clot in three minutes,
but may take ten minutes for a severe wound, and
may need stitches to stop spurting.

If there is hemorrhage with massive blood loss
(there may be weak pulse and falling blood pressure) you should attempt to stop the hemorrhage
by applying pressure (or a tourniquet) between the
wound and the heart. If a tourniquet is used, be
careful not to cut off all circulation, as that can be
very damaging to the tissue below the wound. (See

discussion of use of tourniquets under "Snake Bites" emergency treatment.) Remember that one can lose up to 50% of his blood and remain functionally efficient, so you have time to apply this emergency treatment.

If internal hemorrhage is suspected—complete rest and immobility is urgently required for one to two days, and surgery may be necessary.

Blood Transfusions: Blood transfusions should never be used. There is no exception to this rule. A person who may have lost over 50% of his blood will produce new blood more quickly without, than with, transfusions.

Transfusions can cause many serious problems or death:

(a) When there is a hemolytic reaction (reaction between the two bloods), there is a 50% mortality rate. (There are 15,000,000 possible blood combinations.)

(b) Too great a quantity of blood can cause death.

(c) Air in the blood can cause death.

(d) The blood may be contaminated in handling.

(e) Serious diseases, such as hepatitis and renal poisoning are contracted through transfusions of blood from infected donors.

(f) Cancer, insanity and alteration of personality traits have also been attributed to blood transfusions.

Don't use blood plasma or saline solutions either —they are also subject to many of the same dangers. If you are the victim of an accident, and are taken to a hospital, apply Hygienic principles to whatever extent is possible. Many Hygienists carry cards in their wallets reading "No drugs or transfusions while unconscious". (See my booklet "Don't Get Stuck!")

(C) *Sprains, Torn Ligaments, Strains*

Fix limb to maintain in position and immobilize joint for initial period. Hydrotherapy can relieve pain in some cases. Immerse in cold water (not ice water) a minute or two and take out. Do this five or six times. Repeat in an hour and each hour or so as long as there is pain.

(D) *Wounds:* Cleanliness is important. Clean thoroughly with plain water. Get dirt out with nippers or wash or even scrub to get out particles. If deep cut, cover with porous bandage (not band-aid). If large wound or bleeding is profuse, get to a physician; it may require suturing.

(E) *Puncture Wounds:* Allow to drain, bleed and heal spontaneously. If it is a small slender puncture, or punctured by a rusty nail, let it bleed freely by gently pressing and kneading. No anti-tetanus injection should be used—the introduction of poison into the blood stream can be of no possible benefit.

(F) *Cuts, Burns, Scalds:* Keep clean, protect open wound with light moist covering (moistened with water). Expose to air, but not sunlight, especially for a large burn. Do not use salves or ointments. Hospital treatment is not recommended even for third degree burns. Cool compresses, or immersing burns and scalds in cool water will alleviate pain.

3. *Fever:* Don't check fever, even if over 106 degrees. To thwart Nature by bringing down fever is a dangerous thing to do. After all these many years of advocating trying to reduce high fevers, science has recently come to the conclusion that the substance the body makes, known as "Interferon", functions at its best in the presence of fever, and that temperatures up to 104 degrees will actually kill the deadly polio virus.
Action: Fast

4. *Vomiting* and *Diarrhea:*

Watch for dehydration if vomiting and diarrhea persist. Call a Hygienic doctor. Go on a fast. *Fast.*

5. *Pain:* Don't Move. Pain is a useful guide. If suppressed, it is like throwing the map away. Hydrotherapy (cool or warm water) may sometimes be used for pain, if recommended by a Natural Hygiene doctor.

6. *Appendicitis (Acute):* Extremely painful. Drawing legs up toward abdomen may relieve pain somewhat. At first sign of trouble, call a Natural Hygiene doctor.

(A) Bring knees up as high as possible to relieve pain and relax abdominal muscles. Lie as still as you can.

(B) Don't drink

(C) Don't eat

(D) No heat, no cold, just wait—do not interfere by using packs and enemas. There should be no outside interference, and no poking, pushing and pressing (examining).

If the appendix should rupture as the result of outside interference, or if it ruptures after a period of chronic appendicitis, aggravated by continuation of dietary errors and excesses, and peritonitis occurs, then certainly surgery would be necessary to drain the abdominal cavity. It is a question of judgment. Usually, if there is no interference, a capsule may form around the appendix to protect the peritoneal cavity. But where there has been neglect or much interference, and peritonitis does develop, Dr. Burton considers surgery the only rational approach.

(In peritonitis, there is tremendous rigidity of abdominal muscles, and enormous increase in fever.)

7. *Epileptic Convulsions:* To avoid biting the tongue, place a rolled wash cloth or a wooden stick or pencil, which has been padded with cotton or adhesive tape, between the teeth at the first sign of a convulsion. Waiting may make it impossible to get it between the teeth. *Wait.* It may take 30 seconds to an hour for seizure to pass. Don't recommend to an epileptic that he stop medication, except under competent Natural Hygiene supervision.

8. *Convulsions* (Other Than Epileptic): Don't do anything. Brain damage can only result from trying to interfere with the convulsions, not from the convulsions.

9. *Electrocution* and *Drowning:* Artificial respiration and resuscitation are necessary. In electrocution, it could take four or five hours to revive the victim, though usually there is not much chance after the first hour. Artificial respiration for a drowning victim usually produces much quicker revival than in electrocution.

    Artificial Respiration: Place on back, turn head to side, remove dentures, gum,—open upper clothing. See that tongue is not in back of mouth. Hold victim's nose and blow into mouth every four seconds.

10. *Poisoning* (By Ingestion): Speed is of the utmost importance, since you have only 20 to 30 minutes time in which it is possible to neutralize the poisons. While awaiting the arrival of a professional or other person who may be able to administer an antidote, copious quantities of water may be taken; however, milk is better. Milk will neutralize both strong acids and alkalies.

    Don't check spontaneous vomiting or diarrhea or fever, even if it gets to 106 degrees or more. Usually it is not advisable to induce vomiting, especially if person is unconscious or having convulsions.

Producing vomiting by using an emetic is not the same as spontaneous vomiting, and the condition may be worse afterwards than before.

Try to ascertain the identity or nature of the poison. Vomiting should never be induced if the mouth appears to be burned or damaged. Any products vomited containing lye or petroleum can damage the esophagus or lungs.

Antidotes for Poisoning: If vomiting is dangerous, Syrup of Ipecac (dried root of a South American shrub) can be administered as an antidote. (An antidote is, of course, another foreign substance, but a strong acid or alkali has to be dealt with and neutralized.)

Other Antidotes When Vomiting is Dangerous:

For Acids: Milk, Baking Soda, Egg White, Milk of Magnesia, Olive Oil

For Alkalis: Milk, Butter or Other Fats, Vinegar or Lemon Juice, Raw Eggs

Rest and *Fast* afterwards to provide the body with the most favorable conditions to deal with the poison and heal internal damage.

11 *Poison Ivy, Poison Oak, Etc:* Immediate bathing and copious application of cold water.

12. *Snake Bites:* (Coral, Rattler, Cobra) (A poisonous snake makes fang marks. A non-poisonous snake makes a U-shaped mark.) Immediate attention is necessary.
Action:
(A) Lie down and keep calm so as not to release adrenalin.
(B) Tourniquet. Someone else should apply as quickly as possible on upper arm, leg or thigh. Twist tight with stick until pulse virtually disappears in limb. Leave on 20 minutes, release for 5

minutes and tighten again. This can be done for
several hours, but watch the circulation. Anti-
venom should not be used. (The Red Cross First
Aid Courses previously advised the use of tourniquets for hemorrhage, etc., but has recently
changed this advice to "Never use a tourniquet,—
use pressure instead".)

(C) Don't move victim—he must be transported
in vehicle.

(D) Fast afterwards.

13. *Spider or Insect Bites:* (Mosquitoes, Wasps, Hor-
nets, Bees, Scorpions, Tarantulas, Black Widows)
Most of these insect bites are only slightly poisonous. Do nothing and forget them—a fast is not
necessary unless multiple stings are suffered and
signs of poisoning ensue. Scorpions and black
widow spiders cause a numb feeling for perhaps 24
hours. If you desire to do something, fast till the
numbness passes. A stinger can be removed with a
knife or razor—run the sharp edge along the surface and the stinger will come right out. Use
nothing for relief of itching or pain.

14. *Asphyxiation:* (in Fires, etc.)—Unconsciousness
from smoke or gas. Take out of room—crawl along
the floor. Throwing cold water on the face is not
necessary. Resuscitation method as in drowning.

15. *Dog Bites:* Rabies treatment could be more dangerous than the bites. Do not become fearful.
Wash the wound well. Let it bleed freely if deep
and forget about it. Do not get Rabies treatment.

16. *Something in Your Eye:* Wash hands and pull
upper lid down over lower lid, wipe out corner of
eye gently with sterile cotton; never rub eye; that

may drive object deeper into tissues. If irritation continues, get professional help.

17. *Nosebleeds:* Have patient sit in a chair with head tilted forward, moisten a cotton ball and insert into the bleeding nostril, press nostrils together for at least five minutes. After bleeding stops, cotton should remain in place for several hours.

18. *Stings of Stingrays and Jellyfish:* These venomous denizens of the deep inject a neurotoxin into the victim that produces a stinging sensation. Usually pain is the most serious effect of the attack. A paste of baking soda will relieve the pain and swelling. (St. Petersburg Evening Independent 5/13/75)

19. *Some Constructive or Emergency Surgery:* Surgery may be advisable or unavoidable for:
    1. Repair after Accidents
    2. Repair of Congenital Defects
    3. Concealed Strangulated Hernia in Infant
    4. Some Caesarian Sections
    5. Some Cataracts
    6. Repair of Extensive Damage to Joints and Cartilage
    7. Tubal Pregnancy
    8. Some Hernias
    9. Large Tumors Causing Obstruction or Pressure on Nerves or Organs.
    10. Repair of Opening in Wall of Stomach Eaten Through by Peptic Ulcer of Long Duration
    11. Transplant Where Accident has Destroyed an Organ
    12. Some Other Repairs
    These and other contemplated surgery should be evaluated by a Professional Hygienist.

20. *Emergency Procedure to Save Choking Victims:* (from "Dear Abby", St. Petersburg Independent,

12/28/74) "After reading that 2,600 Americans choked to death last year on food or other objects, Dr. Henry Heimlich, a Cincinnati surgeon, worked out a procedure for saving choking victims. . . .

"Standing behind the victim, place your arms around his waist, slightly above the waist. Allow the victim's head and torso to bend forward. Then tightly grasp your own wrist with your other hand and press into the victim's abdomen forcefully and rapidly, repeating several times. This will push up the diaphragm, compress the air into the lungs and expel the object that is blocking the air passage.

"Until now, choking victims have often died unless a doctor was handy to cut an air passage into the throat, or use a special instrument to remove the block."

An article in June 1975 Prevention Magazine also describes this lifesaving procedure, known as the "Heimlich Maneuver", for Henry J. Heimlich, M.D., Director of Surgery at the Jewish Hospital in Cincinnati, and specialist in the surgical and medical management of esophageal and swallowing problems. Dr. Heimlich says that food-choking kills approximately 4,000 Americans every year and such asphyxiation is now the sixth major cause of accidental death, which occurs in four or five minutes, and is sometimes called "cafe coronary" because it is frequently confused with a heart attack.

If the person has passed out, you can adapt the procedure by pushing down with your fists but angling the pressure towards the chest. If you're the victim, perform this maneuver on yourself, or try throwing yourself over the back of a stout chair.

July 1968—Dr. Esser recommended the book "The Art of Survival", Doubleday Publishing Co.

VI. The Medicine Show

1. *Causes of Disease Ignored*

The use of drugs and surgery ignores the cause and treats the effects, and this is accepted by the public as efficient treatment of disease. This confidence in drugs and surgery might be amusing were the consequences not so tragic.

In a book recently published in England, "Need Your Physician Be So Useless?" by Andrew Malleson, M.D., he writes: "The treatment of established disease is a most inefficient way of ensuring that we survive in good health. . . . The leading causes of death in advanced countries like our own are heart disease, cancer, stroke, accidents, flu, pneumonia, bronchitis, diabetes, birth injuries, sclerosis of the liver, congenital malformations and suicides. Our vices catch up with us. *Cigarettes, alcohol, physical inactivity* and *overeating* are the *major contributors of the causes* of these killing diseases. *Medicine has little help to offer for these self-induced conditions of ill health. . . . In hard statistical terms, we could abolish all treatments and treatment doctors, and our life expectancy would still increase. . . . Most of the standard treatments prescribed in general practice for minor physical illnesses not only confound the principles of scientific medicine, but are even contrary to common sense. Recovery takes place not because of, but in spite of, medical treatment."*

(Italics by author)

Dr. Alec Burton, D.O., D.C., N.D., Hygienic Professional in Australia, reviewed this book, and states:

34

"Hygienists have been saying this for years, but the situation must be reaching a critical point when a member of the medical profession takes such an un-orthodox and honest view of his own practices."

"Physicians Strike—Morticians Beg For Bread"— (From the September, 1973 Hygienic Review reporting on the strike of physicians in Israel, which was accompanied by a marked fall in the general death rate). A similar strike of Israeli physicians about twenty years previously was also marked by a decline in the death rate. Similar declines in death rates accompanied strikes of physicians in Montreal and Holland.

In his column in the San Antonio News, November 26, 1973, L. M. Boyd wrote: "There are more medical doctors per capita in Washington, D.C. than any place else in the country, yet the 'premature death rate' is higher. Alaska, with the fewest medical doctors per capita, is lowest in 'premature death rate'."

From the St. Petersburg Independent, October 10, 1973, captioned "Nutrition: Medical Deficiency" by Marian Nott, "Only about a dozen of the approximately 120 medical schools in the United States have full departments of nutrition, it's reported. Five local physicians were asked to comment on the new Vitamin A and D regulations and the extent to which they used vitamins and minerals in their treatment of patients, and related matters. Two of the physicians refused to talk at all. A gastroenterologist and a gynecologist-obstetrician sent word through their office assistants that they weren't qualified to speak on nutrition. Three physicians did speak. The three agreed they received very little nutrition education in medical school." The three physicians did make some comments in the direction of awareness that nutritional errors and deficiencies may be the proximate cause of disease. The preventive medicine physician said he suspected that his patients were getting too many nitrates which were blocking enzyme systems. The family- and preventive-medicine physician said that almost any American is malnourished. The pediatrician said "It is getting more and more difficult, with the packaged processed food for a person to get a balanced diet containing what he needs for optimal function", and said it would be a good thing for physicians to be more nutrition conscious.

2. *Every Drug Is A Poison*

When a drug is taken, the action that follows is produced by the body, not by the drug. The drug interferes with enzyme activity in the cells, and the adaptations the body is forced to make for its elimination may so impair function as to lead to chronic disease and death.

"The body acts on food to digest it—it acts on poison to expel it. If the organism does not succeed in rejecting the drug, it combines or unites chemically with tissue, and the tissue is damaged or destroyed. No matter how efficiently the body acts in expelling the drugs, some chemical union with tissue will occur."— Dr. Alec Burton, July, 1970 Hygiene Health Conference, "Simplified Biochemistry".

From the Hygienic Review, January, 1974: "It has been repeatedly admitted by both physicians and pharmacologists, especially since the Thalidomide holocaust, that *every drug is a poison and no drug is safe.*"

Dr. Alec Burton, states: "There is no such thing as a 'substance possesssing curative or remedial properties' (definition of medicine). Healing is a biological process accomplished by the lawful and orderly processes of the body, in continuous operation immediately there is any deviation from the normal, until recovery or death.

"Medicines (drugs) may be used for a variety of reasons: to modify bodily function in disease, to relieve pain, to destroy bacteria, etc., or in the 'prevention of disease'. Drugs are said to have pharmacological action, therapeutic action, physiological action, toxicological action, side action, etc., etc. The action which follows the taking of a drug may be stimulation, depression, relaxation, anaesthesia, diuresis (urination), diaphoresis (sweating), etc. . . .

"Drugs are in their very nature poisonous; this is their intrinsic quality. Were they not so they would not occasion the 'therapeutic' effect which occurs when they are used. It is because they are poisons that defensive, expulsive action follows their ingestion. . . . Chemical action is the only action of which drugs are capable; the 'therapeutic', etc. actions are all appearances. We are deceived because we persist in ascribing the actions of the body to the action of drugs. The many actions, such as vomiting, diarrhea, sweating, sedation, stimulation, etc. are defensive, remedial and eliminative actions of the body defending itself against the poison. . . . Drugs are inimical to life . . . and permanently damage the body. Every action performed by the body against drugs weakens it. We cannot poison people into health."

In the May 1974 Hygienic Review is a report by Harry Clements, N.D., D.O., "The Changing Drug Scene", relative to the radical change in the climate surrounding medical drugs, from the adulation of "wonder" and "miracle" drugs to adverse criticism of their potential dangers, being voiced increasingly on radio and television and in the press, including the medical journals. He says: "Surely no one now believes there is such a thing as a safe medicine, and thoughtful people know that drugs are no safer under medical prescription than otherwise. The ever-increasing number of patients who are admitted to hospitals because of the side effects of medicine amply proves this fact. Most people are aware today that the last experiment with medicine is always on the patient. . . . People have been told that aspirin and other household remedies were innocous; today, it is admitted that they are potentially dangerous drugs.

"In the London Sunday Observer we read that 'Aerosol inhaler may have killed 3,500 asthmatics' which was, the report said, a far greater disaster than the thalidomide tragedy. In the London Sunday Times, September 30, 1973, we were told of 'the dangers of an aspirin trip' and were informed that 'at least 7,000 people are treated every year in hospitals for blood vomiting'; that pain-killing drugs cause at least 500 cases of kidney disease (annually), and that stomach ulcers and anemia arise from the same cause, and that aspirin may trigger-off asthma and other allergies. . . .

"It was the claim, when the antibiotics were discovered, that the problem of sepsis in the larger hospitals would be solved. In Medical News (London) October 22, 1973, the statement is made by a leading American surgeon that just the opposite has happened: 'Indeed, today we find our hospitals the very centre of sepsis. . . .

The use and overuse of antibiotics, although life-saving in selected cases, has in the long run contributed to, rather than solved, the problem of infection.'

"W. W. McDermott, who is described as a foremost authority on the subject, wrote: 'A surprising proportion of the disease load in our hospitals today is microbial disease, but unlike those of a few decades ago, today's diseases are caused by the very microbes we have long been accustomed to regard as essentially harmless inhabitants of our tissues. . . . In short, man is beginning to fall prey to what we have hitherto regarded as his "own" microbes.' "It is now the medical view that microbes that were formerly harmless have been transformed into pathogenic bacteria by antibiotics and other drugs used in combating microbes held responsible for diseases."

3. *A Drug-Treated Person Has to Get Well Twice*
(From the Hygienic Review, January 1974): "In the early 1900's, Sir William Osler stressed the fact that a drug-treated person has to get well twice, first of the disease that sent him to the physician, and second, of the disease caused by the drugs prescribed by the

physician, catalogued as untoward side effects, adverse reactions, allergies, allergic reactions, anaphylaxis shock, iatrogenic disease, drug addiction and death, all resulting from dosing with the theoretically 'safe small dose'.

"The problems created by the rising incidence of Iatrogenic Disease (caused by treatment) are causing many patients and physicians to question the sanity of the whole medical system.

"Medical News (London), June 4, 1973, carried this item: 'Iatrogenic Disease in Great Britain seems to be reaching new heights in general practice. . . . In hospitals there is evidence that the building programme could be cut by 10% if Iatrogenic Disease were eliminated.

In medical wards, it runs 16.4%, and 10.2% of all patients receiving drug therapy (digitalis, ampicillin and bronchodilators particularly), have been found to be suffering from drug reactions.' "

4. *Drugs Mask Symptoms*

(From the Hygienic Review, January, 1974): "Drugs mask symptoms and disguise the condition of the sick individual. After the first twenty-four hours of drugging, no physician on earth can tell the true state of his patient. Drugs rob the symptoms of all meaning. A writer in the Saturday Review, October 7, 1961, discussing the first voyage of a human being (Gherman Titov) around the earth in outer space, says of the suggestion that he must have been drugged before the take-off: 'Drugs would have defeated the main purpose of Titov's flight, which was to discover how the human organism responds to prolonged weightlessness and loneliness. Tiny instruments were taped to his body to measure his heart beat, breathing and other indications of mental and physical functioning. Administration of drugs would have removed all meaning from these readings.' "

5. *Results of Suppressing Symptoms*

Drugs suppress the symptoms, lower the fever, stop the pain, and you pay the price later on for interfering with the wisdom of the organism: chronic disease evolves—cancer, heart disease, hardening of the arteries, stroke, arthritis, and other degenerative diseases.

6. *Hospital Deaths Due to Drugs and/or Surgery*

On August 20, 1973, Medical News (London), quoting from an article in the World Health Organization Chronicle (a medical organization and publication of high standing) said: "Surveys in various hospitals have shown that up to 25% of all deaths were ascribed to drugs. The therapeutic risk has reached a magnitude comparable to major surgery."

7. *(A) Sub-Lethal Drug-Created Casualties*

To the high death rate ascribed to drugs and surgery should be added the greater number of drug-created casualties that are short of lethal, and the great number of drug-caused birth defects.

(B) Surgery Aftermath

From the St. Petersburg Independent, May 24, 1974—William J. Welch, M.D.: "A disconcerting and often dangerous problem for a patient who has just been operated on is the difficulty encountered in trying to empty the urinary bladder in the first few days after the abdomen has been cut open. The bruised and recently stitched-up belly muscles are reluctant or unable to provide the tension necessary for the normal expulsion of urine, and the bladder passively balloons up with its accumulated briny contents. The 'easy answer' . . . to this potentially dangerous situation is to slide a catheter into the bladder and draw off the accumulated urine. Often quite casually ordered to be done, this invasive procedure usually hurts and is always humiliating, but, more seriously, accounts for about 50% of infections in post-operative patients.

"In spite of the most impeccable aseptic precautions, the invading catheter, in addition to the welcome relief it brings to the aching bladder, often brings with it bacteria that can set up an infection in the urinary tract. Consequently, lots of tricks to stimulate the bladder-emptying reflex have been tried: injections to make the bladder contract, a few drops of ammonia in the urinal to make fumes that will stimulate the urethra to respond, or, more simply, turning on a near-by water tap." Dr. Welch goes on to tell about a recent ingenious project by Dr. Reese Alsop of Huntington, Long Island, utilizing "sound effects" recordings to induce post-operative patients to urinate, referred to as a "rich melody of aquatic phonetics" which provides a "symphony of sparkling, gurgling, running water". The device is called an "audiocatheter".

In addition to the above described and other difficulties in resuming normal bodily functions after surgery, an all-too-common denouement is the necessity for more surgery, to remove adhesions from the original surgery. Other post-surgery problems include the necessity for the body to recover from the shock and to adapt to the loss of the missing organ or part.

8. Drug Addiction Caused by Physicians

"Under a physician's narcotics, patients often mistakenly believe they are being cured of the ailment which produced the pain. Patients are suing physicians for causing their addiction, and winning." ("Toward Solution of America's Pressing Problems" by Melvin Kimmel, B.A., Juris Doctor, "Hygienic Review", December, 1970.)

9. Flood of Malpractice Suits

In the St. Petersburg Independent of May 7, 1974, was a news item about a malpractice award of $734,300 in damages to a Baltimore, Maryland boy, who was the victim of a faulty circumcision in 1965. There have been a flood of malpractice suits against physicians and surgeons, with heavy damages assessed. In March,

1974 the Sacramento, California Medical Society held a press conference after the third malpractice trial of drug-popping surgeon, John G. Nork. (Forty-eight Sacramento physicians had quit private practice.)

More recent developments have created veritable emergencies in this area, with skyrocketing malpractice insurance premiums, strikes by physicians and surgeons, and desperate attempts to find solutions. It has been repeatedly brought out that very small percentages of the astronomical malpractice awards actually reach the injured patients.

One doctor-hospital "solution" to this dilemma (recently publicized in the Tampa Bay area) was the use of a multiplicity of tests and procedures, on a man admittedly dying when he arrived at the hospital. After his death in less than 24 hours, the bill submitted to the survivors was approximately $1,000. The doctors involved said they were practicing "defensive medicine".

Sincere, conscientious physicians and surgeons need to take the reins, make themselves heard and police their ranks, if the "shadow of fear and suspicion on doctor-patient relations" complained about by the Sacramento County Medical Society is ever to be eliminated. Physicians and surgeons have the answer to malpractice suits in their own hands: simply end the malpractice.

10. *Suicides, Drug Addiction and Alcoholism of Physicians*

From the Medical World News, a weekly for physicians, 4/25/69, Page 44: "In the United States alone, more than 100 doctors commit suicide every year. Drug addiction, estimated to be 15 to 100 times greater in the medical profession than in the general population, probably removes even more doctors from practice."

From the St. Petersburg Times, April 21, 1974: "It may come as a surprise, because they should know better, but physicians suffer the highest rate of alcoholism of any profession in America. Dr. Charles E.

Becker, head of alcoholic detoxification at San Francisco General Hospital, says it's because physicians have the type of personality that lends itself to alcoholic addiction, and they they lack knowledge of C_2H_5OH (ethyl alcohol) and its gradual, long-term effects on people, including themselves. Like so many others, physicians are not sufficiently aware of the gradual, insidious, addictive qualities of the most widely sold drug in the nation."

11. *Unnecessary Surgery*

(From the St. Petersburg Independent, 12/26/73) "Melvin Gold, a New Jersey consulting actuary for insurance companies, in a speech at an insurance conference in September, 1973, asked, 'Why don't insurance companies try to do something about unnecessary surgery, which occurs far too often—especially with regard to tonsillectomies and hysterectomies? Why is there a conspiracy of silence? What is good business for the surgeon is not good business for the insurance company or the patient. We are constantly trying to cure people rather than trying to prevent illness in the first place. More surgeons has only meant more surgery. Insurance Companies should not be afraid of stepping on the toes of other industries and the various professions. The public's health is too important to be left solely in the hands of the medical profession and their allies!"

Which reminds me of something I was surprised to hear on the "Hollywood Squares" on April 12, 1974— (a comedy-information program—they state that their answers to questions are based on authentic information and recognized reference material). They used the following "True or False" statement, and the correct answer was "True": "Nearly a million children have their tonsils removed unnecessarily each year." (My surprise was not at this information about the astounding amount of unnecessary surgery, but at hearing it so casually on the air.) It seemed to be accepted without any particular shock, and they immediately went on to the next question.

(From the Hygienic Review, January, 1974): "It is now admitted that there are more than 3,000,000 useless operations performed every year in this country."

On the positive side: There is no doubt that members of the medical profession, both physicians and surgeons, have saved countless lives through the use of their skills, in emergencies and in the correction of defects, such as described in the following excerpt from a San Antonio, Texas Associated Press Dispatch, which appeared in the St. Petersburg Independent of June 8, 1974: "Tasha La Shay Hudson was born prematurely March 15, weighing one pound, four ounces. . . . The infant now weighs four pounds. Lt. Col. Melvin Baden, Chief of Newborn Services at Brooke Army Medical Center, said: 'Instantly after Tash's birth, doctors and nurses began meeting the intricate respiratory and metabolic needs to keep her alive, despite the almost 100% mortality rate she faced! Eight days after the birth, doctors performed open chest surgery to close permanently a fetal channel connecting the aorta to the pulmonary artery. In full-term babies, the channel normally closes naturally. A hospital spokesman quoted the chief of thoracic surgery as saying it was the first time in his memory 'that so critical an operation has been successfully performed on such a tiny patient.' "

12. *Cancer Caused by X-Ray Treatments*

(From Natural Hygienews, March, 1974): "Fasting, which is Nature's best tool for overcoming inflammation, could have prevented the shocking news March 6 (1974) that 5,000 persons may have thyroid cancer because of x-rays they received twenty years ago for treatment of tonsilitis at Chicago's Michael Reese Hospital. The hospital has issued a call through the news media, offering free treatment to these victims, in the form of surgery. As long as Medicine and the public refuse to accept the fact that the body has built-in power to overcome inflammation, such as in tonsilitis, people will continue to reap the tragic effects of medical treatment."

The Wall Street Journal, June 4, 1974, printed a commentary on this same tragic situation, in an article entitled "Time Bombs". Dr. Eugene Saenger, Professor of Radiology at the University of Cincinnati was quoted: "In medicine today, we are using many stronger drugs and all kinds of esoteric chemicals and machines. There are certain to be some long-term consequences." The article tells about Andria Reisberg, who received x-ray treatments for tonsilitis in 1949, and died of cancer of the thyroid gland in 1972. Since then, the Michael Reese Medical Center of Chicago has been attempting to track down the thousands of patients who also received this treatment.

About 1,000 former patients have been located, 600 to 800 have been examined, and about one-fifth of these had possibly cancerous neck growths, and nodules on their thyroid glands. At least seven cases of thyroid cancer have been positively identified and the thyroid gland removed, after which the patient must use daily doses of hormone pills indefinitely (and suffer the consequences).

13. Over-the-Counter Remedies

Over-the-counter "remedies" may represent an even more potent danger, because of their availability for unsupervised use. In a February 14, 1974 article in the St. Petersburg Independent, Peter Weaver stated: "Under study by the F.D.A. is a possible warning label for aspirin, which could increase bleeding in people who suffer from such things as ulcers and hemorrhoids."

At a press interview (reported in the Independent Press-Telegram, Long Beach, California, October 13, 1973, by Ben Zinser, Medical-Science Editor) Angelo E. Dagradi, M.D. (Chief of Gastroenterology at Long Beach Veterans Administration Hospital and President of the prestigious American College of Gastroenterology) said that physicians are seeing more and more cases of multiple ulcers and bleeding of the stomach lining because of aspirin use and drinking of alcoholic beverages, sometimes serious enough to require an operation to stop the bleeding.

A January 29, 1974, St. Petersburg Independent article quotes the American Pharmaceutical Association as saying that most people suffer some blood loss from the stomach when taking aspirin, and that people with ulcers should not take aspirin. They also warn against using antacids "continuously and indiscriminately", and that "overdosing" with nasal spray can create an adverse effect known as "re-bound" in which the nasal passages become more congested than they were when the nasal spray was initially used. (See Addendum —Laws of Human Life—Law of Dual Effect)

Another article in the St. Petersburg Independent, dated 4/24/74, by E. L. Cole, Jr., M.D.: "Boric acid is absorbed through the skin and mucous membrane. It is interesting that in spite of this, it is an ingredient in the most commonly used mouthwash. Some years ago, an injured telephone lineman's abrasions were treated with boric acid compresses, and he died in three days. Autopsy revealed deposits of boric acid crystals throughout his body, notably in his liver."

14. *Deadly Combinations*

We also find instances where deadly combinations of drugs (or drugs and alcohol) are being taken. Remember the untimely death of Dorothy Kilgallen, prominent columnist and "What's My Line" panelist? The newspapers reported that she had taken a sleeping pill, after having had a cocktail or two during the evening, and expired while reading in bed.

E. L. Cole, Jr., M.D., says (5/1/74, St. Petersburg Independent): "Today patients frequently are served by several physicians or specialists, who are unaware of this fact, and there is potential danger in such a situation, for there may be an accumulative or overdose effect."

The St. Petersburg Independent article of January 29, 1974 also quotes the American Pharamaceutical Association as saying that a drug interaction can occur when two medicines are taken at the same time, and gave as typical examples the effect of taking an antihistamine, cold or allergy preparation while using prescription sedatives or tranquilizers, the combination producing severe drowsiness; and the "blocking" effect occurring when an antacid containing calcium, aluminum or magnesium is used at, or near, the time of taking Tetracycline, a commonly prescribed antibiotic.

From the St. Petersburg Independent, June 21, 1974, Sports Hotline, by Mickey Herskowitz and Steve Perkins: "If a player goes on the operating table and the surgeon doesn't have complete knowledge of every drug he's been taking, the player can die from the anesthesia."

And on June 24, 1974, we found this gem in the St. Petersburg Independent, column by Dr. E. L. Cole, Jr. (M.D.): "Recent literature concerning nephrology— the study of the function and malfunction of the kidney —has raised the question of the safety of combined analgesics over prolonged periods of time. Combined analgesics are pain suppressors such as Excedrin, APCs, and others, where drugs such as phenacetin and acetaminophen are used in conjunction with aspirin. Chronic renal disease is life-threatening and life taking. . . . Chronic interstitial nephritis is one of these diseases. Previously this disease was assumed to be caused by recurrent episodes of bacterial infection of the kidney. Today Mr. Thomas Murray and Dr. Martin Goldberg have reported a study indicating analgesic abuse is a main factor in many cases of interstitial nephritis. . . . The findings of Dr. Paul Balter, director of the dialysis unit at the Central Du Page Hospital in Winfield, Illinois, corrobates the above opinion. . . . He joins other nephrologists in cautioning the physician to avoid prescribing these drugs for relief of pain and warning the public not to buy them over the counter for relief of chronic recurring pain or discomfort."

15. *Caffeine Poisoning*

From the St. Petersburg Independent, May 7, 1974: "Dr. John P. Greden of Walter Reed Army Medical Hospital in Washington, D.C., said too much caffeine in coffee, tea or cola drinks can bring on symptoms of an anxiety state and lead you to a psychiatrist and months of useless treatment with calm-down drugs. Dr. Greden told of reviewing records of 100 psychiatric patients, with no question ever having been asked about caffeine consumption. 250 milligrams daily is considered a large dose. 3 cups of coffee, 2 over the counter headache tablets and a cola drink approximate 500 milligrams, and many Americans exceed that."

16. *Pantyhose Poisoning*

In the "Dear Abby" column in the St. Petersburg Independent of 2/24/75 a new revolting development is exposed. A reader tells of her elderly mother's development of "a dreadful vaginal infection which spread into her bladder, and she was hospitalized in agony." She said that the several doctors who attended her mother said that they had been seeing much too much of similar bacillus infections, mostly among younger women, and concluded there must be something in the dye of the pantyhose that caused the infection, and urged women to wear panties under their pantyhose. Abby consulted several topnotch gynecologists and dermatologists, who confirmed this information.

17. *"I Treat and God Cures"*

From Melvin Kimmell's article (See No. 8 above): "Nathan S. Kline, M.D., head of the research center at Rockland State Hospital, New York, was quoted in the New York Times Magazine, April 6, 1969, Page 54: 'No physician ever cured any patient of anything. As

Paré, the famous 16th Century surgeon said: "I treat and God cures".' "

18. *Read Your Daily Newspaper*
Read your daily newspaper and compile your own list of quotations similar to the above, confirming (wittingly or unwittingly) the Hygienic point of view. (I must confess that in our family it is my husband who "religiously" reads the daily newspaper "from cover to cover" and has "uncovered" many of the surprising and interesting quotes included herein. Orchids to him also for suggesting No. 18 above.)

VII. The Hygienic Diet
(Some Things You Want to Know and Don't Know Whom To Ask)

1. *What to Eat and How and When to Eat It*
The body takes the raw materials of food, sunshine and air, processing and transforming them into its own structures and into energy. It stands to reason that the quality of the raw materials is of prime importance.

The only source of optimal nutrition is from food as provided by the bountiful hand of Nature, the best quality available, and organically grown, if possible. Herculean efforts should be made to grow your own food, or to obtain organically grown food. The advantages of organically grown food cannot be overremphasized. Organically grown lettuce from your own garden is free from chemicals and pesticides, and is loaded with the nutrients you have provided by cooperating with Nature. Among other deficiencies characteristic of plants fed with chemicals, such foods will be deficient in copper, an important trace element necessary for the utilization of iron. Chemical fertilizers prevent this trace mineral from being dissolved and absorbed into the plant, while foods produced from plants free of chemicals will be high in copper. (Independent Press, Booksville, Florida, 4/23/75, "Good Nutrition", J. M. Wiles)

But, if not possible to grow or obtain organically grown food, eat whole, raw, fresh, ripe fruits, fresh vegetables, mostly raw, and raw unsalted nuts and seeds, properly combined, and you will still achieve a much higher state of health, strength, vigor and longevity than conventional eaters. This high-residue fibrous diet has built-in weight control while supplying all your nutritional needs for optimal health.

Studies of rural Africans (Robert Rodale, St. Petersburg Times, April 28, 1974) indicate that such a diet prevents diverticulosis (lower bowel disease), cancer of the colon, appendicitis and ulcerative colitis.

In the St. Petersburg Independent, October 7, 1973, William J. Welch, M.D., says: "If you have had an attack of acute diverticulitis, you probably have been told the way to prevent further attacks is to stay on a 'low residue' diet—one that eliminates fibrous, uncooked vegetables, whole wheat bread, nuts and raw fruits, especially those with seeds. Now it appears that such a diet, except during an acute attack, may in fact do more harm than good. Diverticulitis is an inflammation of the small, sac-like pouchings present in the walls of the colons of at least a third of men and women over 45 years of age. . . . When there is no inflammation, we refer to it as diverticulosis. . . . largely confined to highly civilized man, . . . very rare in primitive societies in which a high residue diet, consisting mainly of coarse grains, fibrous vegetables, nuts and raw fruit, prevails . . . which gives the bowel its proper work to do."

In the St. Petersburg Independent of June 17, 1974, E. L. Cole, Jr., M.D. says: "In the March 1974 issue of 'Consultant', Dr. Steven Bernstein of the University of Miami department of Gastroenterology reviewed some of the present thinking concerning diverticulosis. It is not a pediatric disease, but very well may have its origin in the dietary habits of the family and the child. In the early 1960s a British surgeon, Dr. Neil Painter, using catheters to study intestinal pressure, found that the low residue diet of the urban American and Western European impedes the normal propulsion of material through the colon. Because of this, increased pressures develop which cause a ballooning out of weak spots in this portion of the gut. The result of such repeated and continuous pressure is the adult diverticula—when multiple called diverticulosis. . . . If the British surgeon's findings are valid, and they seem to be, then the pediatrician and family practitioner should be more emphatic about adding bulk and roughage to the diet. . . . Those with symptomatic diverticulosis—belly pain, etc.—need to follow the dietary restrictions of their physician. However, according to Dr. Bernstein, those of us who have diverticula without symptoms should abandon the once fashionable low residue diet, —for it causes a continuation of the abnormal pressures that originally caused the diverticula in the first place and continues to weaken those that already have been produced."

In the St. Petersburg Independent, October 1, 1973, Walter C. Alvarez, M.D. said he has quit using the smooth residueless diet for duodenal ulcer patients and cites Dr. Robert M. Donaldson of the Boston University School of Medicine as also reporting that he has found the bland diet for the ulcer patient doesn't help, and should be dropped. Dr. Donaldson said that if a person gets any kind of gastric upset from eating a certain food, he obviously should avoid that food. Dr. Alvarez is of the opinion that ulcers come as a result of some emotional or mental stress and improve when the stress is removed.

(See Chapters XI through XX for a variety of palatable foods enjoyed by Hygienists.)

When we study the processes of the body at the cellular level, it becomes more and more apparent why it is of the utmost importance to conserve the body's resources by using foods that have not been changed from their natural forms by heating and processing, and in combinations that can be efficiently processed by the digestive system.

Foods should be eaten in their whole form, including skins, whenever possible. If your digestive limitations cause problems with some skins, discard the thin skin only, carefully retaining and eating all the food immediately under the skin.

Serve whole leaves of lettuce, and don't cut other vegetables into small pieces. When there is a dental or digestive problem,—blended salad, ground nuts or nut butter may be used temporarily, but don't settle for these "crutches" for long periods. See a Professional Hygienist and do what is necessary to make it possible for you to eat whole foods.

Eat foods at room temperature, and chew throughly. Your stomach has no teeth. Chewing insures thorough insalivation of food and assures that the food will be tasted and thus send the proper signals for the adaptation of the digestive juices to the character of the food. This communication system in our bodies is complicated and refined and sensitive and far more sophisticated than the most elaborately programmed computer. (See Chapter X—Food Combining) Chewing breaks up the food into fine particles so that the digestive juices may act efficiently. And chewing and tasting our food prevents bolting, we enjoy it more and digest it better, are better nourished, and less likely to overeat.

Eat only when hungry; eat raw food before cooked food; eat only when relaxed and not under time pressure. Never eat when emotionally upset. Skip the meal, or wait until equilibrium has been reestablished. Emotional disturbances can impair digestion, stop gastric secretions, and turn the food into debris.

Don't initiate or tolerate any but pleasant conversation at meal time. Postpone important decisions, contentious discussions, criticism or chastisement.

Don't eat before or during activity; wait at least two and one-half hours after eating for vigorous exercise. After a meal, the blood is needed by the digestive viscera.

Don't overeat! Stop while the food still tastes wonderful, and well before you are surfeited. Overeating or frequent eating create as many or more problems as (if not more than) wrong foods or combinations; no more than two or three meals a day, and no between meal snacking should be the rule; and no food at all when you are ill—just go to bed until you feel better, and then eat sparingly until vigor returns.

2. *What Not to Eat*

There are a good many "don'ts" and "no-nos" in this section, and the first is: Don't accentuate the negative! Learn what are the worst influences, so that you may eliminate them from your life and forget about them. For the rest, when you make occasional exceptions to the ideal (and you will!) don't make a big deal out of it and don't worry about it. And don't concentrate on what you will be giving up, but what you will be gaining.

This is the rule to remember: "Anything you eat that cannot be utilized by the cell is a poison." This includes all drugs, most beverages and many adulterated foods. We must include in this list: salt (even "sea salt"), sugar (even so-called "raw sugar"), vinegar (even cider vinegar) and all condiments. None of these are foods, and the body is forced to make adaptations to eliminate them. After a month or so, you will wonder why you ever wanted them, as your foods begin to taste better and better.

Don't use foods that have been changed by any method other than preparation in your own kitchen—with the exception of sun-dried fruits without preservatives. This eliminates all frozen, processed, packaged and canned foods.

Off limits is anything containing preservatives. Read the labels—although many foods are not required to show additives on the labels, i.e., the twenty or thirty (or more) additives in commercial ice cream. The potential cumulative poisoning from additives and pre-servatives in food (along with chemical sprays and pesticides) is staggering to contemplate. Many of the foods that are eaten require the expenditure of more energy defending the body against the substances con-tained in the food than we can possibly get from the food.

On September 3, 1974, the "Jeopardy" Television program asked the question: "What problem do aller-gists say may be caused in children by artificial color-ings and food additives?" and the answer accepted as correct was hyperkinesis or hyperactivity.

Don't eat strong tasting foods, such as garlic, onions, radishes, parsley, watercress,—but if young and mild, very small amounts may be used. Garlic and onions may be used to season cooked foods (if you use them) —after twenty minutes' cooking, the irritant (mustard oil) disappears.

Some varieties of chestnuts have a bitter skin and are somewhat toxic when raw; if you use these varieties, they should be roasted. Non-bitter varieties may be eaten raw. Mushrooms are probably not toxic, but they are indigestible—they leave the body unchanged. Dr. William L. Esser, in his "Dictionary of Man's Foods" says of mushrooms: "Though fairly rich in nutritive value, little of it is usable."

Rhubarb and cranberries should not be used, as they contain such an excess of oxalic acid (a calcium an-tagonist) as to be more or less poisonous. Spinach and Swiss chard and beet greens are also high in oxalic acid, and should seldom, if ever, be used. Young ten-der spinach may be used raw in salads, sparingly.

Don't cook with butter or any fat or oil. Butter or

cold pressed oil may be added just before serving. The oil may be used as a salad dressing, if you wish. (Try to cultivate the habit of eating your salad vegetables without dressing.) *Never* use oleomargarine or the hard white hydrogenated so-called "vegetable shortenings" which are extremely difficult for the body to process and cause many circulatory and other problems. Commercial peanut butter is also hydrogenated (to keep the oil from rising to the top) and should not be used.

Steer clear also of the aerosol spray used to keep food from sticking to the pan, as it is 97% Freon, a propellant used in air conditioners, deadly when inhaled.

Don't use anything containing white (bleached) flour. Anything containing any kind of flour (even whole-grain) should not be used regularly. If you do occasionally use some whole grain bread, it would be best to combine it with only a large raw salad, and perhaps a steamed, non-starchy vegetable. Whole grains, not ground into flour, but changed only by cooking (as a casserole dish, see Recipes) may be used for variety occasionally (not oftener than once ever week or two). The best way to use whole grains is by sprouting them. (See Chapter XV)

Don't use warmed-up leftover foods—they are twice cooked and have deteriorated. Try to prepare just enough for the current meal.

Honey is not a good food for man—but it is not a serious matter to use it very rarely. However, it is a concentrated sweet and contains harmful acids, and leaches minerals from the body in much the same way as does white sugar. When combined with starches, it causes indigestion and gas formation.

3. *Dairy Products*

The use of dairy products should be minimal—some people should not use them at all. Particularly pernicious is the usual commercial ice cream, with its twenty or thirty or more harmful additives. Dairy products, when taken in large amounts, cause excretion of mucus in enervated and toxic individuals.

Cow's milk is an ideal food—for calves; but when consumed by humans forms a large tough curd, difficult to digest. The growth factor in cow's milk, intended for the maturing of a calf, causes excessive height in young people and complicated problems in adults. The use of goat's milk by humans may be preferable to the use of cow's milk in some respects, since it is easier to digest, and the growth factor problem would not be present. But animal milk is still not an ideal food for man, especially for adults. Man is the only animal that is never weaned.

Dr. E. L. Cole, Jr., M.D., in the St. Petersburg Independent, 5/20/74, states: "Since so many children are allergic to milk, and because of the fact that 10% of the white population and 40% of the black population have a lactase deficiency (the enzyme necessary to digest the sugar lactose found in cow's milk), this raises the question of whether or not it should be eliminated from the school lunch program."

Since adults may have a deficiency of rennin, an enzyme which initiates the digestion of milk, they do better with clabber (See recipes), buttermilk or unprocessed cheese—preferably from unpasteurized milk. Pasteurization changes the milk protein and makes it more indigestible, and destroys the enzymes and much of whatever nutritional value might be available. But even these dairy products are not ideal foods but are tolerated by some adults better than others. And what about dairy products from unhealthy animals, and bad methods of pasteurizing and handling bulk supplies, and additives and drugs (including antibiotics) in practically all dairy products? Fruits, vegetables and nuts are better sources of calcium than milk could ever be, and a Hygienic diet provides an abundance of this vital element.

4. *Meat*

The natural food of a primate is from the plant kingdom, determined by his digestive system and other features of his anatomy. All animals have the anatomy and physiology for getting and using the kinds of foods that Nature intended for them, and on which they will best survive. The carnivores have sharp claws, teeth for killing and tearing, and padded feet for stalking their prey. Their intestinal canals are only three times the length of their bodies, so that meat is quickly digested and waste products expelled—man's is twelve times the length of his body, and the average human digestion can handle not more than four ounces of meat at a time without some putrefaction, in addition to the putrefaction which has already taken place since the animal was slaughtered.

Flesh eating animals secrete hydrochloric acid about twelve times as strong as that of humans. According to Dr. Alec Burton: "Flesh eating animals have an enzyme called Uricase, which breaks down uric acid into allatoin. Man does not possess this enzyme. Vegetable proteins, including nuts, contain enough carbohydrates to make this enzyme unnecessary."

The carbohydrate content of nuts also prevents a process called de-amination. Since the carbohydrate content of flesh foods is negligible, conventional nutritionists advocate eating protein with a carbohydrate (an abominable combination), since it is thought that the presence of carbohydrates is necessary for the digestion of protein, and, when none are present, the liver will break down some of the amino acids and convert them to carbohydrates. If this is indeed true (and the experiments have not been conclusive), then it is obvious that the nuts supplied to us by Nature are completely packaged, along with their digestive requirements, while flesh foods are not. (See "Proteins In Your Diet" by Alec Burton.)

If you eat this second-hand, concentrated protein,

you derive the amino acids (the constituents or building blocks of protein) that were derived by the animal from the plant kingdom. When you eat the plant yourself, you receive the amino acids in ideal combinations with other indispensable substances which are essential to the full utilization of protein (minerals, vitamins, carbohydrates, enzymes, hormones, and chlorophyll, such as only plants can supply), and in a form readily and efficiently broken down by the human digestion.

Protein in its undigested form is a toxin, and proteins in flesh are more complex and difficult to break down into their constituent amino acids. First hand or plant protein has a higher biological value, and a smaller amount is required to supply needs.

Meats contain waste products that the animal would have eliminated, and toxins released into the bloodstream and tissues at the moment of death. Beef contains about fourteen grains of uric acid per pound. Putrefaction in meat eaters is evidenced by the foul stool and odorous emissions absent in frugarians and vegetarians.

Meats and fish that are smoked or pickled are even worse, as a result of the chemicals and added poisons. And all this without even considering the prevalence of diseased animals and the feeding of antibiotics and fat producing hormones. ("Why I Don't Eat Meat" by Dr. Owen S. Parrette, M.D.)

Many readers may have been surprised to see an extensive report on meat in the Wall Street Journal of October 25, 1973, indicating that meat contributes to the development of cancer and other potentially fatal diseases.

A more recent article, in the February 1975 Readers Digest, entitled "Do We Eat Too Much Meat?" condensed from Today's Health, published by the *American Medical Association,* seems to indicate that some members of the medical fraternity may be at last becoming aware of the dangerous impact of flesh foods on human health.

The sub-caption of the article reads as follows: "Americans are meat eaters by tradition. Yet statistics show that vegetarians in this country are thinner, in better health, with lower blood cholesterol, than their flesh-eating fellow citizens. They may even live longer."

Dr. Fredrick Stare, chairman of the department of nutrition at the Harvard School of Public Health, and Dr. Mervyn Hardinge, now dean of the Loma Linda, California School of Health, are mentioned in the article as having shown, by a study of serum cholesterol, that vegetarians have consistently lower levels of cholesterol.

The article goes on to say: "Meat eaters also may be bothered by poor elimination. Food with a low fiber content, such as meat, moves sluggishly through the digestive tract, making stools dry and hard to pass. Vegetables, by contrast, retain moisture and bind waste bulk for easy passage."

The article cites documentation of the excellent health and longevity enjoyed by the Hunzas of Pakistan and the Otomi Indians of Mexico, confirmed by field investigations of these non-meat cultures. Reference is made to the experiences of Denmark and Norway, where the general health of the people improved when vegetarian diets were adopted during World Wars I and II, including a significant reduction in heart disease. "Both nations, however, reverted to meat diets as soon as the crises passed, and subsequent studies showed that the temporary health advantages apparently subsided."

The closing paragraph of the article follows: "It may be helpful to remember that the word 'vegetarian' is derived from the Latin word 'vegetus' which means 'whole, sound, fresh, lively'. 'Vegetarianism is a humanitarian crusade', sums up Jay Dinshah, president of the North American Vegetarian Society. Perhaps it is. From a nutritional standpoint, it may not be a bad idea, either."

Earl Aronson, in the St. Petersburg Times, April

28, 1974, states: "People living in the Caucasus Mountain Range on the Eastern Shore of the Black Sea have one of the world's best longevity records, and Russians believe diet is the most important factor. They eat mostly vegetables. In that particular region of Southern Russia, there are an estimated 5,000 persons more than one hundred years old. The oldest is believed to be almost 170 years old. 70% of their caloric intake is of vegetable origin, and fresh green vegetables are a large part of every meal.

"Also cited as areas of longevity—with a high number of centenarians—are Vilacamba in the Ecuadorian Andes, South America and the Hunza Region of Pakistan. In those two areas, fresh vegetables are even more important. The report is that meat and dairy products constitute only 1.5% of the total diet in both regions. The rest comes mostly from vegetables."

It is interesting to note that the usual life span of animals is seven times their maturity age. Using this criterion, the average life span of man should be seven times twenty or 140 years.

When we speak of man in his pristine state as a vegetarian, many people protest that primitive man was a hunter. In the St. Petersburg Independent of June 21, 1974, in Perry Fulkerson's preview of the third episode of the "Primal Man" television series, subtitled "Struggle for Survival", he says that this episode shows how primal man left his lazy, vegetarian existence of the forest, and learned to survive in a hostile, barren world, watching the animals around him.

Note the following pertinent quotations from "Why I Don't Eat Meat" by Owen S. Parrette, M.D.:

"During the First World War in 1918, Denmark was blockaded by sea and land, and the nation was faced with a food shortage. To feed a cow, kill the cow and eat the meat meant a loss of 90% of the food fed the cow. Dr. Hindehede, a notable authority on nutrition, was called to the emergency by the King of Denmark. He put the nation on a meatless program for a year.

Many thought it would be disastrous. Instead, it established a world record for lowered death rate— around 34%. Eating meat the next year sent the death rate back to its prewar level."

"Some years ago a well-known Yale professor, Dr. Irving Fisher, showed that when vegetarian rookie athletes were pitted against the best athletes of Yale, the untrained men had more than twice the endurance of meat-eating athletes."

"Johnny Weismuller, the Tarzan of the movies and world swimming champion, who had made fifty-six world records, had made no new ones for five years. After several weeks on a well-selected vegetarian diet, he was able to hang up six more world records in the swimming pool."

"The swimmer, Murray Rose, of Australia, world champion and a winner in the Olympic games, has been a vegetarian since he was two years old. His ability to spurt ahead at the finish demonstrates that superior endurance accompanies a fleshless diet."

One of today's athletes, Bill Walton, former star center for the U.C.L.A. championship basketball teams (now with the Portland Trailblazers of the National Basketball Association) maintains his optimal degree of health through vegetarianism.

Athletic prowess maintained by flesh-eaters is often accompanied by other types of stimulation (followed by early aging).

One of the favorite arguments of flesh eaters is that proteins from the plant kingdom are "incomplete", because no one plant food contains all of the 23 identifiable amino acids. Studies of man's physiology, and the effects of his consumption of foods from the plant kingdom, show that it is not necessary to consume all of the amino acids at one sitting, not even the eight "essential" amino acids that are not fabricated within the body. (See list in Chapter XVIII)

The foods we eat are processed by the organism, and the amino acids, vitamins, minerals and other nutrients are reserved in a pool for later use as needed. When we eat, we replenish the reserves in this circulating pool, to be drawn upon by the cell as required. We do not live upon one protein food, but upon the protein content of our varied diet, which supplies all the portein needs of the body.

Nuts are subject to few contaminating influences; they supply everything that we can get from flesh foods, in better form, better condition, cleaner, more easily used, and without the risk of eating diseased flesh.

(See end of "Menus" section for Chart of Hygienic foods containing the essential amino acids, so that you may be convinced that the Hygienic diet adequately supplies them all, as well as all the other amino acids not classified as "essential", since these will almost inevitably be included in these same foods.)

Also see "Special Menus—Hygienic Meals Containing All Essential Amino Acids"—to accommodate those who are not yet ready to subscribe to the "Circulating Pool" hypothesis. However, as they progress in Natural Hygiene, they will discover the validity of the "Circulating Pool" theory, and will abandon this unnecessary preocupation with amino acids.

Nowhere in Nature is there any evidence of the necessity for such complicated maneuvering (striving to include all the amino acids at each meal) to obtain optimal nutrition, and the superior health and longevity of vegetarian peoples are well documented. If your over-all diet consists of a variety of fruits, vegetables and nuts, you will be getting all the nutrients you need, and all the amino acids.

5. *High Protein Diet*

The tremendous amount of protein frequently recommended—75 to 100 grams daily (or more)—is far in excess of the body's needs, and the source of much trouble. The whole system becomes overcharged with poisonous products of protein metabolism, which are not eliminated, commonly resulting in gout, arthritis, and other degenerative diseases.

About 28 grams of protein equals one ounce: most nuts contain around 17% to 25% protein, some higher, some lower. No food is pure protein. Around 25 to 30 grams of protein daily has been found to be adequate if derived from raw unprocessed food. This amount of protein can be secured from eating four ounces of nuts daily along with small amounts of plant proteins, which are of high biological value, obtained from raw whole fruits and large green salads.

The use of whole grains, occasionally, supplies some supplementary protein. But a total of 20% concentrated protein in the diet (the amount commonly used) is far too much, and even 10% is in excess of the body's needs and ability to process. In abnormal conditions, as after a prolonged fast, or during lactation or pregnancy, a greater supply of amino acids may be indicated, necessitating an increase in the protein intake, *if not in excess of the digestive capabilities of the body.* Immediately after a prolonged fast, the body cannot handle a large quantity of protein foods. Concentrated protein foods are more difficult to digest than most other foods, and must be consumed within individual capacities, rather than according to charts. Protein is the most complex of all the food elements, and its breakdown and ultilization is the most complicated.

Dr. Robert R. Gross, Ph. D., in Natural Hygienews, May, 1974, says that the well-known Stillman high-protein diet, originated by Irwin M. Stillman, M.D., "is based on the specific dynamic action of foodstuffs. Protein, as opposed to carbohydrates and fat, is a dynamic action complicated foodstuff, requiring the use of much more body energy and loss of its innate calories for digestion and metabolism. . . . Therefore many people will lose weight initially on such a diet. The hitch is that the end-products of protein digestion are acidic—urea, uric acid, adenine, etc. . . .which beyond a certain normal range cause degeneration of body tissues, producing gout, liver malfunctions, kidney disorders, digestive disturbances, arthritis and even hallucinations. Each individual has his own threshold of ability to cope with these toxic materials."

Some of the symptoms of protein poisoning are burning of the mouth, lips and throat; skin disorders; nasal disorders; "allergies" (manifestations of intolerance for certain foods or substances); excessive fatigue; kidney disorders; hyperacidity; headaches and body aches. (See my booklet "The Happy Truth About Protein" for a more detailed discussion of Protein Poisoning and Allergies.) These symptoms will vary from one individual to another, and develop when the cells seek to establish their defensive action against undigested proteins, in order to sweep them out of the body.

Dr. Alec Burton, Australian Hygienic Practitioner, is of the opinion that, since an adequate amount of protein is necessary, a protein intake 50% to 100% in excess of adequate (around 40 or 50 grams) would be less damaging than an inadequate amount *over a prolonged period of time*. But the 75 to 100 grams daily (or more) high protein diet is beyond anyone's needs or capacity to process without toxicity.

If you are eating plenty of raw food plus four ounces of nuts and/or seeds daily, you can forget about protein, because your needs will be met adequately. Otherwise, you may need to know that some of the symptoms of protein deficiency are dizziness, lightheadedness and lack of energy (similar to the symptoms of Hypoglycemia—low blood sugar).

Dr. D. J. Scott, states: "Too much protein acidifies (like coffee) and has the same stimulating effect, and a high protein diet will eventually destroy the glandular system, and damage the liver, adrenals and kidneys. Some extra protein is required for the following special needs: (5 ounces of nuts daily instead of four ounces)

    1. Growth
    2. Reproduction

  3. Lactation
  4. Recovery from Debilitating Disease
  5. After a Fast
  6. Weight Training

Many people who think they need extra protein are toxic instead, and have already had too much protein."

An interesting sidelight on the high protein diet, which may help to pinpoint some of its ominous implications: In the St. Petersburg Independent, May 29, 1974, Dr. E. L. Cole, Jr., M.D. answered a question about keeping a baby from getting fat by using a high protein, low carbohydrate diet. He said that such a diet in an infant who is supposed to be growing at a relatively rapid rate, might be equivalent to slow starvation and cause irreversible harm to the child. (See my booklet, "The Happy Truth About Protein.")

6. *Cooked Foods*

To the extent that we cut, cook, season and flavor foods, they are changed to substances with reduced potential value to the cell. Foods which can only be eaten after being softened, changed and seasoned, are the poorest foods. Deleterious changes occur in cooking: all of the enzymes are destroyed, plus many of the vitamins and minerals; amino acids are changed or destroyed and proteins are coagulated. Cooking alters fats and they become less digestible, sometimes toxic. Organic substances are converted to inorganic and the balance of Nature is changed.

Raw foods (without flavorings, seasonings, sauces or dressings) cannot be disguised if wilted or spoiled.

When you eat raw food, there is a several hundred percent gain in the available nutrients, because cooking has not destroyed them, and you therefore require less food.

Quick-cooked vegetables lose smaller amounts of their vitamins and minerals, and should be eaten soon after cooking. Starches should be steamed just long enough to become tender and palatable and slightly dextrinized.

If you use cooked food at all, use it no more than once a day, always with a large salad, and comprising no more than 10% of your diet.

Try for more and more days on all raw foods.

7. *Vitamin Pills or Food Supplements*

Vitamin Pills or Food Supplements should not be used. Missing elements in food cannot be replaced by a dried and crystallized tablet, even if it were possible to determine "adequate" amounts. And the potential damage and artificial deficiencies that may thus be created are considerable. Just as an excess of nitrogen in the plant will create artificial deficiencies of other elements and prevent fruiting, so stimulation to the human organism produced by supplementation will disturb the balance of Nature.

This is the "Law of the Minimum": The development of living beings is regulated by the supply of whichever element is least bountifully provided. (Long known in plant life) Using supplements, by creating an over-abundance of some elements, creates an artificial shortage of other elements, known and unknown, and the element in shortest supply determines our development. The ideal is to provide the organism with all the essential factors, but no surfeit of any of them.

E. L. Cole, Jr., M.D., in his column in the St. Petersburg Independent, 11/25/74, states: "Two research physicians, Dr. Elizabeth Jacobs and Dr. Victor Herbert of a New York Medical Center, report in the current issue of the Journal of the American Medical Association, a new finding regarding the taking of Vitamin C. Large doses of Vitamin C destroy much of the Vitamin B-12 we get in our diet. Their interest in the subject was stimulated when it was found that four paraplegic veterans receiving large doses of Vitamin C —ascorbic acid—for treatment of chronic urinary infections—had low serum (blood) levels of Vitamin B-12."

Quoting from another of Dr. Cole's articles in the St. Petersburg Independent 5/26/75: "Dr. I. J. Wilk of the University of the Pacific in San Francisco has just issued a warning concerning the use of large doses of Vitamin C. . . . Vitamin C tablets break down when stored at room temperature and to a lesser degree when refrigerated . . . a degradation of up to 46% in those refrigerated. One of the first products that occurs when Vitamin C deteriorates is oxalic acid . . . which retains Vitamin C qualities . . . oxalic acid has been implicated in triggering diabetes.

"In the second step of the Vitamin C breakdown, apparently sugars are formed which are undesirable for the diabetic. Oxalic acid has been known to cause urinary infections and may accelerate a buildup of kidney stones."

A very fine dentist and his wife, who are staunch advocates of "natural" supplementation, told me that they know the supplements are beneficial and necessary, because "if they don't take their supplements, they just drag around." What better proof could there be of the stimulating effect and addictive nature of supplementation? Of course, when you use any type of stimulation, you are, in effect, "whipping the tired horse". Vitamins are acids and irritants which stimulate and whip the body into a temporary increase of activity. A Hygienist can skip meals, or eat fruit only for several days, or eat his regular diet of fruit, vegetables and nuts, and continue to be his vital, sparkling, indomitable self, with no "crutches" and no pills.

Manufactured concentrates are sold by commercial interests, who are determined, at all costs, to maintain the position that substitute and compensatory substances can provide superior nutrition. These substances are unnecessary, expensive, stimulating, addictive, create artificial deficiencies, are not usable by the cells of the body, and burden the elimination system with their excretion.

Dr. Alec Burton, at the July 1968 Hygiene Health Conference, commented: "When taken over long periods, vitamins produce pathological changes."

The richest sources of vitamins and minerals (including trace minerals) are in the living food: fruits, vegetables and nuts (including seeds), eaten raw, and it is here that they are found in ideal combinations with other substances (known and unknown) essential to their full utilization. If you cannot grow or secure organically grown foods (please keep trying), get the best quality obtainable, and eat the fresh, whole, raw foods—there is no better way! When you eat a variety of whole raw foods, in accordance with Hygienic principles, you need not be concerned about vitamins or minerals or amino acids or anything else—everything will be adequately supplied.

As an example, consider the sunflower seed—a superior source of Vitamin D, richer in B complex than an equivalent amount of wheat germ, and containing liberal amounts of Vitamins E and K, calcium, phosphorus, sillicon, magnesium, fluorine, lecithin and trace minerals, along with large amounts of high grade proteins, all in ideal association for proper utilization. At the July, 1970 Hygiene Health Conference, Dr. Alec Burton said that in the average Natural Hygienic diet, we take five to twenty times as much Vitamin B as we need (in the food we eat). With Vitamins A, B, and C and the other vitamins (known and unknown) abundantly provided by raw fruits and vegetables, along with a plethora of all kinds of minerals, enzymes, chlorophyll and carbohydrates, and the large amounts of oils and proteins in avocadoes and nuts and seeds, what remains to be desired?

If you make no other changes, give up the supplements and eat more raw fruits and vegetables; this will actually supply the nutrients you are seeking from the pills. Be prepared to experience withdrawal symptoms, if you have been saturating your bloodstream with these concentrates and their consequential by-products, but I hope you will abandon them before pathological changes have taken place.

8. *Juices and Elimination Diets*

Foods should not be juiced, but should be eaten in their whole state. Some exceptions may be made. Four ounces of vegetable juice may occasionally be taken twenty to thirty minutes before the evening meal at which a salad and some cooked food are eaten. If carrot juice is consumed in large quantities, it may color the skin and cause carotinemia—the liver cannot handle it. Fruit juice may occasionally be used prior to a fruit meal, preferably freshly made at home.

The habitual use of copious quantities of canned, frozen, or even freshly squeezed orange or other citrus juices is an injurious practice, as that results in over-consumption of this fruit acid, which may cause canker sores, skin symptoms, and other "allergic" reactions. Many authorities believe that these problems are triggered when acid fruits are consumed beyond the body's ability to convert the fruit acids to an alkaline ash. Habitual consumption of large quantities of citrus juices or fruits may also cause erosion of the dental enamel, and, for this reason, Dr. William L. Esser recommends rinsing the mouth after eating citrus fruit.

I have been unable to find substantiation for J. I. Rodale's theory that the oil from the citrus rind, some of which inevitably enters most citrus juice, may be harmful. However, the bitter taste seems to be a sufficient warning against it, and I never bite into the rind, preferring to use a knife to start peeling my orange. (Of course, "candied" orange peel is an atrocity.)

Juices are, of course, used in breaking a fast, and may perhaps be the only food taken for several days after a prolonged fast. Fasts can also be broken on solid foods. For more than a year now, Dr. Vetrano has been successfully breaking fasts on solid foods, and reports much better results; bowel movements commence normally sooner, and there are fewer digestive problems. Decisions on just how to break a prolonged fast should be made by the Professional Hygienist.

Juices are also useful when urgent symptoms require the temporary cessation of food intake, and it is not possible to go to bed and fast. However, the substitution of a long-term juice diet when a fast is indicated may be unwise and wasteful of the body's energy, because this does not accomplish the striking long-term benefits of the fast with nothing but water. However, a juice diet may be indicated in some cases, and only the Professional Hygienist should make this decision.

This also applies to the so-called "fruit fasts", which are, of course, not fasts, but elimination diets. Elimination diets are diets low in proteins, carbohydrates and fats, which cause the cells to use the stored reserves and to eliminate toxins and waste matter (but to a lesser degree than while fasting).

Going on a monotrophic fruit diet (one kind of fruit at a meal) for a day or two or three sometimes serves a useful purpose, when the individual cannot go to bed and fast, and some immediate action is necessary to relieve urgent symptoms; or, a lengthy monotrophic fruit diet may also be used as an elimination diet; or, vegetable broth, uncooked or cooked, may sometimes be used in elimination diets.

Another type of elimination diet is sometimes recommended by Professional Hygienists to patients, to be used in preparation for a fast, or even instead of a fast for certain individuals. These are rather Spartan fruit and vegetable diets, and usually also include small amounts of nuts. There are advantages and disadvantages to elimination diets. Consult a Professional Hygienist before deciding.

9. *Water*

Drink no beverages except pure water, only when thirsty, and not with meals, as drinking at meal time dilutes the digestive juices and retards digestion. Most of the beverages commonly consumed are loaded with poisons, and a threat to your health. Caffeine-containing beverages such as coffee, tea and cola drinks are addictive and can be destructive of vital organs.

"Caffeine-free" coffee can be even worse, because of the poisonous chemicals used in extracting the caffeine. All "soft drinks" are loaded with sugar or chemical sugar-substitutes, and numerous poisonous additives.

The least harmful "beverages" are some of the milder "herb teas" but they are unnecessary and do not contribute to your nutrition and health. (See No. 8—Juices)

No particular amount of water is necessary: thirst is your best guide. Hygienists usually drink very little water, because no spices or seasonings are used, and there is so much liquid in foods as provided by Nature. If thirsty, you may drink ten to twenty minutes before meals, one-half hour after a fruit meal, two hours after a vegetable or starch meal and four hours after a protein meal. Sip, don't gulp. If you ignore the feeling of thirst that sometimes follows a meal, it will be satisfied with digestive secretions and accomplish good digestion. If you feel very thirsty, and *must* drink, try a few sips, instead of gulping large quantities of water.

Drinking water should be as pure as possible. Avoid chlorinated city water, if you can, or boil to evaporate the chlorine. However, boiling the water causes a concentration of other poisonous minerals. Don't drink fluoridated water; do whatever you must to avoid it. Using fluoridated water in cooking is even worse, as it concentrates the florides (rat poison). Osteoporosis can occur from drinking fluoridated water. Sodium fluoride will also inactivate magnesium and some amino acids, and inhibit enzyme activity.

I have a wealth of quotable material on anti-fluoridation, and had decided not to belabor this point by using any of it, leaving that to another time and place. But an article from the Indianapolis News of May 2, 1970, by Ralph de Toledano, is irresistible, and I quote from it:

"Some of my readers will want to wash out my typewriter with soap, but here I am agreeing with Ralph Nader. . . . It must have taken considerable courage on his part to take on the fluoridation lobby. . . . His was not the strongest statement on the subject, but coming from Ralph Nader, it showed that more and more Americans are beginning to realize that compulsory fluoridation of the water supply has been the biggest put-on since they stopped selling gold bricks. Looking back, the gold brick salesman wasn't too bad a character. He took a few people, but he wasn't acting the way the American Dental Association and the American Medical Association have been doing. They calmly admit that they have no independent research on fluoridation, then try to stampede the country into going ahead with it. . . . There is much more that Nader might have said about fluoridation, including an explanation of his failure to raise his voice as loudly over this insidious poisoning of the nation's water supply as he has over less serious matters. He might have noted the pressure tactics of the Public Health Service and the American Dental Association —and their opposition to experts who have attempted to speak up, on the basis of sound research, against a practice that was begun before all the facts were in. . . . Perhaps compulsory fluoridation will not get the public scrutiny it warrants until the fed-up 'silent majority' announces that it will not pay municipal taxes unless that pernicious practice ceases."

Minerals in water inhibit the absorption of the water. The minerals are inorganic substances and must be eliminated by the body. These inorganic minerals are usable only by the plant, which converts them to organic minerals, making them usable by man. Pure water from a rock spring is excellent; fresh rain water (if it could be gathered unpolluted) and distilled water are best. Never drink artificially softened water, in which the miscellaneous inorganic minerals have been replaced by salt.

10. Digestion Time and Food Time Table

Digestion Time:	Fruit and Vegetable Juices	15 to 30 minutes
	Whole Fruit	1½ to 2 hours
	Vegetables & Concentrated Starches	2½ to 3½ hours
	Concentrated Proteins	3½, 4½ or even 5 hours

Food Time Table: It is better not to eat around bedtime, but exceptions may be made, if this is not an extra meal, but one that you couldn't schedule any other time, or because of a party. It is better to go to bed with the stomach empty, so that your whole body may be at rest. A late evening fruit meal, having the shortest digestion time, is better than a protein or starch meal at this time. The ideal Hygienic Food Time Table is No Breakfast, a Fruit Lunch, and Supper in the early evening after the day's work is done and you may relax while the meal is digesting and retire for the night after the meal is digested, or almost completely so.

Please be warned against fad diets, reducing diets, liquid diets, supplementation diets, high protein diets, low calorie diets, macrobiotic diets, complicated "vegetarian" diets imitating meat diets, and who knows how many others, usually based on anything except a knowledge of human physiology. Even the exponents of these diets, themselves, frequently warn against using them for long periods of time.

Why not reach a higher plateau of vibrant health by partaking of Nature's offerings and ignoring the hucksters?

Author's recommendation: Read Volume II (Orthotrophy) of the Hygienic System, by Dr. Herbert M. Shelton, a 591 page hard cover book on Food. I have

said that if I have to part with all my books but one,
this is the one I would choose to keep.

VIII. The Changeover

1. *Getting It Together*

We should avoid overemphasizing food, because a
Hygienic diet by itself will not achieve optimal benefits.
Natural Hygiene is not a system of diet, but a total
way of life. But it is also true that food selection is a
critical area, and the one subjected to the greatest
abuses, due to indifference or misinformation.

We can avoid over-preoccupation with health and
with food by developing patterns of living and eating,
in accordance with our own needs and limitations,
which will produce positive results almost automatically.

Realizing only too well the initial impact of a line
of thought that calls for a revolutionary change in
habits, and with the confusion and bewilderment
engendered by "Nutritionists" and diet exponents on
all sides, it is recommended that the neophyte first investigate Natural Hygiene to satisfy himself as to its
validity and credibility, by reading, and by association
with members of local chapters of the American
Natural Hygiene Society, in person or by mail. He will
find that Hygienists have no vitamins or "cures" to sell,
that they welcome the opportunity to help. He may
then find himself willing or even anxious to learn more
about this unusual and rewarding way of life by living it.

Consider this observation of the Roman sage, Seneca:

"There is nothing against which we ought to be
more on our guard than, like a flock of sheep, following
the crowd of those who have preceded us, going, as we
do, not where we ought to go, but where men have

walked before. We live, not according to reason, but according to mere fashion and tradition. . . . Let us ask what is best, not what is most customary."

Some compromises may be made with total adherence to Natural Laws. Occasional exceptions can be dealt with by a healthy body. It is what we do daily, habitually, that will determine what benefits we achieve.

But here is the other side of that coin, worthy of your serious consideration, as you progress in Natural Hygiene.

Occasional exceptions may become more and more frequent, ultimately becoming habitual. And you are faced with the necessity of making so many decisions! If you eliminate the exceptions, you eliminate the necessity for making countless difficult and frustrating choices. Shall I do it this time? When did I do it last? How often is occasional? If you follow the rule of not even one, life is really easier.

But the choice is still your own, and many Hygienists make exceptions now and then, with full realization of what they are doing, and are able to keep the situation under excellent control.

However, this applies only in relationship to the health of the individual. Physiological limitations and pathological conditions may make indulgences and exceptions inadvisable and even dangerous.

Changes for improved health may be made at one's own pace. Each one must decide what he wants to accomplish. What he gains will be in direct proportion to what he invests—and the more information he acquires, the better his chances.

If you want to make changes along Hygienic lines, and make improvements as you go along (many Hygienists have taken this path, though it is long and circuitous), you will note improvement to the extent you discontinue devitalizing practices and replace them with more Natural living. The best time to start making these changes is before you are 25 years old. The second best time is right now.

To quote from an ancient Moslem prayer: "For yesterday is gone, and tomorrow is only a vision. But today well lived makes of every yesterday a dream of happiness and every tomorrow a vision of hope."

2. *Head Start*

A head start is to eliminate entirely the worst of these basic causes of ill health:

   a. Overeating
   b. Smoking
      The heavy smoker may find a short fast or elimination diet a good tool to get "over the hump"; —See Chapter VII, Section 8 and this Chapter VIII, Section 8.
   c. Drugs
      Your Professional Hygienist will advise you as to how to eliminate prescription drugs.
   d. Alcoholic Beverages

3. *Opening The Door*

Next, consider the following additional Un-Hygienic practices and how far you are willing to go to correct them:

   a. Wrong foods and combinations of foods
   b. Stimulating beverages, hot and cold
   c. Food Supplements (Vitamins) See Chapter VII, Section 7
   d. Lack of sufficient exercise
   e. Neglect of other basic needs, such as fresh air, pure water, sunshine, sufficient sleep and rest, emotional poise, rewarding activity, recreation

4. *What Do You Want to Accomplish?*

Remember, if we expect a significant difference, we must make a significant change. Once we are convinced of the truth and value of Natural Hygiene, what is there to gain by "cutting off the dog's tail an inch at a time"?

5. *Changes At Your Own Pace*

The following "Starter" program is suggested (along with the elimination of smoking, drugs and alcohol):

a. Less food—try to eliminate snacking—try to eliminate beverages other than pure water.

b. An increasing percentage of your diet should be raw fruits, vegetables, and nuts and seeds.

c. Try to eliminate "cheat" foods from your diet as much as you can, particularly products containing white flour and sugar, salt and condiments.

d. Learn about and practice proper Food Combining. *This is important.* Instances have been noted where much improvement was obtained through Food Combining only, without a radical change in diet.

e. Get sufficient rest, sleep, recreation.

f. Enjoy sunshine on all or most of your body regularly, but not to excess (See Chapter III).

g. Breathe fresh air by day and by night.

h. Get regular exercise.

i. Cultivate emotional stability.

j. Engage in rewarding activity.

6. *What to Expect* (Withdrawal Symptoms)

If you make the recommended basic changes in your eating and living habits, particularly the use of higher quality foods and the elimination of toxic substances, you might experience a period of withdrawal symptoms while your body is "cleaning house", and a feeling of less energy, due to the redeployment of your forces and power for the rebuilding of vital organs.

In "What Symptoms to Expect When You Improve Your Diet", Stanley S. Bass, D.C., says in the January, 1973 issue of the Hygienic Review: "The amazing intelligence of the body and this Rule of Nature becomes manifest: When the quality of the food coming into the body is of higher quality than the body tissues, the body discards the lower-grade materials to make room for the superior materials which it uses to make new and healthier tissue. The cellular intelligence is saying, 'Look at all these fine materials coming in. Let's get rid of the old garbage and build a beautiful new house.' It is important at this time for the person to rest and sleep more during this crucial phase, not to resort to stimulants of any kind, and have patience and faith and just wait it out."

You must also realize that nutritional adaptations occur when changing from a conventional diet to a Hygienic diet, and there may be impairment of digestive efficiency for a period of time. For this reason, the new diet should be introduced carefully: the best way is to abandon the old diet and then eat small quantities, and very simple meals, during the transition period.

[For further ref. see "Food Combining Made Easy" by Dr. H. M. Shelton, also Vol. II, "The Hygienic System".]

As the body becomes cleaner, self-discipline becomes easier, and you have fewer reactions, until you reach a level plateau of vibrant health.

7. *Going Forward*

The biggest and most meaningful step towards adopting the Hygienic way of living is mental. Once that door is opened and we realize that we have been the victims of our own bad habits, misinformation and/or indifference, the vista that appears before us may be almost overwhelming in its magnitude. But it is then that we might decide to do whatever is necessary to achieve for ourselves a better, healthier, lengthier future.

8. *The First Short Fasts*

If you are one of these determined individuals, you may decide to start with a fast. If you are not on prescription drugs, and have no established serious disease, short fasts without supervision may be undertaken. It cannot be emphasized too strongly that prolonged fasts should not be undertaken without supervision. Certain developments and changes during the fast must be assessed, and the blood pressure, blood sugar level and nitrogen balance must be observed. The Professional must also determine whether adequate water is being taken.

Another word of caution: Short fasts, *taken at too frequent intervals,* produce enervation and exhaustion, and create nutritional deficiencies. Serious problems cannot be corrected in this manner.

How frequently should one fast? Some individuals fast 36 hours every week. Some fast 36 hours at intermittent intervals, when indicated or convenient, one to four times monthly. Three day fasts should be spaced farther apart, depending on individual programs and needs, about every 60 to 90 days, if desired. Seven to fourteen day fasts may be undertaken twice a year, but the first such fasts should be supervised. Generally, fasts of about 30 days or longer should not be taken more than once annually. However, there may be exceptions; the Hygienic doctor may advise another long fast without waiting for a year to elapse.

Under some conditions, short fasting periods are always indicated, as:

a. When you feel ill, go to bed and don't eat until you feel better. Take no food where there is fever or diarrhea, or in the acute stages of a cold.

b. When you have eaten some food or a meal that disagrees with you, skip the next meal or meals until you return to normal.

c. Do not eat when tired, or under stress or emotional strain.

If you do contemplate a short fast on your own for perhaps three days or so, it would be well to first read "Fasting Can Save Your Life" and/or "Fasting for Renewal of Life" (both by Dr. Herbert M. Shelton), and/or my book "Your First Fast—What To Expect."

Then plan ahead for it, so you may withdraw from

your normal activities and take a complete rest. If you have not been on a Hygienic diet for at least two or three months prior to the fasting period, it might be wise to go on a monotrophic fruit diet (one fruit at a meal) or a juice (freshly squeezed orange juice is good) (See Chapter VII, Section 8) for a day or so before the fast. Following such a procedure reduces the possibility and/or intensity of any withdrawal symptoms.

A plentiful supply of oxygen is particularly important during a fast because oxidation is increased. The first fasts may produce headaches or other symptoms, and a small percentage of people may experience some vomiting. The body is simply trying to release poisons. Various drugs taken in the past are tasted in the mouth during a fast.

Drink when thirsty; sip, don't gulp; take small quantities at a time. It is necessary to take some water to avoid dehydration, but it is not necessary or advisable to use large quantities of water, which may overwork the kidneys and actually interfere with the elimination of toxic material.

Breaking the fast initiates processes of digestion that have been resting for varying periods of time, and changes in physiology must take place to accommodate to the new situation. Consequently, breaking the fast must be done very carefully.

After a three day fast, you should go on freshly squeezed orange juice for one day. (Eight ounces of juice every three hours—room temperature.) Longer fasts would require even more careful and gradual return to eating, and, for the neophyte, should only be undertaken under competent supervision.

If you do not decide on a three day fast, skipping a meal or two, or fasting 24 to 36 hours will help.

If you are afflicted with a serious pathological condition, Natural Hygiene offers you the only rational approach to its improvement, and the only real hope for recovery. I hope this book will inspire you to seek the help of a Professional Hygienist.

IX. Classification of Foods

Proteins

—Nuts—	—Seeds—
	Sunflower Seeds
Pecans	Sesame Seeds
Almonds	Pumpkin and Squash Seeds
Brazil Nuts	
Filberts or Hazelnuts	
English Walnuts, Butternuts, Heart Nuts	
Black Walnuts	
Macadamias	
Pistachios	
Pignolias (Pine Nuts)	
Indian Nuts	
Beechnuts	
Hickory Nuts	
Cashews (not really a nut, but classified as a nut)	

—Other Plant Proteins—	—Animal Proteins—
Soy Beans	Cheese (raw milk or unprocessed)
Olives	Eggs (not recommended)
	All Flesh Foods (except fat) (not recommended)

—Low Protein—	—Starchy Proteins—* (Combine as Starch)
Avocado (may also be classified as a neutral fruit)	(See Chapter X—Food Combining)
Milk (not recommended)	Dry Beans
	Dry Peas
	Lentils
	Peanuts
	Chestnuts
	Coconuts

—Green Vegetable Proteins—* (Combine as Starch)	—Sprouts— (High in Protein, especially in early stages)
Peas in the Pod	Soy Sprouts
Lima and other Beans in the Pod	Mung Bean Sprouts
Mature Green Beans in the Pod	Alfalfa Sprouts (may be combined as green vegetable)
	All Seed & Bean Sprouts
	(See Chapter XV, Sprouting)

*Classified as Starches for Purposes of Food Combining

Starches

—Starchy Proteins—
(Classified as Starches for Purposes of Food Combining)

Peanuts	Dry Beans	Peas in the Pod
Chestnuts	Dry Peas	Lima and other Beans in the Pod
Coconuts	Lentils	Mature Green Beans in the Pod

Wild Rice

Brown Rice
Buckwheat Groats
Millet
Oats
Wheat } All Grains,
Rye } Foods Containing Grains, and
Barley } Sprouted Grains

Sprouted Grains

—Starchy Vegetables—

White Potatoes
Yams and Sweet Potatoes
Winter Squash (Acorn, Butternut, Hubbard, etc.)
Pumpkin
Jerusalem Artichokes

—Mildly Starchy Vegetables—

Globe Artichokes
Cauliflower
Beets
Carrots
Rutabaga
Salsify (Oyster Plant)
Parsnips
Corn (Green Vegetable Until Two Hours After Picking, Then Starchy)
Water Chestnuts

Non-Starchy and Green Vegetables

Lettuce	Dandelion Greens
Celery	Turnip Tops
Cabbage (young, sweet)	Mustard Greens
Celery Cabbage	Okra
Cucumber	Kohlrabi
Snow Peas	Turnips
Escarole (if not bitter)	Eggplant
Endive (if not bitter)	Green Corn (if not mature, and if eaten less than 2 hrs. after picking)
Sweet Pepper	Green Beans (young & tender)
Broccoli	
Rappini (similar to broccoli)	Zucchini } and all other
Brussels Sprouts	Yellow Crookneck Squash } Summer
Kale	Chayote } Squash
Collard Greens	

Spinach
Swiss Chard } Use seldom if at all—too high in oxalic acid
Beet Tops } (a calcium antagonist)
Rhubarb

Parsley
Watercress
Chives
Scallions } Irritant foods (unless very young and sweet)—should not
Onions } be used often or in large quantities
Leeks
Radishes
Garlic

Fats

Butter
Cream

Olive Oil
Sesame Oil } All Oils (Use unrefined Cold Pressed Oils, preferably
Sunflower Seed Oil } stable oils like olive and sesame oil, less
Corn Oil } likely to be rancid)
Peanut Oil } (Oils are fragmented, concentrated foods,
Cotton Seed Oil } and are best omitted)
Safflower Oil

Nuts and Avocados (Proteins) may also be included in this classification, since they are high in fat content.

All Meat Fats (not recommended)

Butter Substitutes (not recommended)—Oleomargarine and the hard white hydrogenated "vegetable" shortenings commonly used in frying and baking are particularly pernicious substances, which the body is not equipped to handle.

(Fats delay digestion—may take up to four to six hours. The need for fat is small, and the best sources are whole foods like nuts and avocados.)

Sweet Fruits

Bananas
Persimmons
Thompson Grapes (Seedless)
Muscat Grapes
All Sweet Grapes
Carob

Dried Fruits: Dates
Figs
Raisins
Prunes
Apricots
Peaches
Apples
Cherries
Bananas
Litchi "Nuts"
All Dried Fruit

Some unusual or tropical fruits not listed—
Sweet taste is a good indication of its classification.

Subacid Fruits

Sweet Apples (Delicious)   Fresh Figs
Sweet Peaches   Fresh Litchi "Nuts"
Sweet Nectarines   Sweet Plums
Pears   Blueberries
Sweet Cherries   Raspberries
Papayas   Blackberries
Mangos   Mulberries
Apricots   Huckleberries
                            Cherimoyas
                            Some Grapes (neither sweet nor sour)

Some unusual or tropical fruits not listed

Acid Fruits

Oranges   Kumquats   Limes
Grapefruit   Loquats   Sour Apples
Pineapples   Carambolas   Sour Grapes
Strawberries   Loganberries   Sour Peaches
Pomegranates   Gooseberries   Sour Nectarines
Lemons   Cranberries (not Sour Plums
                   recommended)   Sour Cherries

Tomatoes—Acid fruit, without the sugar content of other acid fruits.
    Used with vegetable salad or any green or nonstarchy vegetables, but
    not at a starch meal. May be used with nuts or cheese, but not with
    meat, milk, or eggs.

Some unusual or tropical fruits not listed—
Acid (or Sour) taste is a good indication of its classification.

Melons

Watermelon   Crenshaw Melon
Honeydew Melon   Pie Melon
Honey Balls   Banana Melon
Cantaloupe   Persian Melon
Muskmelon   Christmas Melon
Casaba Melon   Nutmeg Melon

Syrups and Sugars

Brown Sugar ⎫
"Raw" Sugar
White Sugar
Milk Sugar
Maple Syrup ⎬ None of these substances are recommended.
Cane Syrup
Corn Syrup
Honey   ⎭

X. Food Combining—Rationale, Rules, Charts

Food Combining is as important as the selection of your food, perhaps more so. Even if you do not change to a Hygienic diet, adherence to the rules of Food Combining will often result in noticeable improvement in health and remission of digestive problems.

The usual "Russian Roulette" eating patterns do not take into account the physiological limitations of man's digestive system. If you have no discomfort after this type of eating, that is no criterion as to whether the food is being properly utilized, or whether future problems are being incubated.

There is scientific evidence for food combining, and its value is easily demonstrated by a study of the action of enzymes and digestive juices. An enzyme is a rather complicated protein molecule, which initiates or speeds up chemical reaction by catalytic action without itself being used up in the process. The digestive glands supply different enzymes and juices, of varying strength and character, and with careful timing, depending on the different foods ingested. The digestive juices may be more or less liquid, of different degrees of acidity or alkalinity, with complex and elaborately contrived variations. No computer could ever be programmed as efficiently.

Chewing and tasting the food sends the proper signals for the adaptation of the digestive juices to the character of the food. The glands react to the foods eaten to the best of their ability; they interpret the signals they receive and supply the best secretions they can muster to preserve health and the integrity of the organism, until a saturation point is reached. When foods are eaten in incompatible combinations and fermentation occurs, alcohol is produced in the digestive tract, with the same consequences as imbibing it, and with the same potential for liver damage.

A good example is the rule against combining proteins with starches, or acids with starches. Starch digestion starts in the mouth, with the action of the enzyme ptyalin, in a neutral or alkaline medium. Even a very mild acid will inhibit, halt, or destroy the ptyalin, resulting in impairment of starch digestion, and, consequently, fermentation. The starch must then be digested in the duodenum and the digestion will probably not be completed.

So the first food combining rule is:

1. Do Not Combine Starch With Acid.

Since proteins must be digested in an acid medium, HCL (hydrochloric acid), to activate pepsinogen, is secreted when protein is eaten; this immediately stops the digestion of starch. So the second rule is:

2. Do not Combine Protein With Starch.

Some foods contain both protein and starch, but when they are eaten as grown by Nature, we find that the body is capable of handling them, providing the right amounts of acid at the proper times during digestion.

There is some protein, however little, in every living thing—in all foods—but when we refer to protein in food combining, we mean *concentrated* proteins like nuts, cheese, eggs, or flesh foods—if you use them.

Sweet fruits, such as bananas, persimmons, etc., and dried fruits (like dates, figs, raisins, etc.) are extremely high in sugars, which should be out of the stomach in one-half hour to an hour, but if delayed by combining with foods that have a long digestion time, will ferment. Therefore, the third rule is:

3. Do Not Combine Sweet Fruits With Protein.

4. Two Concentrated Proteins Of Different Characters And Compositions Should Not Be Eaten At The

Same Meal, as the gastric acidity produced for different proteins is not uniform.

Since concentrated protein is more difficult to digest than other food elements, incompatable combinations of two different concentrated proteins should be avoided.

For example, you may combine two or three varieties of nuts and/or seeds, if you wish. But don't combine nuts with cheese or legumes (or nuts or cheese with flesh foods).

5. Do Not Combine Sweet Fruits With Acid Fruits. The digestion of the sweet fruits will be delayed and fermentation will occur.

6. It is best not to combine Vegetables, Proteins or Starches with Fruits, because the fruit digestion will be delayed and be subject to fermentation. Exception: Lettuce and celery may be combined with fruit and cause no problem.

7. Tomatoes (an acid fruit, without the sugar content of other acid fruits) may be used with the vegetable salad, or with any green or nonstarchy vegetable, but not at a starch meal. Tomatoes may be used with some proteins, such as nuts and cheese.

8. Avocados are best used with salad or subacid fruit, and are a fair combination with starch or sweet fruit. They are high in fat and contain small amounts of excellent protein, and should not be used at the same meal with nuts, which are also high in fat.

9. Melons should be eaten alone; one kind at a meal is best, but some people have no problem when combining two kinds at a meal, or combining with other fresh fruits. They are about 90% liquid and leave the stomach very quickly if not delayed and fermented by combining with other foods. When eaten in this way, many people who complain that melons do not agree with them have no trouble.

Acid fruits (citrus, strawberries, pineapple) are a fair combination with nuts and seeds, and many Hygienists thrive on this type of meal. Some people with impaired digestions find they do very well by delaying thirty minutes after the fruit before eating the nuts. In any event, the acid fruits should be eaten first.

Sweet fruits combine quite well with subacid fruits. It is best to have these fruits at a fruit meal, without combining with other types of food, though some exceptions may occasionally be made, as with using some types of acid or subacid fruits at the beginning of a meal. Such vegetables as lettuce and celery combine very well with most fruits. If you use clabber (soured milk, of a custardy consistency—See Recipes), it may be used with the fruit meal.

Salads combine very well with proteins or starches, as do nonstarchy raw or cooked vegetables. Do not have tomatoes with a starch meal, as mentioned heretofore (but it will bear repeating), as this is a particularly bad combination.

So, to quote Dr. John M. Brosious, at the July, 1973 Natural Hygiene Health Conference, "Simplicity seems to be the name of the game, with sufficient variety over the long range to get all the nutrients."

Occasional indulgence in incorrect food combinations will not do great harm; a healthy body can cope with some exceptions. It is what we do daily, habitually, that will make the difference. Dr. Herbert M. Shelton, Page 320, Volume II, The Hygienic System, quotes Major Austin: "It is certainly everyone's duty to have the courage of his convictions, but a cause is not benefitted by unreasonable advocates. So when at a friend's table do not deliver a homily on food combinations, and critically select and refuse, causing the host embarrassment. Take what is offered, and do not think about it unless sick or uncomfortable; then do not eat. No one should eat when seedy or out of sorts—no, not to please anyone."

DETAILED FOOD COMBINING CHART
Also See Next Page:
SIMPLIFIED FOOD COMBINING CHART

Nonstarchy & Green Vegetables

Lettuce	Cucumbers	Globe Artichokes	Okra
Celery	Sweet Peppers	Greens (Kale, etc.)	Kohlrabi
Celery Cabbage	Snow Peas	Summer Squash	Green Corn
Cabbage	Broccoli	Eggplant	Green Beans
	Brussels Sprouts	Turnips	

Protein		Starch	Mildly Starchy
Nuts		Peanuts	Cauliflower
Seeds	EAT NONSTARCHY	Coconuts	Beets
Beans	& GREEN VEGS.	Chestnuts	Carrots
Peas	With *EITHER*	Wild Rice	Rutabaga
Lentils	PROTEIN or STARCH	All Grains	Salsify
Olives	DO NOT COMBINE	Potatoes	Parsnips
Cheese	PROTEIN & STARCH	Swt. Pots.	Mature Corn
Eggs		Wint. Sqsh.	
Flesh Foods		Jer. Artcks.	

DO NOT COMBINE VEGETABLES, PROTEINS OR STARCHES WITH FRUITS

Except:
Nuts with Citrus   —Fair Combination
Lettuce & Celery with Fruit—Fair Combination

Acid Fruits		Sweet Fruits
Citrus		Bananas
Pineapples	EAT SUBACID FRTS.	Persimmons
Strawberries	With *EITHER* ACID	Thompson Grapes
Pomegranates	Or SWEET FRUITS	Muscat Grapes
Sour Apples	DO NOT COMBINE	All Sweet Grapes
Sour Grapes	ACID FRUITS	All Dried Fruits
Sour Peaches	& SWEET FRUITS	
Sour Plums		
Sour Cherries		

Subacid Fruits

Sweet Apples	Subacid Grapes	Apricots	Blueberries
Sweet Peaches	Pears	Sweet Plums	Raspberries
Sweet Cherries	Papayas	Cherimoyas	Blackberries
	Mangos	Fresh Figs	

Tomatoes:	Use with Green & Nonstarchy Vegetables & Protein
Avocados:	Best with Salad or Subacid Fruit
	Fair with Starch or Sweet Fruit
Melons:	Eat Alone

SIMPLIFIED FOOD COMBINING CHART
Also See Previous Page:
DETAILED FOOD COMBINING CHART

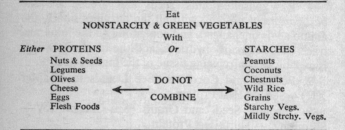

Eat
NONSTARCHY & GREEN VEGETABLES
With

Either PROTEINS   *Or*   STARCHES

Nuts & Seeds		Peanuts
Legumes		Coconuts
Olives	**DO NOT**	Chestnuts
Cheese		Wild Rice
Eggs	**COMBINE**	Grains
Flesh Foods		Starchy Vegs.
		Mildly Strchy. Vegs.

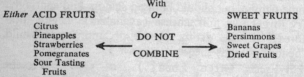

Eat
SUBACID FRUITS
(All Fruits Not Sweet or Acid)
With

Either ACID FRUITS   *Or*   SWEET FRUITS

Citrus		Bananas
Pineapples	**DO NOT**	Persimmons
Strawberries		Sweet Grapes
Pomegranates	**COMBINE**	Dried Fruits
Sour Tasting		
Fruits		

**DO NOT COMBINE VEGETABLES, PROTEINS OR STARCHES
WITH FRUITS**

Except: Nuts with Citrus   —Fair Combination
          Lettuce & Celery with Fruit—Fair Combination

Tomatoes: Eat with green and non-starchy vegetables and Protein

Avocados: Best with Salad or Subacid Fruit
          Fair with Starch or Sweet Fruit

Melons: Eat alone

XI. Protein—Scales of Quality

1. Raw unsalted nuts, seeds and greens are the *best source of protein,* with all the enzymes intact, the amino acids unchanged, and containing all the minerals, trace elements, carbohydrates, and the life force which is capable of reproducing tissue of the highest quality.

2. Peanuts and Coconuts (See Details in Chapter XII)—Second Best Protein

3. Sprouted Seeds and Grains (See Chapter XV—Sprouting)—Third Best Protein

4. *Unsalted Raw* Milk Cheese—Fourth Best Protein

Cheese is a useful source of additional protein for some people, but should be used seldom and sparingly. Try to get raw milk cheese (available at health food stores), or use ricotta cheese or unprocessed mild Cheddar or Swiss cheese.

5. Fresh Green Lima Beans (esp. Baby Limas), Tender Green Peas, Edible Podded Peas (Snow Peas) (eaten raw).) A Good Protein Source When Eaten At The Same Meal With Raw Leafy Vegetables.

6. Lentils, Split Peas, Chick Peas, Beans) Fifth and Sixth Best Protein Sources

Some people have digestive problems with legumes, but find that if these are eliminated from the diet for

---

All of the above are superior, in all the nutrients needed to rebuild health, to any of the flesh foods.

a time and then restored (sparingly), small portions are handled very well.

7. Chestnuts (Roasted)—Some varieties are Toxic When Raw.

8. Olives are protein foods, but it is difficult to obtain olives that are acceptable. You might find some in a Health Food Store that have not been chemicalized, but they would still not be raw or unsalted.

9. Eggs are best omitted. The albumen is toxic when raw and difficult to digest when cooked. The yolk is relatively innocuous and may be used raw or cooked, if desired, but is not a necessary or superior food. If you do use eggs, use strictly fresh, and fertile eggs.

XII. Proteins—Nuts and Seeds Raw and Unsalted

Nuts and seeds, the finest quality protein, may be combined with green and nonstarchy vegetables. They also may be eaten with acid fruits—a fair combination and agreeable to most people. Some people find it advisable to wait twenty to thirty minutes after eating the acid fruit before eating the nuts. Shell them yourself, if possible. It is best to eat one kind at a meal, but many people eat mixed nuts and get along with them quite well. If you have any digestive problems, you might experiment with one kind at a time, and see which ones agree with you best.

At a recent Natural Hygiene Health Conference, Dr. Virginia Vetrano, B.S., D.C., shared the results of one of her inspired experiments, relative to facilitating the use and digestion of nuts by people whose physical impairments caused difficulties. She found that many such people experienced little or no discomfort after a meal of salad and nuts, eaten intermittently—that is, a bite or two of salad, then a bite or two of nuts, chewing thoroughly, continuing this pattern throughout the meal.

In the case of extremely oily nuts like brazils and macadamias, it might be best to eat a few along with some other nuts or seeds. All nuts and seeds should be properly combined and thoroughly masticated.

Brazil nuts and filberts are excellent sources of methionine, a relatively rare amino acid in the plant kingdom.

Most varieties of almonds should be blanched (see Recipes), as their brown skins contain a strong astringent (prussic acid). Almond skins which do not have a bitter taste are safe to consume. Almonds are also harder to chew than other nuts, but they are valuable nuts and worth a little extra trouble. Dr. William L. Esser, D.C., N.D., in his "Dictionary of Man's Foods" says: "The almond is one of the best of all nuts, and, for the vegetarian, one of the richest sources of protein." After blanching, chew very thoroughly (or you may grind them into a meal, or make almond butter— immediately before using, if possible). To prepare almond butter, grind in blender or mill, and add a very small amount of oil. (Sesame oil is a pleasant tasting and stable oil.) Some people may prefer to scrape off the brown almond skins with a sharp knife blade, as an alternative to blanching.

Pecans are easily-digested, fine flavored nuts of high nutritive value. Dr. Esser's "Dictionary of Man's Foods" states: "According to Carque, one pound of pecans has more than three times as much nutritive value as the average cuts of meat. On full grown pecan tree can easily keep an adult man constantly supplied with more proteins and fats than he needs. Pecans can be safely and beneficially given to infants in the form of nut milk, and to children in the natural state or as nut butter (See Recipes). Pecans are in the same class as the almond for their high nutritive value and their easy digestibility. No other proteins offer such a fine source as these nuts." (Author's Note:

Pecans are not as hard as almonds, and considerably easier to masticate thoroughly.)

Filberts (or Hazelnuts), Walnuts (all varieties), Macadamias, Pistachios, Pignolias, Indian Nuts and Beechnuts are all excellent, nutritious nuts, each with its own pleasant and characteristic flavor.

Cashew nuts are classified as nuts, but are not really nuts. The so-called cashew nut is the pistil of the cashew apple. It is toxic when picked and must be heated slightly to be made edible, which is done before they are marketed. Do not combine cashews with other nuts, as they are not quite compatible. Cashew butter, if desired, may be made without the addition of any oil,—just grind in blender and pat into a butter.

Sunflower seeds and sesame seeds are very nutritious. (See Chapter VII, Section 7, for details about the superior nutrition contained in the sunflower seed.) Pumpkin and squash seeds are also available, and are good foods.

Peanuts and Coconuts are not really nuts. They must be combined as starches, with no acid foods included in the meal. (See Chapter X, Food Combining)

Some people enjoy raw peanuts, some do not like the taste at all, when eaten out of hand, but enjoy raw peanut butter. If made at home, and eaten soon after preparing, this is a fairly good food. Just grind in blender or grinder, and pat into butter—no oil necessary. A better textured peanut butter may be made in the Champion Juicer, using the homogenizing blank. The commercial roasted, salted, hydrogenated peanut butter usually available in supermarkets should be scrupulously avoided, as well as other hydrogenated fats. If you want to use roasted peanut butter occasionally, obtain an unsalted, unhydrogenated variety from your health food store. (Progress Report: Some supermarkets now offer "old-fashioned" unhydrogenated peanut butter.)

Coconuts are good food. To open, first drive a clean large nail through two of the three "eyes" or soft spots, and drain off the liquid. You may filter the liquid through filter paper to remove any bits of husk, and it may be drunk immediately, or stored in the refrigerator a short time. Then the shell may be cracked with a hatchet or hammer, or in a vise. If you put the coconut in your freezer for an hour or so before cracking, it will crack and come away from the shell a bit easier, Break up the meat in small pieces and eat out of hand. They may be stored a short time in the coconut liquid or in water. Peel first if you have problems with tough skins. Also coconut may be grated if used shortly after preparing (may be used in salads). Some people use coconut with sweet fruits, and they seem to combine fairly well. Don't use with acid or subacid fruits.

Chestnuts are also to be classified as starchy proteins, and may be lightly roasted, or boiled, as some varieties are toxic when raw.

Protein Content of Nuts and Seeds

Almond	18.6%
Beechnut	19.4%
Brazil Nut	14.3%
Butternut	23.7%
Cashew	17.2%
Chestnut	2.9%
Coconut	3.5%
Filbert	12.6%
Hickory	13.2%
Macadamia	7.8%
Pecan	9.2%
Pignolia (Pine Nut)	31.1%
Pistachio	19.3%
Walnut (Black)	20.5%
Walnut (English)	14.8%
Pumpkin & Squash Seed	24 %
Sesame Seed	18.6%
Sunflower Seed	24 %

XIII. The Fruit Meal

Subsisting on fruit only for limited periods may sometimes be advisible, especially for a temporary elimination diet (See Chapter VII, Section 8), but it is not wise to attempt to live on an all fruit diet, or even almost all fruit (as one enthusiastic young neophyte in the "Health Food" wilderness declared her intention of doing). Fruits may be deficient in calcium, though fruit acids are valuable in maintaining the calcium of the diet in soluble form. Most green leaves contain an abundance of calcium. An all fruit diet will be deficient in protein, and the excess of sugars and free acids will eventually cause problems.

In his lecture on "Simplified Biochemistry" at the July 1970 Hygiene Health Conference, Dr. Alec Burton, D.O., D.C., N.D., warned that people who stay on fruit diets for a very long time effect a change in their internal environment; they become nervous and irritable and do not sleep well, and there is a smell of acetone on their breath. Acetone is a compound sometimes found in the urine, especially in diabetes.

Advocates of a diet of fruit alone may be disseminating dangerous advice. Some few people might make it on fruit alone, but most people would suffer a serious protein deficiency, and could become over-alkaline, thin, neurotic and anemic, and their body chemistries may become so badly deranged that irreversible pathological conditions could result. People who advocate fruit diets, or prolonged juice diets, should carefully qualify such advice as not being applicable to all people.

Eat fruits and vegetables, especially green leafy vegetables, and nuts and seeds, for an adequate diet and optimal health.

Do not partake of unripe or overripe fruit. Unripe fruit is highly indigestible, and usually quite unpalatable. Overripe fruit has started to ferment, and is no longer suitable as food—if in doubt, discard it. Learn to recognize ripe fruit at its peak of delicious flavor, by appearance, touch and taste. Most ripe fruits have lost all traces of hard spots, but are not mushy. Many ripe fruits exude a delightful but delicate fragrance. As a rule, you should buy fruits which are almost ripe, and eat as soon as flavor peak is reached (or refrigerate when ripe and eat as soon as possible thereafter). Bananas and avocadoes are, of course, exceptions— best results for these fruits are obtained by purchasing "green" and ripening at home.

For the fruit meal, which may be eaten daily, see Chapter IX, Classification of Foods, for the variety of sweet fruits and subacid fruits which may be combined freely for this delectable meal. It is best not to combine more than three or four fruits at a meal. Avocado, banana (or clabber, if you use it), combined with some subacid fruit, makes a satisfying repast.

A meal of acid fruit and nuts is a favorite of many Hygienists. Properly ripened acid fruits, particularly organically grown oranges, are among the finest of our available foods. "Oranges are so vital that they cause the cells to immediately go to work excreting."— Dr. Scott, D.C., N.D., July 1973 Hygiene Health Conference. The rich Vitamin C content of citrus fruit is well known.

But like all other good things, their use may be overdone. Do not overeat acid fruits beyond the body's capacity to convert the fruit acids to an alkaline ash. I have heard some imprudent people boast of consuming ten to twelve oranges at a sitting; if this is not done regularly, a temporary excess will do no great harm.

Do not combine melons with other foods. Watermelon parties and picnics are refreshing and great fun.

XIV. Salad Vegetables
(and Salad Dressings—if you must)

Green vegetables are the richest sources of minerals and vitamins, and their liberal use improves the food value of the diet. Green leaves convert sunlight into food by a process called photosynthesis, aided by the green pigment chlorophyll. Since only green plants can do this, they are the most important things on our planet, because they are the originators of life. The analysis of chlorophyll shows it to be identical with the red blood cells of the body, except that the red blood cells contain iron, and chlorophyll contains manganese. An increase in the ingestion of green leafy vegetables is capable of producing a dramatic improvement of an anemic condition.

When Dorothy Brosious became pregnant, she also became anemic. She and her husband, Dr. John M. Brosious, B.S., D.C., N.D., visited a laboratory, and the technician found her hemoglobin count to be about 70% of normal. Dr. and Mrs. Brosious had recently changed from a conventional diet to a mostly raw diet of fruit, vegetables and nuts, and Mrs. Brosious had been eating one fruit meal every day, one meal of citrus fruit and nuts, and one meal consisting of a large salad with nuts, or sometimes with a cooked starchy food like baked potatoes, and perhaps a cooked green vegetable.

Upon the advice of her husband, she changed from the two fruit meals and one salad meal daily to one fruit meal and two salad meals daily, thus doubling her greens intake. They returned to the laboratory about two weeks later.

Quoting from Dr. Brosious' account of the incident:

"When the technician saw the blood sample, he said, 'Oh, boy, she sure must have been taking a lot of iron pills,' and I said 'No'—and he said 'Liver shots, then,' and I said 'No.' The technician scratched his head and asked, 'What *did* she do?' When he heard that all she had done was to eat more green leafy vegetables, he could only scratch his head again, because her blood count had been brought up to about 94% of normal in just two weeks."

Due to the greater abundance of vitamins and minerals in the young plants, and their more alkaline reaction, and because they contain smaller amounts of cellulose, they are better food than matured plants.

Never soak vegetables in water—valuable nutrients are lost. Wash quickly without bruising. The leaves of a tight head of buttercrunch or Bibb lettuce* may be separated without damage by holding under running water. Wash romaine lettuce leaves separately and drain by standing leaves against side of bowl or dish drainer. Do not use anything but plain water in which to wash your vegetables. If you do use other substances, you then have the additional problem of removing those substances from the food. Besides, these compounds may leech nutrients from the food, or cause deterioration.

Use whole leaves of lettuce, whole tomatoes, and don't cut up any vegetables into any smaller pieces than necessary for serving each portion. Serve and eat the salad first (before cooked food, or before nuts or other protein or starch foods).

Lettuce:

1. Bibb Lettuce has a delicious nutty flavor, is crisp, crunchy, has little fibre, and is easy to chew.

2. Buttercrunch Lettuce is an improved Bibb variety, with larger heads, more heat tolerance, and thick, buttery, crisp, deep green leaves.

---

*Named after developer Jack Bibb.

3. Boston Lettuce is a larger-leafed variety, similar to Bibb.

4. Romaine or Cos Lettuce is an excellent, nutritious, sweet-tasting lettuce, with excellent keeping qualities. It is a large-leafed, upright variety.

5. Varieties of Leaf Lettuce (Green, Ruby-Tipped, Bronze Leaf, Oak Leaf and Salad Bowl) are all nutritious and palatable.

6. Iceberg Head Lettuce has the least food value and is inferior to any deep green, young, tender variety of lettuce.

EAT A LARGE SERVING OF LETTUCE EVERY DAY.

It is vitamin- and mineral-rich, and contains small amounts of protein of high biological value.

Celery is one of the best salad vegetables, and some strips should be eaten raw every day, as this is an excellent source of sodium and potassium. When the strong-tasting green leaves, along with some cut-up strips, are used in cooked foods, they serve as a natural seasoning, without the harmful qualities of salt and condiments. The green leaves may also be slightly steamed and use as a green vegetable.

Cabbage—Green, Savoy (which is also green), and Red: Use young, sweet cabbage. Bitter, mature cabbage is high in oxalic acid (a calcium antagonist). Cabbage is a crisp, palatable, nutritious, and potassium, calcium and iodine rich vegetable, when eaten raw, but should be thoroughly masticated. It is extremely hard to digest when cooked.

Chinese Cabbage (Celery Cabbage): Eat raw only when young and succulent. May also be slightly steamed and eaten as a green vegetable, or used in Vegetable Chop Suey (See Recipe Section).

Cucumbers are good mineral-rich vegetables, containing more than 90% water, and an excellent summer food. They should, of course, be eaten raw, and the small young ones are best for flavor and quality. Be sure to peel them, if they are waxed. If not waxed, eat the skins, if possible. (The skins are difficult for some people to digest.)

Carrots should be used regularly for their food value and vitamin content. Scrub well and serve raw and whole. The small, sweet varieties make delicious eating.

Tomatoes are acid fruits without the sugar content of other acid fruits, and may be used freely in salads (but not with starch meals). When picked ripe, they are delicious. When picked grassy-green and ripened afterwards, they are inferior and tasteless. If you grow your own tomatoes, try some of the orange-colored subacid varieties. (Tomatoes are rich in Vitamin C, of course, like other acid fruits.)

Sweet Peppers (Bell and Pimento): Green peppers are not ripe, and are difficult to digest. Sweet Red Peppers (the same peppers allowed to ripen on the vine) are delicious eaten raw, and give a wonderful sweetness when added to steaming vegetables. They are rich in Vitamin C.

The Jerusalem, or Ground, Artichoke is a mineral-rich, palatable, starchy vegetable, and, when used raw and unpeeled, is a tasty, crisp addition to any salad. They taste a little like water chestnuts—only better. However, I have recently learned from Dr. Vetrano that the starch of the Jerusalem artichoke is INULIN, and is indigestible. Because the inulin is excreted from the kidneys in the same form as ingested, it is often used for experimental purposes, such as testing the function of the kidneys. Despite the inulin, you may want to use Jerusalem artichokes (also called sunchokes) for their minerals and good taste.

Sprouts are a wonderful addition to any salad. (See Chapter XV)

Snow Peas (also called Dwarf Sugar Peas or Edible Podded Peas): These are really "scrumptious" (if I may be permitted an eloquent slang expression), and are easy to grow. They are quite expensive to buy and not often available.

Any young, sweet, tender green peas or green beans, or young, tender squash may be eaten raw in your salad; also small amounts of raw broccoli, cauliflower, turnips, beets (if young, tender, succulent and palatable). Also the inside of the stalks of the broccoli makes a wonderful addition to the finger salad. Just peel back the tough outer covering and you will find the tender, juicy, edible part inside. If you have garden broccoli, use the young tender green broccoli leaves in your salad, also young tender leaves of garden kale or collard greens.

SALAD DRESSINGS (If You Must!—or For Company)

Bottled salad dressings should not be used. They contain stomach irritating condiments, and frequently have a mineral oil base. Mineral oil is a coal tar derivative, and a mineral oil coating in the digestive tract blocks the absorption of necessary nutritive factors. The following (for occasional use) are suggested instead:

1. Equal parts Vegebase and Oil

Sesame Oil is a stable oil (not subject to quick rancidity) and has a pleasant taste.

2. Sour Cream, Vegebase, Chopped Cucumbers (to taste)

3. Sour Cream, Mashed Avocado, Vegebase (to taste)

Number 2. and 3. may also be used as dips, with celery strips for dipping.

4. Blended tomatoes with avocado

5. Blended tomatoes with nuts

Do not use numbers 4. or 5. with a starch meal.

XV. Sprouting

Sprouting is fun! It is exciting to watch the growth (in a jar on your kitchen counter) into vitamin-, mineral- and protein-rich green vegetables, loaded with enzymes and chlorophyll. As the tiny seeds multiply in volume (one to two tablespoons of alfalfa seeds fills the jar with sprouts), a wonderful salad ingredient is being grown, with an abundance of Vitamins A, B, and C. Alfalfa sprouts are also a splendid source of Vitamins D, E, G, K and U. Vitamin C is especially high in lentils and mung beans after 3 days. (Vitamin-conscious people please take note, though Hygienists need not be concerned—leaving that to Nature and the Hygienic diet.) Read Catharyn Elwood's chapter on "Sprouties" in "Feel Like A Million".

"Sprouties" are easily grown in all seasons, organically grown seeds are available in health food stores, and they are convenient and economical. I have found alfalfa, mung beans and lentils easiest to sprout, and we like alfalfa sprouts best, using them freely, mostly in salads.

Garden peas, soy beans, garbanzo beans, sunflower seeds, wheat and rye may also be sprouted, with a little experimentation and practice. (Most whole nuts, seeds, beans and grains may be sprouted.) All may be eaten raw after sprouting, and may be stored in the refrigerator a week or so. Sprouted beans, raw or cooked, are less gassy than unsprouted beans, which, of course, must be cooked.

Eat rye in 24 hours or so, when but a short sprout is showing—also wheat or other grains. (Grains sour easily.) Phytic acid in whole grains is antagonistic to calcium and other minerals. Soaking and sprouting neutralizes the phytic acid, so sprouted grains not only provide increased nutrients, but eliminate the threat of the phytic acid.

Sunflower seeds: sprouts no longer than seeds. Eat lentils in 2 or 3 days, sprouts not more than one inch.

Garbanzo and soy bean sprouts are especially high in protein, but are not easy to work with; sprouts should be short: they also may sour. Lentils are high in protein also, and they are easier to handle. Mung beans also are easier to sprout and will be ready in three or four days, sprouts around two inches (and green leaves —see sprouting instructions).

Alfalfa: Ready in 3 or 4 days, sprouts two to three inches (and green leaves—see sprouting instructions).

SPROUTING INSTRUCTIONS:

This is the simplest and easiest sprouting method: Put one to two tablespoons of alfalfa seeds (or beans, 3 to 6 tablespoons; or grains, one-half cup) in quart jar with purest possible water (preferably distilled) three to four times volume of seeds. Soak over night or 6 to 10 hours. Soak longer if cool weather, less if warm weather.

Cover jar with stainless steel mesh and jar ring, or cheesecloth or nylon mesh held on with rubber bands or jar ring. Next morning (or at end of soaking period) drain and rinse and set to drain at an angle (prop up back end of jar about an inch). Rinse two to four times daily through mesh without removing lid. Just fill the jar with water from the tap, empty and shake gently to disperse seeds around jar. Cover with small towel so it will have air and warmth, but no light.

Alfalfa & Mung Bean Sprouts: After 3 days or when leaf appears, remove towel so light (not direct sunlight) will green up the leaves (chlorophyll). This may take 8 to 12 hours or more, after which they may be eaten or stored in refrigerator. Other sprouts are used sooner, without green leaves. See details previously given.

Another simple sprouting method is the use of a

bowl with a plate over the top, but care must be taken to see that some air gets to the sprouts, and to drain off all the water each time it is rinsed.

There are a number of other sprouting methods, involving the use of other paraphernalia. There are special sprouting bowls made of pottery, and tiers of trays may be purchased that grow "straight-up" sprouts, instead of curled up, as in a jar.

Dr. Virginia Ventrano (Director of Dr. Shelton's Health School near San Antonio, Texas) recently suggested (September 1973 Hygienic Review) growing sprouts in well-dampened sand, as being superior in many respects to jar sprouting, notably precluding the osmotic loss into the water when soaking the seeds.

This might possibly be avoided in the jar method by experimenting with utilizing only enough presoaking water so that all the water is absorbed into the seeds. (H. J. Dinshah, Hygienic Review, December, 1973).

Dr. Herbert M. Shelton, suggests (December, 1973 Hygienic Review) that soy beans, being subject to spoilage, must obviously do better when sprouted in sand. He also points out that, while using this "bonus viand" more or less frequently, we should not depend upon them for our chief source of fresh vegetation, which must still come from the garden, because of the free exposure to air, soil and sunlight.

XVI. The Market Basket—My Garden

Even those of us who have a sizeable organic garden must track down and purchase many of the foods we need. When the weather is warm, take along a picnic cooler with ice, for transporting perishable food. Much damage can result from alternately cooling, warming, and again cooling your produce. It is even a good idea to carry a cooler when the weather is cold, because your car will be heated.

Our greatest concern will be produce—good quality fresh fruits and vegetables. It is even sometimes possible to locate organically grown produce, but, if not, get the freshest, best quality obtainable, and you will come out ahead, as there will be much less waste. Sometimes you can, just by trying a bit, locate individuals in your own area, who are growing organically for their own use, and have some surplus to share.

In the Fall of 1973, before we got our own garden going, we bought organically grown produce from Osteen Farm, in Largo, Florida. We located them through the local Organic Gardening Club. We find some organically grown produce and a good line of fruits and vegetables at the Bo-Tree Market in St. Petersburg, Florida. We have also found that some of the local fruit and vegetable stands occasionally have some organic produce. It will be worth your while also to shop the transient roadside truck merchants, whose wares are sometimes excellent, though sometimes very poor. This chapter will include information to help you to learn how to judge. Usually their prices are more economical than elsewhere. As a last resort, shop the supermarkets. Here, too, some of the produce is of excellent quality, some very poor.

If the packaged offerings contain a percentage of "garbage" (at current high prices!), complain to the produce manager or store manager, and they will sometimes make available fresher unpackaged produce, or break open the packages and allow you to select what you want.

Fruit

Citrus: If you live in Florida or California or Texas (or any other citrus producing area) it may be possible to obtain organically grown citrus fruits, if you will take the trouble to locate the organic orchards, and travel a bit to pick up a bushel or two or three. Perhaps you could arrange a cooperative with friends or neighbors, and take turns going. If you live elsewhere, you can have organically grown citrus shipped (in a pool with others to keep the shipping costs down).

If you must buy your citrus from a commercial producer, or at a market, try to get fruit that hasn't been dyed (color added). In some areas, this is almost impossible, but sometimes you can get a produce manager or store manager or health food store interested in the idea of supplying you and your friends with this type of citrus fruit. Some health food stores carry a line of organically grown produce. If you cannot get undyed citrus fruit, it is better to use the dyed fruit than not to use citrus fruit at all, as it is a valuable food.

Other fruits: It will be necessary to use what is available, of course. *It is always best to use fresh fruit in season.* In the harvest season in your area, frequently it is possible to find a variety of organically grown or unsprayed fruits.

Organically grown apples are available from sources in Michigan, Virginia, Ohio, Indiana, Canada, the Pacific Northwest and some other areas. Through the years, I have purchased organically grown apples from Golden Acres, Front Royal, Virginia, from Vita-Green Farms, Vista, California, and from some growers in Michigan, Ohio, and Indiana. If you order a bushel of apples from a distance, order a variety with good keeping qualities. (See "Storing Food—Apples", Chapter XVII.)

As a rule, commercial apples should be avoided. It is my understanding that these contain more poison than any of the other fruits (they poison the tree), and I usually don't eat apples unless I am reasonably sure they are organically grown. When I don't have any organically grown fresh apples. I use dried apples (usually obtainable organically grown from Health Food Stores or from Walnut Acres, Penns Creek, Penn.).

Grapes are available in most areas most of the year,

but should be selected carefully. We try to get a grape to taste before buying, and reject the sour ones. During much of the year, most people must rely on grapes and other fruits shipped from California. Some months out of the year, usually around April and May, grapes are only available from South America, and we have learned not to buy those. They are expensive, and lack flavor, as they are picked green, do not ripen properly and are usually sour. We have found this to be true also of other fruit from South America.

Sometimes it takes quite a bit of hunting, when you start out in a new community, to find places which carry consistently good produce, and sometimes you find that while one fruit stand or market may carry good grapes, you must shop another for good bananas or avocados. The condition in which you find the produce is due primarily to the manner in which it has been handled during picking, packing, shipping and storing, particularly after it reaches the retailer. Ask the cashier and the sacker to handle the produce with T.L.C. Frequently, we do our own sacking.

Here in Florida, we have some excellent fruits available from nearby sources, such as citrus, papayas, mangos and avocados. I have not seen any supermarket papayas that were worth purchasing. They are picked green and rot instead of ripening. I get some organically grown papayas from a friend in Clearwater who has a surplus. Mangos from the supermarket are acceptable, as they will usually ripen satisfactorily, but they are expensive. (But then, what isn't)?

Florida avocadoes, available locally, are sometimes excellent, sometimes not. Organically grown avocados and mangos (and citrus) are available by the case from a source in Miami: All Organics, Inc., 15870 S.W. 216th Street.

Buy your avocados as hard as you can get them, they will usually ripen nicely. Dark avocados are somewhat soft to firm when ripe—if very soft and have black spots, they are usually rotten. Green avocados are soft when ripe.

Bananas should be purchased as green as possible and ripened at home. Usually they will ripen well on your kitchen counter (but not in the sun), if the temperature in the house is warm (at least 70 degrees). If it is cold at night, put them in a tightly closed brown paper bag. When you buy your bananas, notice whether any of those on the stand are ripening properly, with freckles, and not with blotches and dark streaks. Sometimes, you can get bananas which have not been gassed, through your Health Food Store. But if they freckle, they have not received the worst treatment, and will usually be sweet and good. Don't use bananas until they are thoroughly ripe (but not overripe), freckled, with a little give when you feel them, but not soft or mushy.

Japanese Persimmons: The season is all too short for this delicious fruit, which should be purchased when starting to ripen, and ripened at home. If very green, they may not ripen at all, but will rot instead. They should be eaten when quite soft to the touch, almost but not quite mushy. I got some wonderful ones last Fall from a lady in Clearwater, but she has only one tree. I have frequently found some excellent Japanese Persimmons at supermarkets.

Fruits like peaches and apricots must be firm and almost ready to eat when purchased. They spoil quickly, so avoid bruised fruit. Pears will ripen after purchasing.

Avoid grainy pears (unless you like them).

Good quality sweet strawberries must be ripe but not old when you get them—many times they are half garbage.

It is difficult to get or identify a really good pineapple. Sometimes you can tell by the fragrance or the color. Many stores will guarantee a pineapple. The best pineapples—almost fool-proof—are Dole Royal

Hawaiian pineapples—Jet-Fresh—picked almost ripe and flown in from Hawaii.

Don't buy melons out of season. They are expensive and of inferior quality. Buy melons in season, grown locally or from adjoining areas.

Blueberries, Raspberries, Blackberries, are usually not too good, unless available locally in season. Occasionally I have found some excellent ones that have been shipped in.

Excellent sweet dark cherries are sometimes available. Avoid the first expensive shipments of small, pale, sour fruit, and wait for the large, sweeter, darker, less expensive variety.

If you buy fresh fruit in season, you will do better. Don't buy the first shipments of any new fruit; wait a while for better quality and lower price.

Try to find tomatoes that have been allowed to ripen on the vine. All the crates of tomatoes and the signs in the stores are marked "Vine Ripened", but the tomatoes shipped in those crates are frequently picked green as grass. When the seeds in the tomatoes are dark, that is a certain indication they were picked green. A more certain sign is the flat taste and mushy texture. After you have eaten vine ripened tomatoes, you will recognize them by their glowing red color and wonderful taste. In the North, vine ripened tomatoes are only found in the summer, usually at fruit stands.

If tomatoes are picked *almost* fully ripe, they will ripen in your kitchen (not on the window sill or in the sun). Don't buy hydroponic tomatoes. They are grown in water, and chemicals are added to the water, in an attempt to supply the nutrients usually supplied by the soil.

Green, Nonstarchy and Starchy Vegetables

Lettuce is so easy to grow, in season, almost anywhere, that most people ought to be able to have their own organically grown lettuce, at least part of the year. The leafy green vegetables are of prime importance, and a dependable supply of good lettuce is invaluable. If you *must* buy it at the market, look for the darker green varieties: Romaine, Boston, or Leaf Lettuce. Bibb is a wonderful lettuce, but is usually priced much too high. Iceberg head lettuce is an inferior type. (See Salad Vegetables—Lettuce, Chapter XIV) Find out when the supplies of lettuce arrive, and try to arrange to buy it by the pound before it is packaged.

Celery: Look for heads that still have some green leaves—not heads that have wilted and have been trimmed back. Sometimes packages of "hearts of celery" are available; these usually contain three "hearts", which have been trimmed of only the toughest, damaged outer stalks, and still have plenty of green, more tender stalks, and green leaves, and are generally a good buy.

Since cabbage should always be eaten raw (it is highly indigestible when cooked) look for a fruit stand or market that can supply you with consistently sweet (not bitter) heads. (Bitter cabbage is high in oxalic acid—a calcium antagonist). The same would apply to celery cabbage.

Escarole and endive are usually too bitter, unless you grow them yourself, and pick in their earliest stages.

Cucumbers are excellent when very fresh, but spoil rapidly. Waxed cucumbers are usually of poor quality.

Sweet Bell Peppers and Pimentos: Bell peppers and pimentos should be allowed to ripen on the vine until they are bright red and sweet tasting. It is seldom possible to buy these sweet red peppers in the North, except home-grown in season. In our area in Florida, they are available much of the time, usually at fruit stands.

Look for carrots and beets that still have their tops. If you must buy them without tops, be sure they are firm and hard. Kohlrabi, Turnips, Salsify and Parsnips should also be firm and hard. Rutabaga is a very hard vegetable and difficult to cut—usually available only waxed—sometimes available from local gardeners.

Try to find clean, white firm heads of cauliflower, with leaves still attached and still green; deep, dark green full heads of broccoli with lots of fresh looking leaves; and green heads of Brussels sprouts with no yellowing outside leaves.

Globe artichokes should be green with no dark spots. If cut ends are shriveled, they are not fresh. Look for uniformly solid heads with compact leaves. You can tell overmature or poor quality artichokes by their loose, spreading, and discolored leaves.

Kale, Collards, Turnip, Mustard and Dandelion Greens should be crisp, green and fresh looking, not wilted and yellowing. Use only the young and succulent leaves, which do not contain large quantities of cellulose.

Okra should be small and tender and green and clean —not too large and not full of dark spots and stripes.

Buy only firm heads of eggplant, with no soft or damaged spots, and reasonably even in color. A fresh eggplant will not have dark seeds.

Corn is best when fresh picked. Try to buy in the husks. Firm ears with small kernels will be tenderest. Large ears may be tough; small ears may be young and tender, or inferior and stunted. If you can pull back the husks on the smaller ears, you may find some excellent, tender corn.

Buy Green Beans only if firm and green and if they snap when broken.

Select young, tender, firm, fresh zucchini and yellow crookneck squash.

Use asparagus only when fresh and firm.

Immature, fresh, green chives and scallions may be eaten sparingly if sweet, not strong. Parsley, watercress and radishes should be fresh, not wilted, and may be used sparingly if not too strong. (If the tops of the radishes are wilted, they are old.)

Get firm, perfect bulbs of onions and garlic, for use in cooking only. Podded peas and beans should be firm and green. Jerusalem Artichokes, as well as Acorn, Butternut and Hubbard Squash, should be hard and firm. Sweet Potatoes and Yams should be hard and firm, with no color added.

The several varieties of white potatoes should be hard and firm, with few irregularities. Watch for greenish areas (where the root has been exposed to the sun). These are toxic. Green potatoes contain a bitter poisonous alkaloid called solanine. If a small area, cut it off, but avoid purchasing such potatoes. Sprouts on potatoes also contain solanine. Don't buy sprouted potatoes except for seed. If tiny sprouts appear before you use them, take them off; if badly sprouted, use for seed or discard them. Try to get potatoes that have not been treated with a sprout retardant. Practically all supermarket potatoes have been so treated.

Dried Lentils, Peas and *Beans; Grains; Peanuts; Coconuts; Olives*

Good quality and organically grown dried lentils, peas and beans are available in health food stores; also brown rice, buckwheat groats, millet and other grains. Don't use white rice, from which most of the nutritional value has been removed. Brown rice is available in the supermarkets, and is a much better buy. One cup of raw white rice makes three cups of cooked rice, while one cup of brown rice makes four cups of cooked rice.

Wild rice is more flavorful than brown rice and has more nutritional value.

Raw peanuts should be purchased unshelled. Raw chestnuts are sometimes available—some varieties must be boiled or roasted before using, as those varieties are somewhat toxic when raw.

Whole coconuts should be heavy and full of liquid— if dry, don't buy them. Shake to determine whether dry.

Olives are sometimes available canned in health food

stores, but although they may have been organically grown, and do not have added chemicals, they are really not acceptable, since they are salted (and, of course, cooked and canned).

Cheese, Eggs, Oils, Butter

Cheese: Some health food stores have raw milk cheese, some even have rennetless raw milk cheese. (Rennet is an enzyme used for curdling milk and is made from the lining of a calf's stomach.) If unsalted raw milk cheese is not obtainable, you might occasionally use unprocessed mild Cheddar or Swiss cheese, or other unprocessed mild cheeses, or ricotta cheese. Use cheese sparingly and not more than once weekly.

If you use eggs, buy fertile eggs from your health food store, or from a farmer you know doesn't use "modern" methods or poisons. Eggs are not recommended in the Hygienic diet.

If you occasionally use oil, get cold-pressed oil from your Health Food Store. Sesame Oil and Olive Oil are the most stable oils obtainable—other oils become rancid more quickly. Olive Oil is the least subject to rancidity—Sesame Oil is next in line, and has a much better flavor. If you use butter, find an unsalted variety.

Nuts and Seeds; Dried Fruits.

Nuts and Seeds and Dried Fruits are available organically grown, and the best and most economical way to buy them is directly from the growers. Order these easily stored foods in December and January when new fresh packs are available. Dried fruit from California is excellent, as well as many varieties of nuts. We buy from Jaffe Brothers, Valley Center, California. Good quality pecans in the shell are sometimes available from growers in Georgia and Mississippi, and some organically grown are available around October or November. You might find some in your Health Food Store. You can generally find some good quality pecans at Stuckey's Shops, located at numerous interchanges of the Interstate Highway System. When ordering food from great distances, the shipping cost is a very large item, and you can save quite a bit by pooling orders with other buyers and dividing shipping costs.

Good quality, organically grown nuts and dried fruits are also available in the Health Food Stores, and you can usually get a discount if you buy each item in ten pound quantities.

Walnut Acres

There is an excellent mail-order Health Food Farm and Store called Walnut Acres, in Penns Creek, Pennsylvania. The owner, Paul Keene, is trustworthy and forthright. They have an extensive list of foods available. They feature many organically grown products, including fresh produce in season. They will be glad to send you a current price list, upon request.

We have compiled a list of good food sources, accumulated in our travels in the U.S. and Canada, and in our years of Hygienic living. These include some Natural Food Stores and Restaurants, and Local and Mail Order Sources of Produce, Nuts and Dried Fruits (including some organically grown food). A booklet listing these sources has been published.

Fringe Benefit

When we lived in Indianapolis, we had produce shipped in from California by Air Freight, during the long Winter months when it was impossible to grow any organically grown produce, and the shipping costs could be brought down by pooling our orders with other Hygienists. We ordered once a month, and did the best we could between times, but at least we had some good quality organically grown produce part of the time. It was well worth the extra cost, though it was expensive.

One of the fringe benefits of our move to Florida,

in May of 1973, is that it is possible to have a garden for about nine months of the year. For the past several months (I write these lines in May, 1974), we have been eating "high off the garden": five kinds of lettuce, celery, snow peas, carrots, broccoli, cauliflower, cabbage, green beans, yellow crookneck squash, zucchini and butternut squash. We have tomatoes ripening all over the place, some transplants, some planted from seed, and some volunteers in our lettuce garden (from our sheet composting). The sweet potatoes and sunchokes look good and the beets, eggplants and the pimentos and sweet peppers are almost ready to pick. We have some beautiful sunflowers, cucumbers, honeydew melons and watermelons coming along and getting bigger every day. We have used no chemicals or poisons and our garden is the talk of the neighborhood—lush and dark green, and delicious! I must confess I am surprised at the quality of the food we are growing, as I expected to have to go through a frustrating "trial and error" period. So far our only real problem has been a rabbit who likes to eat our young, tender shoots, and we finally put up a fourteen inch fence that we can step over.

We have had some delicious figs and kumquats off our trees, and our young orange trees are starting to bear. We have four grape vines, and three of them have clusters well on their way. Our avocados and papayas and loquats and almonds and filberts and our banana trees are still in their early stages, and our peach tree and red grapefruit tree bloomed and set fruit too early, and lost the fruit in a late February night-time freeze.

So we will have to wait until next year for peaches and grapefruit. But an organic garden is a wonderful experience, and teaches us a lot.

The Law of Homeostasis works here too: "If you give living things the right conditions, they will automatically proceed in the direction of health."

A good "Organic Gardening" library should include:

"How to Grow Vegetables & Fruits by the Organic Method" by J. I. Rodale and Staff

"The Basic Book of Organic Gardening" by Robert Rodale

"The Pfeiffer Garden Book" by Bio-Dynamic Farming & Gardening Assn., Inc.

"Gardening Without Poisons" by Beatrice Trum Hunter

"Getting the Bugs Out of Organic Gardening" by the Staff of Organic Gardening and Farming

"Best Ways to Improve Your Soil" by Staff of Organic Gardening & Farming

"The Bug Book—Harmless Insect Controls" by John & Helen Philbrick

"The Ruth Stout No-Work Garden Book" by Ruth Stout & Richard Clemence

"Sunset Guide to Organic Gardening"—Lane Books, Menlo Park, California

"Down to Earth Vegetable Gardening Down South" by Lacy F. Bullard, with C. Art Cheek

SOURCES FOR NATURAL AND BIOLOGICAL CONTROLS:

Bio-Control Co., 10180 Ladybird Drive
Auburn, California 95603
    Ladybugs and Praying Mantis Egg Cases
Gothard, Inc., P. O. Box 370,
Canutillo, Texas 79835
    Trichogramma Wasp
    Carded Insect Eggs
Fairfax Biological Laboratory
Clinton Corners, New York 12514
    Doom—Milky Disease Spore Powder for
    Japanese Beetle Grub
Palm Beach Nutrition Center
11860 U. S. #1
Palm Beach Gardens, Florida 33408

SM-3 Nutritional
Seaweed Spray
Southern Agricultural Insecticides
Palmetto, Florida
Thuricide:
Thuringiensis—Microbe to fight
about 20 different insects.
(Available in some nurseries)

XVII. Storing Food

One of the first things a Hygienist learns is that one refrigerator is not enough. While the ideal would be to pick or obtain food for each day as needed, most of us cannot readily attain this ideal.

Do not wash, or remove stems from any fruit before storing.

If you can obtain organically grown citrus fruit by the bushel, it will keep well (if freshly picked) in your refrigerator for several weeks.

If you can obtain organically grown apples by the bushel, eat your Delicious apples first, as other apples have better keeping qualities. Delicious apples (if fresh and in good condition) will keep (under refrigeration) for two or three weeks—other varieties may keep for several months or longer, if you keep culling and using them. Do not store apples with other foods, or, if you store them in an uncovered container, do not store other uncovered food in the same refrigerator. Apples give off a kind of gas which tends to spoil other exposed foods.

Other ripe fruits may be stored in the refrigerator (grapes, cherries, peaches, apricots, pears, papayas, mangos, plums, berries) from several days to a week, or longer depending on their condition when you get them. Keep watching, culling and using them.

Melons and pineapples need to be used when ripe, as they do not keep well.

Fruit that is purchased when not quite ripe, for ripening at home, should be moved to the refrigerator as soon as ripe. Soft fruits ripening in the kitchen must be covered at night, as they may attract insects. Fruits with tough outer covering (bananas, avocados, melons) need not be covered.

Bananas should be used when ripe. Ripe bananas may be stored in the refrigerator for a day or two, but they deteriorate rapidly. If you have too many to use up quickly, they may be frozen, but this, of course, is not really Hygienic.

Avocados may be stored in the refrigerator after ripening—but not too long. They may also be stored in the refrigerator before ripening and taken out to ripen as needed. This is the only fruit I know of that will (almost consistently) ripen properly after having been chilled before ripening. Sometimes this can be done successfully with mangos also.

Japanese Persimmons should be eaten when ripe; they do not store well. They may be stored in the refrigerator a day or two after fully ripe. If you have too many to use before they spoil, they may be frozen successfully, but with some loss of flavor.

Coconuts may be stored in the refrigerator for a week or so.

Dried fruits store very well in your refrigerator, and may be purchased in quantity and stored for months. Store in airtight, moisture-proof bags or containers.

Nuts and seeds, shelled or unshelled, may also be purchased in quantity and stored in the freezer section of your refrigerator, well wrapped in airtight, moisture-proof double pliofilm bags. They do not "freeze", but keep their fresh taste a long time, and do not become rancid.

Shelled nuts, when not kept in the freezer, must be kept refrigerated at all times, but nuts in the shell will keep for weeks or months without refrigeration, depending on the temperature.

If you occasionally use cold pressed oil, store it in your refrigerator, and do not keep it too long. Sesame and olive oils are the best keepers.

If you use butter (unsalted), store in the freezer, except for the stick you are using. Fresh vegetables: Buy small quantities and use in a few days. Store in pliofilm bags and don't wash until just before using.

Lettuce may be stored in the crisper drawer, covered with some damp paper towels. Add a few drops of water to the pliofilm bag in which you store your Celery.

Dr. Virginia Vetrano (July, 1968 Hygiene Health Conference) recommended putting a fine mist of water on your vegetables, and putting them in a brown paper bag, and then in a plastic bag.

Cucumbers are poor keepers, unless very fresh. Store in crisper drawer, unbagged. They become slimy when bagged.

Use Broccoli, Brussels Sprouts, Asparagus and Greens soon after buying—they lose color, crispness and quality quite rapidly. Cauliflower keeps a little better. Cabbage keeps quite well for a week or two.

Corn will keep in the refrigerator a few days. Eggplant should be used not more than a few days after buying—also Green Beans, Zucchini and Crookneck Squash.

Root vegetables like Carrots, Potatoes, Sweet Potatoes, Beets, Turnips and Onions are good keepers, and will keep a month or so in your refrigrator, in airtight, moisture-proof bags or containers. Be sure to cut the tops from Carrots, Beets and Turnips, because the roots deteriorate as the greens wilt.

Winter Squash (Butternut, Acorn, Hubbard, etc.) may be kept in the kitchen for a month or so after picking—they "ripen" but do not deteriorate too rapidly, unless the weather is very warm.

Jerusalem Artichokes may be stored in the refrigerator in a pliofilm bag for a few days, if in good condition. Salsify and Parsnips may be stored in the refrigerator in pliofilm bags for a week or so.

Grains and Dried Beans and Peas will keep a long time if stored in the refrigerator in double pliofilm bags.

Fresh eggs (if you use them) may be stored in the refrigerator for a week or two or longer, but not uncovered, as is a common practice. They will pick up odors from other foods; this will hasten deterioration. Slip the egg carton into a pliofilm bag, or store in a covered container.

Raw milk cheese or unprocessed cheese will keep a week or two, if carefully handled. Each time it is unwrapped, rewrap in a fresh piece of pliofilm, so that the pliofilm is in smooth contact with each cut side of the cheese. Do not re-use the old pliofilm that has been in contact with the cheese. After exposure to air, the oily residue on the used pliofilm, if again brought into contact with the cheese, will accelerate deterioration.

XVIII Menus

How many times have I been asked in the midst of a discussion on Natural Hygiene—but what *do* you eat? for breakfast? lunch? dinner?

Mention of the "No Breakfast Plan" usually draws a blank look or a hostile stare out in the never-never land of ham and eggs, toast and coffee.

A Hygienist eats two or three meals a day, with no snacking in between. The following menus give three meals a day for a twenty-one day period, but do try the "No-Breakfast Plan", at least some of the time. You will eventually find that the mornings you skip breakfast will be happier and more productive, and your mind will be clearer. (That is, after you get over the hump, and form the new habit.)

A	Breakfast	Lunch	Supper
Sun.	Honeydew Melon (as much as you want)	Salad: Romaine & Bibb Lettuce, Celery Cabbage, Sweet Red Peppers, Alfalfa Sprouts Wild Rice Casserole Company Squash (baked)	Strawberries Apples (not too sweet) Pears Cheese—4 oz. (unpasteurized, unprocessed, unsalted)
Mon.	One Grapefruit 2 to 4 Oranges 2 to 4 oz. Pecans	Black Grapes One Banana ½ Avocado Dried Soaked Apricots	Salad: Bibb Lettuce, Celery, Red Cabbage, Whole Tomatoes Eggplant Casserole with Cashew Topping
Tues.	One or Two Pints Strawberries 2 to 4 oz. Cashews or Cashew Butter	Large Serving Papaya ½ Avocado, 6-8 Dates	Salad: Salad Bowl & Leaf Lettuce, Celery, Carrots Brussels Sprouts (steamed) Sweet Corn (raw or cooked)
Wed.	6 Sweet Kumquats 4 or 5 Oranges 2 to 4 oz. Filberts	Apples Banana Japanese Persimmons Dried Cherries	Salad: Romaine Lettuce, Red Cabbage, Sweet Red Pepper, Broccoli Fingers Lentil Casserole Steamed Broccoli
Thurs.	Grapes, Pears (as much as you want)	Salad: Bibb Lettuce, Green Cabbage, Celery, Cucumber, Sweet Red Pepper Peanut Butter on Celery Sticks (use unhydrogenated peanut butter, preferably raw)	Salad: Leaf Lettuce, Celery Cabbage, Carrots, few flowerets raw Cauliflower Tasty Cauliflower (cooked) Steamed Green Beans
Fri.	½ Fresh Ripe Pineapple 2 to 4 oz. Black Walnuts	Red Grapes ½ Avocado Figs	Salad: Romaine Lettuce, Celery, a few young tender raw Green Beans, Carrots Baked Potatoes Steamed Green Beans
Sat.	6 to 8 Oranges 2 to 3 oz. Walnuts and a few Brazil Nuts	Peaches Papaya Dried Bananas ½ Avocado	Salad: Bibb Lettuce, Celery, Green Cabbage Freshly Shelled Green Lima Beans, steamed with Broccoli & Diced Celery

	Breakfast	Lunch	Supper
Sun.	Watermelon (as much as you want)	Salad: Ruby & Leaf Lettuce, Sweet Red Pepper, Cucumber, Broccoli Fingers, a few raw Broccoli Flowerets, Tomatoes Eggplant Surprise Steamed Broccoli	Salad: Bibb Lettuce, Snow Peas, Alfalfa Sprouts Vegetable Stew with Garbanzos
Mon.	1 or 2 pints Strawberries Almond Butter Sunflower Seeds	Green Seedless Grapes ½ Avocado Dried Bananas	Salad: Leaf Lettuce, Celery, a few raw asparagus tips, green cabbage Kasha (Buckwheat Groats) Steamed Asparagus
Tues.	½ Fresh Ripe Pineapple 2-4 oz. Cashew Nuts	Pears Japanese Persimmons ½ Avocado 6 to 8 Dates	Salad: Bibb Lettuce, Cucumber, Tomatoes, Alfalfa Sprouts Unprocessed Cheese, 4 oz. Company Squash
Wed.	1 Grapefruit 2 to 4 Oranges 2 to 4 Oz. Blanched Almonds	Black Grapes Dried Bananas ½ Avocado	Salad: Romaine Lettuce, Carrots, Water Chestnuts Baked Beets and Baked Parsnips (or Steamed Oyster Plant) Steamed Kale
Thurs.	Red Grapes Pears	Salad: Leaf Lettuce, Celery, Cucumber, a few raw peas Thick Vegetable Soup with Freshly Shelled Peas	Salad: Lettuce, Celery, Sweet Red Pepper, Tomatoes, Raw Young Tender Zucchini 2 to 4 oz. Indian Nuts or English Walnuts
Fri.	1 Grapefruit 2 to 3 Oranges 2 to 4 oz. Pecans	Papaya ½ Avocado Banana Dried Soaked Prunes	Salad: Bibb Lettuce, Celery, small piece raw Turnip or Kohlrabi, Carrots Baked Butternut Squash, Steamed Turnips or Kohlrabi
Sat.	1 to 2 pints Strawberries 2 to 4 oz. unsalted Pistachios or Filberts	Mangos or Nectarines Banana ½ Avocado Dried Cherries	Salad: Ruby & Leaf Lettuce, Celery Cabbage, Cucumbers, Sprouts Split Pea Soup (Thick)

C

	Breakfast	Lunch	Supper
Sun.	Cantaloupe or Casaba Melon (as much as you want)	Salad: Bibb & Romaine Lettuce, Red Cabbage, Red Pepper Broccoli Fingers, Sweet Red Pepper Baked Globe Artichokes Steamed Broccoli Company Squash	Strawberries Tart Apples Cheese—4 oz. (unpasteurized, unprocessed, unsalted)
Mon.	2 to 3 Oranges Ground Blanched Almonds with Ground Sesame Seeds (Ground fresh in blender)	Black Grapes 1 Banana Pears Dates	Salad: Ruby Lettuce, Celery, Green Cabbage, Sweet Red Pepper Baked Sweet Potatoes or Mashed Rutabagas Steamed Asparagus
Tues.	Red Grapes Japanese Persimmons	Salad: Lettuce, Celery, Cucumber, Carrots Raw Peanuts or Coconut	Salad: Lettuce, Celery Cabbage, Sprouts, a few raw peas Freshly shelled Green Peas steamed with Broccoli & Celery Company Squash
Wed.	1 Grapefruit 2 to 3 Oranges 2 to 4 oz. Filberts	Watermelon (all you want)	Salad: Bibb & Oak Leaf Lettuce, Celery, Cucumber Millet Casserole Mixed Greens with Diced Turnips, Diced Celery, & Diced Sweet Pepper
Thurs.	1 to 2 pts. Strawberries 2 to 4 oz. Filberts	Banana ½ Avocado Apples Figs	Salad: Romaine Lettuce, Celery, Cucumber, Sprouts, Tomatoes Squash Casserole with Melted Cheese Topping Steamed Kale
Fri.	Papaya (as much as you want)	Salad: Bibb Lettuce, Celery, Green Cabbage, Cucumber, Raw Tender Young Squash, Tomatoes 2 to 4 oz. Pecans	Salad: Leaf Lettuce, Celery Cabbage, Carrots, Cucumbers Brown Rice Casserole Steamed Zucchini
Sat.	Watermelon (as much as you want)	Salad: Butter Crunch Lettuce, Celery, Snow Peas, Carrots, a few raw Cauliflowerets Tasty Cauliflower (baked)	Salad: Romaine Lettuce, Celery Cabbage, Cucumber, Tomatoes, Sweet Red Peppers 2 to 4 oz. Macadamia Nuts or Sunflower Seeds

SPECIAL MENUS

Hygienic Meals Containing All Essential Amino Acids
To accommodate those not yet ready to subscribe to the
"Circulating Pool" hypothesis—(Experienced hygienists have
abandoned this unnecessary preoccupation with amino acids).

1. a. Brazil Nuts or Filberts
   b. Any one or more of following nuts:
      Almonds, Pecans, Walnuts, Pignolias, Macadamias, Pis-
      tachios, Indian Nuts
   c. Pineapple or Tart Apples or Tomatoes
   d. Celery and Lettuce
2. a. Lettuce and Celery
   b. Avocado
   c. Carrot
   d. Raw Cabbage or Raw or Steamed Cauliflower or Brussels
      Sprouts
   e. (Add Baked Potato or any starch food, if desired)
3. a. Lettuce or Alfalfa Sprouts
   b. Celery
   c. Tomatoes
   d. Any Nuts (exc. Peanuts, Cashews, Coconut, Chestnuts,
      Sunflower Seeds)
   e. Raw Cabbage or Steamed Brussels Sprouts
   f. (Another Steamed Nonstarchy Vegetable may be added,
      if desired)
4. a. Apple
   b. Papaya
   c. Lettuce and Celery
   d. (Banana and/or other sweet or subacid fruit may be
      added, if desired)
5. a. Apple
   b. Avocado
   c. Lettuce and Celery
   d. (Other subacid fruit may be added, if desired. Bananas or
      other sweet fruit are a fair combination with avocados,
      and may be added, if desired)

HYGIENIC FOOD SOURCES OF
AMINO ACIDS

Name	*Food Sources*		
	Vegetables	*Fruits*	*Nuts*
Alanine	Alfalfa Carrot Celery Lambs Quarters Lettuce Cucumber Turnip Sweet Pepper	Apple Apricot Avocado Grapes Olive Orange Strawberry	Almond
Arginine (Considered Essential by Some Authorities)	Alfalfa Green Vegetables Carrot Beet Cucumber Celery Lettuce Potato Parsnip		
Aspartic	Carrot Celery Cucumber Tomato Turnip Greens	Grapefruit Apple Apricot Pineapple Watermelon	Almond
Cystine	Alfalfa Carrot Beet Cabbage Cauliflower Kale Brussels Sprouts	Apple Currants Pineapple Raspberry	Brazil Nut Filbert
Glutamic	Snap Beans Brussels Sprouts Carrot Cabbage Celery Lambs Quarters Lettuce	Papaya	
Glycine	Carrot Dandelion Greens Turnip Celery Alfalfa Okra Potato	Fig Orange Huckleberry Raspberry Pomegranate Watermelon	Almond

Name / Food Sources

Name	Vegetables	Fruits	Nuts
Histidine (Considered Essential by Some Authorities)	Carrot Beet Celery Cucumber Lambs Quarters Turnip Greens Alfalfa	Apple Pineapple Pomegranate Papaya	Most Nuts
Hydroxyglutamic	Carrot Celery Lettuce Tomato	Grapes Huckleberry Raspberry Plum	
Hydroxyproline	Carrot Beet Lettuce Turnip Greens Cucumber Kale	Apricot Cherry Fig Raisin Grapes Orange Olive Avocado Pineapple	Almond Brazil Nut Coconut
Iodogorgoic	Carrot Celery Tomato Lettuce	Pineapple	
Isoleucine (Essential)	Carrot Kale Cabbage Most Green Vegs.	Papaya Avocado Olive	Coconut All Nuts (exc. Peanut, Cashew, Chestnut) Sunflower Seed
Leucine (Essential)	Same as Isoleucine		
Lysine (Essential)	Carrot Beet Cucumber Celery Turnip Greens Alfalfa Soybean Sprouts	Papaya Apple Apricot Pear Grapes	Most Nuts
Methionine (Essential)	Brussels Sprouts Cabbage Cauliflower Kale	Pineapple Apple	Brazil Nut Filbert
Norleucine	No Reported Plant Sources— Helps Leucine Function Synthesized If Needed		
Phenylalanine (Essential)	Carrot Beet Tomato Most Green Vegs.	Pineapple Apple	Most Nuts

Name   *Food Sources*

	Vegetables	Fruits	Nuts
Proline	Carrot Beet Lettuce Dandelion Greens Turnip Cucumber Kale	Apricot Cherry Avocado Fig Raisin Grapes Olive Orange Pineapple	Coconut Almond Brazil Nut
Serine	Carrot Beet Celery Cucumber Cabbage Alfalfa	Papaya Apple Pineapple	
Threonine (Essential)	Carrot Alfalfa Green Leafy Vegs.	Papaya	Most Nuts
Thyroxine	Carrot Celery Lettuce Turnip Tomato	Pineapple	
Tryptophane (Essential)	Carrot Beet Celery Kale Snap Bean Brussels Sprouts Alfalfa Turnip		Most Nuts
Tyrosine	Alfalfa Carrot Beet Cucumber Lettuce Dandelion Greens Parsnip Asparagus Sweet Pepper	Strawberry Apricot Cherry Apple Watermelon Fig	Almond
Valine (Essential)	Carrot Turnip Dandelion Greens Lettuce Parsnip Squash Celery Beet Okra Tomato Kale	Apple Pomegranate	Almond

XIX. Preparation of Cooked Foods and Recipes

Seasonings

ALL SEASONINGS ARE UNHYGIENIC.

Raw foods require no seasoning.

Lightly steamed or baked individual vegetables require no seasoning.

When several foods are cut up and combined into a casserole, stew or soup, we are getting farther away from the simplicity of Hygienic food preparation, and the pleasant natural individual flavors of foods. It is then that we are confronted with "seasoning" problems.

Many people request "recipes" for such casseroles, stews, or soups, for use during the transitional period to Natural Hygiene, to meet the demands of their families, for variety, and for special occasions.

Such recipes are therefore included in this book, with the admonition that they be used infrequently, and not as a regular part of the diet.

These dishes may be "seasoned" with very small amounts of onions or garlic, if care is taken to cook the onions or garlic for twenty minutes (after which the mustard oil, an irritant, is gone). Parsley and celery tops and sweet red bell peppers may also be used as seasonings. Tomatoes may be used as a seasoning for dishes which do not contain any starches or starchy proteins.

Two seasonings which are available in health food stores are also included in some of the recipes, Vogue Vegebase, and Dr. Bronner's Seasoning, but, if you use these at all, use them seldom and sparingly, and only in the transition period, or to meet the demands of non-conforming family and friends. The sooner you can get away from the use of all such commercial preparations, the greater will be your progress toward the ideal.

The Case Against Seasonings

First of all, all seasonings, even the mildest, are irritants to some extent.

Next, it is important to remember that most of the senses have a role in digestion. Seeing, smelling, touching and tasting the food all help in sending the proper signals for the secretion of the digestive juices, and their adaptation to the character of the food. Complicated mixtures of foods interfere with this process, and make it less efficient, and may cause digestive problems.

When we compound the problem by adding these commercial seasoning mixtures (perhaps required for "fancy" recipes or because of jaded appetites) the true taste of the individual foods is further disguised. Such a situation makes it extremely difficult for the digestive system to supply secretions that can adequately cope with these meals, and digestion is inhibited and impaired.

When you are a "seasoned" Hygienist, you will abandon all seasonings.

Preparation

The less "preparation" foods have undergone, the more valuable they are as foods. Salad vegetables should be washed immediately before serving, and should not be cut up. Eat as a "finger salad".

Cooking a long time at low heat causes more damage to food than quick cooking, and cooking under steam pressure destroys vitamins. Use small amount of water, steam for short periods of time, and use any residual liquid.

Leafy vegetables should never be cooked so long that they change color. Cook as short a time as possible, and serve immediately. The practice of adding bicarbonate of soda to vegetables to preserve their green color destroys their food value, impairs their digestibility, and is certainly not necessary.

Carrots, beets, parsnips, turnips, squash, potatoes and sweet potatoes should not be pared and cut up before cooking. Scrub them, cook whole and serve whole.

Butter, cream or oil should be added to vegetables when serving and not while cooking—fats should never be cooked. Try using a piece of avocado when serving or eating (instead of butter or oil). Avocado is tastier, and far superior nutritionally.

Eggplant is an excellent and tasty vegetable, but requires a little extra care in preparation. (See Recipes)

Soups (if used) should not be too watery; better a bit thicker.

Salsify, Rutabaga or Kohlrabi may be baked or steamed.

Fresh Green Lima Beans (or other fresh beans and peas): Buy in the pod, shell them yourself, and steam until tender.

Young tender Okra (raw or cooked) is a good green vegetable, combines well with tomatoes, and is a good thickener for mixed vegetables, or vegetable stews or soups.

Steamed Vegetables: Broccoli, Cauliflower, Green Beans, Yellow Crookneck or Zucchini Squash, Brussels Sprouts

Add diced celery and sweet pepper to any vegetable, if desired. Steam in small amount of water until just barely tender. Do not overcook. Or use Steamer (Steamarvel) which may be inserted in any size pot so vegetable does not lie in water and can't scorch or burn.

Add small amount of butter before serving, if desired. If not overcooked, no seasoning should be necessary.

Globe Artichokes (Green Vegetable)

May be baked in oven in covered casserole—no water necessary. Just wash and put in casserole wet. Bake at 400 degrees, approximately one hour, longer if quite large. May also be steamed, using Steamarvel, or as small an amount of water as possible.

Corn on the Cob

Green Corn, freshly picked, is delicious eaten raw, if not too mature, and is classified as a green vegetable. Several hours after picking, it is a starchy vegetable. Steam until just tender and serve with small amount of butter, if desired.

Greens: Kale, Turnip, Mustard, Dandelion, Collard (for greatest nutritional value, eat young tender greens raw)

Steam in very small amount of water until just tender. Add small diced turnips to turnip greens. You may add diced celery and sweet pepper. No seasoning or butter necessary.

Cooked spinach should not be used: it is too high in oxalic acid, a calcium antagonist. Use beet greens seldom, for same reason. Same applies to Swiss Chard. Kale is an excellent green.

Steamed or Baked Potatoes

Steamed potatoes retain more nutrients (lower heat). Scrub clean and steam in skins.

Bake without foil or any coating. Scrub & bake in open pan in 400 degree oven. Small potatoes take 45 minutes or so, large ones 1 hour. (If baked in closed pan, baking time is reduced.) Preheat oven.

Baked Beets or Parsnips or Carrots

Scrub and clean well. Bake in covered dish. Select beets about 2 inches in diameter. These will all bake in about 45 minutes and are delicious; no seasoning required. Small amount of butter O.K.

Baked Yams, Sweet Potatoes, Butternut or Acorn or Hubbard Squash
Bake Sweet Potatoes and Yams whole. Cut Squash in half and remove seeds. Serve with butter if desired. Baking time varies—about 30 minutes.

Asparagus—Raw asparagus tips are delicious.
To cook, place in pan at an angle so tips are not in water. Steam till barely tender. Serve with butter, if desired.

MODIFIED HYGIENIC RECIPES

Eggplant Surprise (Protein)
   8 oz. Cashew Nuts
   2 Small to Medium Tomatoes, Peeled & Cut Up
   2 Strips Celery, Cut Up
   4 Small Comfrey Leaves (If Available)   } Topping
*½ Tablespoon Vegebase (Optional—Not Hygienic & Not Recommended)
   ½ to ¾ Cup Water

Blend all, start with ½ cup water, more water if necessary; mixture should be quite thick. Spread thickly on broiled eggplant slices, and brown very slightly in broiler. Enough to cover slices from two medium sized eggplant. Can also be used as a topping for other non-starchy vegetables.

Broiled Eggplant Slices: Slice eggplant about ½ inch thick. Peel if desired (peeling gets a little chewy in broiler). Spread out on cookie sheet. Run water on slices so they are quite wet on both sides. Sprinkle both sides sparingly with Vegebase*. Broil lightly on

*See Chapter XIX, No. 1, Seasonings

both sides, spread with topping and brown in broiler per above directions.

Easy Eggplant Casserole (Protein)

    2 Medium Diced Eggplant (Unpeeled) (Dice in Rather Large Pieces)
    2 Medium Tomatoes, Peeled and Cut Up
    4 Strips Celery, Sliced
    ½ Sweet Pepper, Diced
    *½ Tbsp. Vegebase (Optional—Not Hygienic & Not Recommended)

Place all in casserole, add about 1 inch of water. Steam (covered) on top of stove about three minutes. Add 8 oz. ground cashew nuts (on top). Bake uncovered in 375 degree oven about 20 minutes or until cashews are slightly browned. May be dotted with butter just before serving. Serves 3 or 4.

Crumbly Eggplant Casserole (Protein)

Broil Eggplant slices lightly (same as for Eggplant Surprise, but do not spread with any topping).

Prepare desired amount of Spanish sauce (see recipe). Grind desired amount of cashew nuts.

Put Spanish sauce, ground cashews and broiled eggplant slices alternately in casserole (in layers), ending up with Spanish sauce and light sprinkling of ground cashews over the top. Bake in 375 degree oven until lightly browned.

Suggested quantities to serve 3 or 4:

1 large or 2 medium Eggplant
1 recipe Spanish sauce
10 to 12 oz. ground cashews

Eggplant Steaks

Slice in ½ inch slices, spread out on cookie sheet. Run water on slices so they are quite wet on both sides.

---

*See Chapter XIX, No. 1, Seasonings

Sprinkle Vegebase* sparingly on both sides. Broil lightly on both sides. Turn off broiler and let slices remain in hot oven about ten minutes longer to become slightly more tender. Can be eaten plain as a non-starchy vegetable, just dotted with butter before serving, or. . . . If desired, put a thick slice of raw tomato on each steak and a slice of Swiss or unprocessed mild Cheddar cheese. Serve when cheese is barely melted or very lightly browned. (Protein)

Lentil Casserole (Protein)
    1 Cup Lentils
    4 Strips Celery, Cut up Small
    ½ Diced Sweet Pepper
*½ Tblsp. Dr. Bronner's Seasoning
    2 Cups Water

Steam approximately 20 minutes or until tender. Do not overcook. Add small amount butter before serving. (Soaking lentils an hour or so before cooking will shorten cooking time.) Serves 2 or 3.

MODIFIED HYGIENIC RECIPES

Zucchini Cheese Casserole (Protein)
    4 Medium Zucchini or 2 or 3 Large
    2 Medium Tomatoes, Peeled and Cut Up
    4 Strips Celery, Sliced
    ½ Diced Sweet Pepper
*½ Tblsp. Vegebase (Optional—Not Hygienic & Not
       Recommended)

Place all in Electric Skillet (or Casserole on top of stove). Steam until tender, about 15 minutes. Turn off heat. Dot with butter and lay slices of unprocessed cheddar cheese over top. Cover and serve when cheese is just barely melted. Serves 3 or 4.

---

*See Chapter XIX, No. 1, Seasonings

Split Pea Soup (Protein)
1 Cup Dried Green Split Peas
4 Cups Water
1 Small Chopped Onion
1 or 2 Small Cloves Minced Garlic
   Combine and simmer for approximately 1 hour. If
desired, mash before adding other ingredients. Add 2
strips sliced celery, one sliced small yellow crookneck
squash, one small sliced zucchini squash, plus approx.
½ tbsp. *Dr. Bronner's seasoning. Simmer 15 minutes
longer. Add small amount of butter before serving.
Serve with sprinkling of alfalfa sprouts. Serves 3 or 4.

Brown Rice Casserole (Starch Meal) or
Wild Rice Casserole (Wild Rice is higher in Protein
   than Brown Rice, but is still classified as Starch, or
   Starchy Protein)
   ¾ Cup Wild Rice or Brown Rice (or Mixed if you
      get a variety of Brown Rice that cooks as quickly
      as Wild Rice, or you may precook the Brown
      Rice before adding)
   4 Strips Sliced Celery
   2 Diced Carrots
   ½ Diced Sweet Pepper
   8 Water Chestnuts, Cut Up (If Available)
*¾ Tblsp. Dr. Bronner's Seasoning (Optional—Not
      Hygienic & Not Recommended)
   Pour boiling water over combined ingredients. (Wild
Rice approx. 2½ cups water, Brown Rice approx. 3½
cups water). Put in 350 degree oven. Wild Rice takes
approx. 45 minutes to one hour; Brown Rice approx.
1¼ to 1½ hours. Check to be sure whether additional
water is necessary about ¾ way through. Add small
amount of butter before serving. Serves 3 or 4.

Kasha (Buckwheat Groats) (Starch Meal)
   ¾ Cup Brown Buckwheat Groats, 4 Strips Celery,

---

*See Chapter XIX, No. 1, Seasonings

Sliced, 2 Diced Carrots, ½ Diced Sweet Pepper, 1 Tblsp. *Dr. Bronner's Seasoning (or less). Pour approx. 4 cups boiling water over combined ingredients. Simmer until tender—do not overcook. Be watchful so it won't burn, may need more water. Serves 3 or 4.

MODIFIED HYGIENIC RECIPES

Millet—Squash Casserole (Starchy Protein)
½ Cup Millet, Browned Slightly (Dry) in Skillet
2 Cups Boiling Water
Cook about 10 minutes, then add 4 Strips Sliced Celery, 3 Small Sliced Zucchini Squash, add more water if necessary, and cook about 15 minutes more, until tender and all water absorbed. Add ½ tsp. Dr. Bronner's Seasoning*, 1 tsp. Vegebase*, and small amount butter before serving. Serves three or four.

Vegetable Soup or Stew (Soup should be very thick, even less water for Stew) (Vegetable Meal, Slightly Starchy)
A few soaked (see Bean instructions) Garbanzos or Split Peas (not enough to make it a Protein Meal)
Yellow Crookneck Squash
Zucchini
Carrots
Celery
Green Beans
Cauliflower
Raw Parsley
*Vegebase (Optional—Not Hygienic & Not Recommended)
Any Combination of These Vegetables.
Cook Parsley in Soup, or add small amount raw chopped parsley before serving.
Add Butter before serving.

---

*See Chapter XIX, No. 1, Seasonings

Company Squash (Green Vegetable)

Use tender young yellow crookneck or zucchini squash or both. Slice slantwise (oval slices) about ¼ inch thick. Place in casserole with enough water to wet slices throroughly. Pour off most of excess water. Sprinkle wet slices with Vegebase*. Sprinkle with Paprika. Bake at 375 degrees 10 minutes covered, 10 to 15 minutes uncovered till slightly brown. Dot with butter before serving.

Tasty Cauliflower (Slightly Starchy Vegetable)

Break or cut into small flowerets. Steam on top of stove about 10-15 minutes until just barely tender. Then toss with Vegebase* and brown lightly under broiler. Add butter before serving. (May be sprinkled with Paprika before broiling.)

Spanish Sauce (May be used wtih Protein, not Starch Meal)

4 or 5 Medium Sliced Tomatoes
1 Chopped Sweet Pepper
4 Strips Diced Celery

Simmer 20 to 30 minutes (add small amount of water, if necessary) and add small amount of butter. Serve on plain eggplant steaks, plain baked soy beans, steamed zucchini or yellow crookneck squash, or broccoli.

Okra Casserole (Protein)

    1 Cup Sliced Okra
    3 Medium Tomatoes, Peeled and Cut Up
    1 Small Sweet Pepper, Diced
    1 Medium Zucchini Squash Sliced
    4 Strips Celery, Sliced
*½ Tbsp. Vegebase (Optional—Not Hygienic & Not Recommended)

*See Chapter XIX, No. 1, Seasonings

Simmer okra, tomatoes, onion and pepper in enough water to barely cover about twenty minutes. Add remaining ingredients, plus a topping of eight ounces ground cashew nuts. Bake uncovered in 375 degree oven about twenty minutes or until cashews are slightly browned. May be dotted with butter just before serving. Serves 3 or 4.

Okra-Tomato Vegetable Soup or Stew

Broccoli
Yellow Squash
Zucchini Squash   Any or All
Celery   of these
Okra   to your
Tomatoes   taste.

Less Water for Stew.
Vegetable Meal—no starch.
May be used with protein.
Add butter before serving.

MODIFIED HYGIENIC RECIPES

Instructions and Information re Soy Beans (Protein) (and other Beans, Dried and Fresh)

Soy Beans contain about three times as much protein as other beans, and little or no starch. Dried Soy Beans take a long time to cook—they may take 3½ to 5 hours. Dried Soy Beans should be soaked over night in water (preferably distilled) to cover, in refrigerator. Next day, add more water to cover (use the soaking water), and cook until desired softness is attained, adding more water as necessary. If the soy beans are to be used in a baked casserole, or ground, or chopped, they should not be cooked until soft, but removed when still rather firm and chewy. Cooking time may be shortened (perhaps halved) by freezing after soaking (in soaking water) several hours or over night. Some nutritionists advocate longer soaking of soy beans (24 to 48 hours) and the discarding several times of the soaking waters, in order to be certain of the destruction of the toxic anti-enzyme factor that is said to block the digestion of proteins. The longer soaking shortens the cooking time. (All dried beans should be soaked, preferably over night, before using.)

Green Soy Beans will take much less time to soften, probably from 15 to 30 minutes, depending on variety and condition, and need not be soaked. Other beans fresh from the pod (limas, black-eyed peas, etc.) will soften more quickly, and only need a brief cooking period—no soaking.

Plain cooked Soy Beans or other beans may be seasoned with *Dr. Bronner's seasoning to taste, butter may be added when serving, or they may be served with Spanish sauce (see Recipe). They may also be added to steamed nonstarchy vegetables.

Sprouted Soy Beans (or other sprouted beans) may be eaten raw, or steamed a short time to improve their palatibility.

MODIFIED HYGIENIC RECIPES (Protein)

Soy Bean Casserole

Soak 1 cup Dried Soy Beans over night in two cups water (in refrigerator). See Soy Bean Instructions for Cooking (not until soft, but still rather firm and chewy). Add 2 strips diced celery, a few chopped celery leaves, one diced sweet red pepper, and *Dr. Bronner's Seasoning to taste, about 2 tsp. Add enough water to cover. Cover casserole and bake in 375 degree oven until done, with lid removed during last half hour of baking (may take one to one and one-half hours). Serves 3 or 4.

This recipe may also be used for any dried beans.

---

*See Chapter XIX, No. 1, Seasonings

(All dried beans should be soaked, preferably over night, before using.)

MODIFIED HYGIENIC RECIPES (Protein)

Crunchy Soy Bean Treat

Soak and cook dried Soy Beans as usual (see Soy Bean Instructions)—not too soft, should still be rather firm and chewy.

Grind or chop to consistency of coarsely chopped nuts. Add diced celery (about 2 strips per three servings); a few chopped celery leaves; one diced sweet red pepper. Add *Dr. Bronner's Seasoning to taste (about 2 tsp. per three servings). Place in casserole or loaf pan. Add the soy bean liquid and/or water to almost cover. Bake uncovered in 375 degree oven until lightly browned and liquid is absorbed. Add butter when serving, if desired.

MODIFIED HYGIENIC RECIPES (Protein)

Soy Bean Loaf (or Garbanzo Bean Loaf)

Soak and cook dried Soy Beans or Garbanzo Beans as usual (See Bean Instructions)—not too soft, should still be somewhat firm and chewy.

Grind or chop to consistency of chopped nuts (not too coarse). Add diced celery (about 3 strips per three servings); a few chopped celery leaves; one diced sweet red pepper; about ½ cup broccoli flowerets, cut up in small pieces, and about ½ cup zucchini squash, cut in thin half slices (per three servings); *Dr. Bronner's Seasoning to taste (about 2 tsp. per three servings). Mix ingredients together lightly and add enough soy bean liquid and/or water so it will hold together. Put in loaf

---

*See Chapter XIX, No. 1, Seasonings

pan, top with slices of raw tomato and strips of sweet red pepper or pimiento. Bake uncovered in 375 degree oven until lightly browned, but still somewhat moist (about 20 to 30 minutes).

Bean Pot (Protein)

Use any beans fresh from the pod: Limas, Soy, Black-Eyed Peas or any other freshly shelled beans.

Cut up in bottom of pot: 4 strips Celery, 2 Medium Yellow Summer Squash or Zucchini Squash. Sprinkle with 1 tsp. Vegebase.* On top of cut up vegetables, put 1 cup beans which have been pre-cooked for 10 to 15 minutes until almost soft. Over top sprinkle 1 tsp. Vegebase.* Add water carefully around side about half way up. Cover and bake in 375 degree oven for one-half hour. Uncover and bake until a little drier. If you like it quite dry, use less water. Serves 2 or 3.

MODIFIED HYGIENIC RECIPES

Two Protein Soups or Stews

1. 1 Cup Freshly Shelled Blackeyed Peas, Lima Beans or Green Peas; Add 2 Cups Water for Stew (3 Cups water for Thick Soup.) Simmer 15 minutes. Add 4 strips Diced Celery, 1 Small Sliced Zucchini Squash, and simmer 10 minutes more. Add Vegebase* to taste and butter before serving. If desired, sprinkle servings with alfalfa sprouts. Serves 2 or 3.

2. Simmer 1 Diced Onion in 3 Cups Water for Soup (2 cups Water for Stew) for 10 minutes. Add 4 Strips Sliced Celery, ½ Small Head Broccoli, cut-up, 2 Small Sliced Zucchini Squash. Simmer 10 minutes more. Add 4 ounces Ground Cashew Nuts (add more water, if necessary). Simmer a few minutes and add Vegebase and butter to taste, before

*See Chapter XIX, No. 1, Seasonings

serving. If desired, sprinkle servings with alfalfa sprouts. Serves 2 or 3.

Chewy Potato Casserole (Starch Meal)

Plain Baked Potatoes are a lot less work, but this potato dish has some advantages:

1. Good company dish—Serve with plain eggplant steaks and steamed broccoli
2. Different chewy consistency
3. Short cooking time
4. All skins are eaten

3 Unpeeled Medium Potatoes
3 Unpeeled Medium Carrots
3 Strips Celery, Diced
1 Small Diced Sweet Pepper
1 tsp. Dr. Bronner's Seasoning (or more, if necessary)
1 tsp. Vegebase

Shred the potatoes and carrots coarsely and blend balance of ingredients and combine. Or for an easier method, shred half of the potatoes coarsely and blend balance of the ingredients and combine. The coarse shreds provide the chewy consistency. When blending these ingredients, use the minimum amount of water possible. Bake about 30 minutes in covered casserole, then uncover to brown top slightly. Serve with butter. Serves 2 or 3.

Beet Borsht (Slightly Starchy)

Cook Sliced Beets slightly (about 10 minutes). Put in blender with small amount of raw beets. Suggested amount: Two large beets cooked, two small beets raw. Add to blender mixture 2 strips raw celery, 2 small raw carrots. Use water from cooked beets and add more water as necessary to blend. Should not be too thin. Add 1 tsp. Vegebase* or more. Chill. Add sour cream to taste before serving.

---

*See Chapter XIX, No. 1, Seasonings

MODIFIED HYGIENIC RECIPES

Protein Vegetable Chop Suey

  A Few Pieces of Celery Top
1 large Sweet Pepper, Sliced
4 Strips Sliced Celery
2 Large Strips Sliced Celery Cabbage and an equivalent amount of Broccoli Flowerets and Green Leaves
¾ Cup Freshly Shelled Green Peas
*1 tsp. Dr. Bronner's Seasoning (Optional—Not Hygienic & Not Recommended)
*1 tsp. Vegebase (Optional—Not Hygienic & Not Recommended)
1 Cup Mung Bean or Soy Bean Sprouts

Steam celery tops 10 minutes. Blend half of the green peas in one cup water and add to the steamed celery. Add the whole green peas, half of the sprouts, and the balance of the ingredients. Water level should be about half way up. Steam 10 minutes more. Add the seasoning and a small amount of butter and cover. Sprinkle the remaining raw sprouts over the top when serving, or serve over the raw sprouts. Cooked unsprouted soy beans may be substituted for the bean sprouts, served with alfalfa sprouts and raw Snow Peas (if available) sprinkled over the top of each serving. Serves 3 or 4.

Starch Vegetable Chop Suey

  A Few Pieces of Celery Top
1 Large Sweet Pepper, Sliced
4 Strips Sliced Celery
2 Large Strips Sliced Celery Cabbage or an equivalent amount of Broccoli Flowerets and Green Leaves
¾ Cup Freshly Shelled Green Peas

---

*See Chapter XIX, No. 1, Seasonings

2 Large Carrots, Cut Up in Bite Sized Pieces
½ Cup Cauliflower Flowerets
½ Cup Jerusalem Artichokes, cut up in
   chunks, or   } Optional
¼ Cup Water Chestnuts, cut up in chunks
*1 tsp. Dr. Bronner's Seasoning (Optional—Not Hygienic & Not Recommended)
*1 tsp. Vegebase (Optional—Not Hygienic & Not Recommended)

Steam carrots, celery tops (and water chestnuts, if used) for 10 minutes. Blend half of peas in one cup water and add. Add the balance of the peas whole, and the other ingredients. Water level should be about half way up. Steam 10 minutes more. Add the seasoning and a small amount of butter and cover. Serve over cooked or baked brown rice. Sprinkle alfalfa sprouts and raw Snow Peas (if available) over each serving. Serves 3 or 4.

Plain Cooked Brown Rice (for Vegetable Chop Suey—Starchy Type)
1 Cup Brown Rice and 2 Cups Cold Water
Boil for one minute. Cover tight, turn flame down low, and cook 45 minutes covered till water is absorbed and rice is fluffy. If not dry, put in warm oven uncovered for a few minutes.

Plain Baked Brown Rice (for Starch Vegetable Chop Suey)
1 Cup Brown Rice and 1½ Cups Boiling Water
Cover and bake one hour in 375 degree oven until dry and fluffy. If not dry, uncover for 5 minutes or so.

MODIFIED HYGIENIC RECIPES

Potato Broccoli Soup (Smooth!) (Starch)
Blend one medium-sized unpeeled potato with one

---

*See Chapter XIX, No. 1, Seasonings

small onion in 3 cups water. Heat until it thickens. Add optional amounts of cut-up broccoli, diced celery and celery tops, and cook over slow burner for approximately 15 minutes, stirring frequently. Add more water if necessary. Add ½ tblsp. *Dr. Bronner's Seasoning and ½ tblsp. *Vegebase. Add a chunk of butter before serving.

MODIFIED HYGIENIC RECIPES

Vichysoisse (Starchy)

Cut up 2 Leeks or 4 Large Spring Onions (white part only) and put in blender with 2 Medium cut up Potatoes, 1 Large cut up Carrot, and 2 cut up Strips Celery. Add 1 Cup Water. Blend. Put in saucepan. Add 1 to 1½ Cups more Water and 2 tsp. *Dr. Bronner's Seasoning. Heat to boiling point and turn down to barely simmer for 10 minutes or so until thick. Add ½ cup Heavy Cream (preferably raw). Serves 2 or 3.

Clabber or Cottage Cheese

Put whole raw milk in individual cups or glasses (covered with thin cloth or paper towels) in a warm place (about 75 to 85 degrees) about 30 to 48 hours (may take less or longer, depending on milk and temperature) until thick and custardy. (Don't move it, mix or stir.) Sour cream will be on top. This will keep in refrigerator about five days. The secret of successful clabber is an even warm temperature. Clabber may be eaten with the fruit meal.

For Cottage Cheese, put Clabber in cheese cloth or nylon net bag and let drip all night.

Faster Recipe: Clabber can be made in 12 to 24 hours by adding 2 or 3 tbsp. Borden's Buttermilk per

*See Chapter XIX, No. 1, Seasonings

quart to the sweet milk, or by adding lemon juice to the sweet milk to start the souring or clabbering process.

Coconut Milk (See Chapter XII for Instructions for Opening Coconut)

Some people who find coconut meat difficult to chew may enjoy using this palatable coconut milk occasionally.

Blend 2 cups warm water with ½ cup fresh peeled coconut, and cool in refrigerator. Blend again and strain through cheesecloth or Nylon mesh. If stored in refrigerator, it will separate, but may be stirred with a spoon before drinking. Do not store too long.

Coconut Milk Shake
1 Cup Coconut Milk
Blend with 1 Small Banana
and/or 1 tbsp. Carob Powder
and/or Several Dates
and/or 2 oz. Sweet Cherry or Sweet Grape Juice—adds an extra "fillip"

Depending on how sweet you like it

MODIFIED HYGIENIC RECIPES

Blanched Almonds

Almonds should be blanched, as their brown skins contain a strong astringent. To blanch, put almonds in a large strainer (with a handle) and dip in boiling water for about one minute, and then dip in cool water. If this does not loosen the skins sufficiently, repeat the process. Skins should slip off easily.

Almond Butter or Pecan Butter

Grind in blender or mill and add a very small amount of oil. (Sesame oil is a pleasant tasting and stable oil.)

Cashew Butter

Grind in blender or mill and pat into a butter. It is not necessary to add any oil.

Peanut Butter

Grind raw or slightly roasted peanuts in blender or grinder, and pat into a butter. It is not necessary to add any oil. A better textured peanut butter may be made in the Champion Juicer, using the homogenizing blank.

Brazil Nut Butter with Walnuts

Grind in blender or mill and pat into butter. It is not necessary to add any oil.

Nuts 'n' Seeds Butter

 1 Cup Nuts (any kind except cashews)
½ Cup Sunflower Seeds
½ Cup Sesame Seeds

Grind in blender or mill. Add a very small amount of oil.

Nut Milk

 2 Cups Water
½ Cup Nuts

Blend as thoroughly as possible. If this is to be used for an infant, it may be necessary to strain it through cheesecloth.

XX. Special Recipes for Entertaining

Many of the recipes in Chapter XIX are excellent for use in entertaining guests, both for convenience and palatability.

However, some of the recipes in *this* chapter would

not be used by a Hygienist in his regular diet, but they might work out better for parties and groups of people, because they are perhaps:

1. More economical
2. More convenient
3. More liberal for conventional friends

See end of Chapter XIV for Salad Dressings and Dips.

Serve trays of finger salad with salad dressings on the side.

Or serve large bowls of salad cut up as little as possible, with salad dressings on the side. Or serve celery sticks with dips.

Fruit Salads For Entertaining

Fruits should be served whole and should only be peeled, cut or broken immediately prior to eating. The Hygienic Fruit Meal with its trays of beautiful colorful whole fruit served with a sharp knife cannot be surpassed. But serving an attractive cut-up fruit salad is a good compromise when entertaining your conventional friends.

A good fruit salad for this purpose may be prepared in advance as follows: Start with eight ounces of cherry juice or grape juice. For this purpose, you may use bottled juice, usually obtainable in Health Food Stores, frequently from organically grown fruit, and of quite good taste and quality, although it is, of course, pasteurized. Add whatever fresh subacid fruit is obtainable: peaches, apricots, sweet apples, pears, papayas, sweet grapes, cherries. If you don't have enough fresh fruit (three or four kinds would be ample), add some dried cherries and/or apricots (soaked over night). Don't cut up the fruit into too small pieces, and be sure there is enough juice to cover. Add sliced bananas just before serving.

You could serve this fruit salad along with an avocado dip (mashed avocado and sour cream) with celery sticks for dipping, and rice crackers for your conventional friends who just must have some kind of "bread".

Another good fruit salad to serve your guests, if you are serving a protein snack like cheese, is the following:

1 Whole Grapefruit, segmented
3 Oranges, segmented
1 Small Ripe Pineapple, Cut Up, or Libby's unsweetened canned Pineapple
1 Quart Whole or Sliced Strawberries (Fresh)

If there is not enough liquid from the fresh fruit to cover, add some Libby's unsweetened canned pineapple juice.

Two other attractive fruit salads for entertaining (really the best ones except that they cannot be prepared too far in advance) are:

1. Subacid and Sweet Fruit

   Arrange on a large platter whole cherries, small bunches of sweet grapes, whole apricots, quartered peaches, apples and pears, papaya and avocado slices, surrounded by dried dates and figs. A separate platter of whole bananas may be served. No other refreshments should be necessary with this sumptuous repast.

2. Acid Fruit

   Cut pineapple in quarters; cut away each quarter from skin and slice downward; serve in the shell (pineapple boats). Arrange on platter surrounded by whole fresh strawberries and orange sections. This may be served with assorted nuts and/or cheeses.

Individual Salad Bowls (Protein)
Meal - in - One

Medium-sized pieces of lettuce (2 or 3 varieties): Boston, Bibb, leaf, Romaine

Cut-up Red Cabbage
Sliced Sweet Red Pepper
Sliced Celery
Quartered Tomatoes

Choice of $\left\{ \begin{array}{l} \text{Sliced young tender Zucchini or other} \\ \text{Summer Squash} \\ \text{or} \\ \text{A few small Broccoli Flowerets} \end{array} \right.$

Choice of $\left\{ \begin{array}{l} \text{A few Snow Peas or young tender Green} \\ \text{Peas} \\ \text{or} \\ \text{A few Olives} \end{array} \right.$

Garnish with:

Pignolia Nuts and   Raw Milk Cheese Slices and
Sunflower Seeds and OR Avocado Slices and
Alfalfa Sprouts   Alfalfa Sprouts

Serve with Vegebase and Oil Dressing or Cucumber Sour Cream Dressing, if desired.

Coconut Treat
Combine optional amounts of:

> grated coconut
> grated carrot
> grated cabbage
> chopped celery
> (if desired, a few raisins
> may be added)

Moisten with coconut liquid or coconut milk.

May be served with a large green salad and globe artichokes for a satisfying company meal.

Ambrosia Sweet Potatoes
Cut baked sweet potatoes in half lengthwise just before serving, add a bit of butter, and sprinkle with shredded fresh coconut.

Date Coconut Pie
Moisten fresh grated coconut with water and pat into pie plate for crust. Chill for an hour or so.

Blend bananas and pitted dates in as little water as possible (mixture should be quite thick) and pour over the crust.

Put coconut liquid in blender and added small pieces of peeled coconut until you have a thick blended mixture, and spread over the pie.

Top with shredded coconut and pitted dates, whole or slices. Chill for at least two hours.

Fruity Banana Coconut Pie

Mix equal amounts of fresh grated coconut and chopped dates, and pat into pie plate for crust. Moisten with water, if necessary. Chill for an hour or so. Fill with sliced bananas. Blend any subacid fruit with raw cream and pour over sliced bananas. (Mixture should be thick.) Top with whipped cream and sprinkle with grated coconut. Chill for 2 hours before serving.

Compote

Blend bananas with small amount of sweet grape or cherry juice, and with other sweet or subacid fruit. Serve immediately, or keep very cold until served.

Apricot-Prune Whip

Soak over night dried apricots and pitted prunes, and blend the next day with the soaking water. Serve plain or with sliced bananas.

Frozen Bananas

Roll ripe bananas in carob syrup (carob powder mixed with water) and then in grated coconut and freeze.

Raw Apple Sauce

Wash, quarter and core sweet juicy apples with skins on. Put in blender a few pieces at a time with a small amount of apple or grape juice. Other fruits may be combined with the apples. Should be prepared immediately before serving, to keep color and flavor, or keep very cold until served.

Strawberry-Citrus Fruit Cup

Combine peeled orange and grapefruit sections with sliced or whole strawberries.

Ice Cream

Put 1 quart cream (preferably raw) in blender, add two bananas and/or other sweet fruit. Add enough pitted dates to make a thick mixture. If frozen in regular ice cream freezer, mixture need not be thick. If frozen in refrigerator-freezer, make as thick as possible, so ice crystals will not form, and stir up two or three times during freezing. Carob may be used for a flavor and color similar to chocolate.

Or whip the cream until stiff and fold the blended fruit into the whipped cream and freeze in refrigerator-freezer.

Coconut-Carob Ice Cream

Blend two cups of warm water with 1 cup of fresh coconut and cool in refrigerator. (Use more water if necessary.) Blend again. Add twenty or more cut-up soft dates and 4 tablespoons carob powder. Freeze in regular ice cream freeze.

CREAMY ICE FRUIT
(Successor to Ice Cream!)

½ Cup Sweet Cherry Juice or Sweet Grape Juice or Sweet Apple Juice

¾ to 1 Cup Water (or a little more, if needed)

1 Large or 2 Small Bananas

1 Large or 2 Small Avocados

4 Tablespoons Carob Powder

15 to 20 Soft Pitted Dates (depending on size)

Blend dates in juice and water. Add pieces of avocado a little at a time, while blending, then add slices of banana and carob. If more liquid is needed to blend, add as little more water as possible. Should be very thick and creamy. Will freeze in refrigerator-freezer without ice crystals (if served shortly after freezing). If not served same day, thaw slightly before serving.

Rice Crackers

Rice Crackers made of Brown Rice and water only (no salt or leavening) can be purchased in Health Food Stores, or you can make them yourself.

Grind brown rice in blender or grinder, add a little *Vegebase, if desired, and add enough water to hold it together into a dough. Roll very thin between two sheets of wax paper. Place on cookie sheet, and mark off into cracker size with knife. Bake at 325 degrees for about 10 minutes or until golden brown.

---

*See Chapter XIX, No. 1, Seasonings

XXI. Guest Menus
Luncheon, Dinner, Evening, Weekend

For Luncheon:
1. Fresh whole fruits.
2. Citrus and strawberry fruit cup and an avocado, lettuce and celery salad, or a ricotta, lettuce and celery salad.
3. Quartered tomatoes filled with ricotta cheese and topped with sour cream and alfalfa sprouts.
4. Trays of finger salad, tomatoes, and bowls of sunflower seeds and/or nuts, alfalfa sprouts and salad dressings.

For Dinner:
Serve trays of finger salad as usual, but include

some bowls of cucumber-sour cream dressing, and some Vegebase and oil dressing.

Select an attractive protein casserole dish as your entree (Eggplant with Cashews or a Lentil Casserole, perhaps) and serve two other vegetables, like Broccoli and Yellow Crookneck Squash.

You might also make an exception, and serve dessert. After a protein meal, you could serve whole fresh strawberries and/or pineapple boats.

Or, how about (after the salad) a gourmet starch meal of a Wild Rice and Brown Rice Casserole, and some Globe Artichokes? And maybe even home made Ice Cream for dessert, just this once.

Even without the desserts, your guests probably won't miss their meats. My guests usually eat so heartily of these meals, they don't have any room for dessert, so I usually don't bother.

For the Evening:

When we have guests for the evening, we serve no snacks during visiting or cards, but serve a repast after the cards or conversation or pastime of the evening. Usually an attractive assortment of fruit is well received, and enjoyed by all.

When the occasion or party seems to call for a spread, we go a little farther, and the following is a sample of the variety you might offer:

- Assorted unsweetened fruit juices: apple, grape, cherry (available bottled at your Health Food Store) or Dole unsweetened canned pineapple juice from your supermarket.
- Avocado Dip (mashed avocado with sour cream)
- Ricotta Dip (ricotta cheese, with sour cream, chives and Vegebase)
- Celery for dipping
- Rice Crackers and/or Rye Crackers for those who just must have them.
- Assorted Unprocessed Cheeses
- Fresh Strawberries and/or Fresh Pineapple or

- Acid Fruit Salad or
- Subacid Fruit Salad with no sweet fruit.

Overnight or Weekend Guests:

When we have Hygienic guests, that's velvet! For conventional family and friends, we lay our cards right out: This is what we eat—you may share, or meet us half way, or we will go all out your way for you.

Some elect to share our regular diet, as an interesting experiment. Others just must have their coffee and/or some kind of bread, but will make out without eggs or meat.

When they "must" have their flesh foods regularly, we do our best for them, and usually resolve the matter by eating out for the evening meals (sometimes after a large salad at home) at places where we can eat our way, and they can eat theirs. But we handle it as quietly as possible, without fuss or embarrassment, and, once it is settled, it need not be discussed again, and we can settle down to enjoying our company.

XXII. When You Are The Guest

When you are invited out for the evening (an evening of bridge or visiting and the inevitable snack or spread afterwards): In the case of a "new" friend, it is best to "play it by ear". Sometimes it is prudent and politic to brief your hostess before hand, so she can get her initial "shock" out of the way in advance. We just say we'd love to visit, but would appreciate being allowed to pass up the goodies. She usually insists on knowing what she can serve that we would eat, in which case we suggest perhaps some grapes and/or other fresh fruit.

Sometimes, if we have not been able to make such

advance arrangements, we eat sparingly of one or two foods provided by the hostess, especially if she seems too distressed by our abstinence. We try to be as gracious as possible, and, after the first time, *if* you are invited back, there is no problem. Friends worth having will go along with you.

When you are invited to Luncheon or Dinner, brief your hostess—we usually start by jocularly saying: "We'll allow you to withdraw the invitation, since we might cause you a problem." So far, no one has "withdrawn", and they are happy to provide a large salad, baked potato and green vegetable, and are usually so interested in the whys and wherefores, there is animated conversation about it all evening. When it gets too lengthy or burdensome, especially during the meal, we usually suggest postponing the discussion till later, and frequently end up giving them a leaflet, and suggesting books they may read.

When you are Overnight or Weekend Guests: We avoid accepting such invitations, but sometimes a loving relative or friend just won't be refused. Usually, they know our requirements in advance, so there is very little need for us to deviate. Our needs are simple, and, with a little planning ahead, it works out very smoothly.

At this juncture, I am reminded of the question some years ago (in the "Dear Abby" column, I believe) about the problem confronting a hostess when inviting a "health nut" to dine, who would eat only fruits, vegetables and nuts. The answer was (and I quote from memory): "Usually 'health nuts' are far from nutty. Prepare whatever menu you wish for yourself and your other guests; just pass the fruits, vegetables and nuts to him."

XXIII. Eating Out

While admitting that the meals prepared in our own kitchens are perhaps the only dependably, consistently Hygienic ones, there are times when, for some reason, we decide to eat in a restaurant (usually when it is impossible or inconvenient to eat at home).

If you are fortunate enough to be reasonably close to one of the better "Natural Foods" Restaurants (frequently managed by dedicated young people), you may be able to get an excellent fruit or vegetable salad, sprouts, nuts, avocados, and even some excellently prepared cooked vegetables and casseroles.

The next choice would be a good cafeteria. In Florida, we have many cafeterias, a few where it is possible to get a green salad without dressing (not a Hygienic finger salad, by any means, just some cut up head lettuce with a few pieces of other raw vegetables, but at least it is usually fresh and crisp), or a wedge of head lettuce, and/or some sliced tomatoes. A variety of cooked vegetables is always available, including baked potatoes every day, and a selection from the following (varying from day to day): broccoli, green beans, carrots, okra, eggplant, turnips, rutabagas, cauliflower, greens, squash, green lima beans, black-eyed peas and some others. Most of the vegetables are simply prepared and frequently they are not *too* overcooked. Fresh strawberries without sugar are frequently available, and a variety of fresh melons. Anyway, you can "make out"!

Sometimes, when we leave the house in the morning and know we will be gone all day, past the dinner hour, —we eat our citrus and nuts before we leave, and take along our picnic cooler, with a bag of our beautiful salad from our garden. We spend the day doing our shopping or errands (or whatever) and around 4:30 or 5:00 we eat our bag of salad and head for one of the good cafeterias for a baked potato and a green vegetable or two.

If you are "trapped" in an area without a decent cafeteria, and you must eat out there, try settling for a large wedge of lettuce and a baked potato, to tide you over (these are usually available almost anywhere in most of the better steak houses).

Some Chinese restaurants will prepare, upon request, vegetable chop suey without starch, lard, or seasonings, served over raw mung bean sprouts, and topped with raw or slightly steamed snow peas (edible podded peas).

If a Jewish delicatessen and/or restaurant is available, they usually serve "Farmer's Chop Suey", which is a large serving of fresh raw vegetables, topped with sour cream. They may also have thick lentil or split pea soup or plain "kasha" (buckwheat groats).

Sometimes it is possible to develop a rapport with a local restaurant, whose management will agree to serve whatever you want (within their capacity) upon one or two or three hours notice. They may be able to supply an acceptable salad without dressing, a baked potato, and you may have to settle for some lightly cooked frozen green vegetables. The very best restaurants are sometimes able to provide a variety of *fresh* vegetables, especially if notified in advance, and you will eat economically even in an expensive place, since the meat is the highest priced item.

Occasionally it is possible to make a connection with a small family type restaurant, whose cook or owner will take an interest, and be willing to go along on a regular basis, if you want to "eat out" once a week or so.

Don't give up! You can line up such places in your own area, if you keep trying.

If you occasionally want to "dine out", perhaps

with friends at a special place, or at a Dinner Theatre, these might be the times to deviate from your Hygienic program (and maybe fast the next day, if you feel too bad about it—otherwise, forget it!). Most of the time, though, we manage to entice our friends into places where we can do our thing, and they can do theirs.

XXIV. Travelers' Aide

The food expense for the traveling Hygienist is far less than for the conventional traveler. We carry a picnic cooler, with two tall plastic containers of ice (readily renewable at motels), in which we carry a supply of nuts and dried fruits, replenished frequently at Health Food Stores. We do other food shopping, as required, at fruit stands or markets.

Breakfast (if we have it) is citrus and nuts before leaving the motel in the morning. Lunch—usually a picnic at a rest park—if we have not had breakfast, we might have our citrus and nuts now. Or we might buy some tomatoes and unprocessed cheese, or some ripe bananas, grapes and/or other fresh fruit and/or eat some of our dried fruit.

Supper: We try to find a Natural Foods Restaurant (we carry an Organic Foods Directory, so we can often plan ahead). Sometimes we can find one by consulting a local telephone directory—in the Yellow Pages under Health Foods or Restaurants. Or we phone the local Health Food Store and may get a good tip on a local cafeteria or restaurant where a "vegetarian" can get an acceptable meal. Or we might ask a local resident or business person.

One of the best meals we ever ate in a restaurant was "uncovered" through the good offices of a delightful sales girl in Kamloops, British Columbia, Canada, from whom we purchased a $2.00 scarf. She phoned around and we made a reservation at a top-flight hotel-restaurant, where we had a beautiful large fresh salad, and some very lightly cooked *fresh* broccoli, *fresh* green beans, and a perfect fresh baked potato, at a very economical price.

Some evenings, for whatever reason, we might decide to just check into a motel (perhaps get a room with efficiency or kitchenette) and shop the local grocery. We might settle for a fruit meal, or a salad with nuts, or bake some potatoes or artichokes or some other vegetables. We carry a few utensils. Our traveling food budget is small, and, by and large, we do very well.

Our need for, and interest in, locating suitable sources of food supply adds an extra dimension to our travels, and is an additional area of interest, anticipation and fulfillment, when we "track down" exceptional markets, eating places, and the interesting people we find in these oases—both operators and patrons.

Some areas of the United States (and Canada, too), especially in the West, have a good many excellent Natural Foods restaurants; some areas have good cafeteria chains. In the South, there are some excellent cafeteria chains, among which are Davis Brothers, Morrison's, Piccadilly and Wyatt. You will find Chinese and Jewish restaurants "sprinkled around". (See Chapter XXIII, Eating Out.)

When we were in Banff (Alberta, Canada) in August 1973, we found a little Natural Foods Restaurant in very limited quarters, but serving quite good food to order. We don't remember its name, or even whether it had a name. It was located on the North Side of an East and West street, about a block West from the bus terminal, and doing a thriving business. We enjoyed our meals there.

We recall another good Natural Foods restaurant in Vancouver, British Columbia, Canada, whose name we did not note. The others we liked in our travels are listed in the "Food Sources" booklet referred to in Chapter XVI.

The Vegetarian Hotel, in Woodridge, New York, is worthy of special note, as a place where it is possible to spend a delightful vacation in the Catskill Mountains, and partake of Hygienic meals. Their food is excellent and all vegetarian, and a Hygienist may order each meal in advance, and select his own variety, in accordance with his needs and desires.

The Florida Spa, at Orlando, Florida, is another vegetarian resort, where it is possible to obtain Hygienic, meals, while spending a restful vacation in attractive surroundings.

Be sure to note the list of Hygienic Resorts in the Addendum. Shangri-La at Bonita Springs, Florida, is a beautiful, luxurious, outstanding place for a Hygienist to spend a vacation. The Bay 'n' Gulf Health Resort, St. Petersburg, Florida (Redington Shores, on the water) has lovely, restful vacation facilities, as does Esser's Hygienic Rest Ranch at Lake Worth, Florida.

The Villa Vegetariana Health Resort at Cuernavaca, Morelos, Mexico, is a lovely place to spend a Hygienic vacation, and the Orange Grove Health Ranch, where a Hygienic community is being built, is worth a visit.

When traveling, especially on long automobile trips, or any trips involving long periods of inactivity, it is more important than ever to be sure to get some vigorous exercise every day. It is also a good idea to eat lightly while en route.

XXV. Foods for Pleasure and Health!

If you will give the Hygienic system of eating and living a trial in the scientific laboratory of your own body, you will be able to determine for yourself what remarkable results can be achieved. Don't concentrate on what you will be giving up, but on what you will be gaining. And please be assured that you will not be surrendering the pleasant interludes associated with meal time.

While I am not preoccupied with food between meals, and never snack, I cannot remember any time in my life when I have approached my meals with more anticipation and keener appetite, or experienced more gustatory pleasure. The role of pleasure in eating should not be underestimated. Tasting and enjoying your food induces you to linger over each mouthful and prevents you from gorging.

I remember reading a news item about a man who could maintain a reasonable weight only by eating foods that he didn't like. Otherwise, his gluttony was uncontrollable.

The Hygienist has no such problem. As mentioned elsewhere in this book, the cleaner the body becomes, the easier is self-discipline. The Hygienist develops the happy ability to enjoy his food and develop Epicurianism in its higher sense, without becoming a slave to gluttony. He contemplates other dietaries with no envy and no sense of deprivation, but rather with a sense of elation for himself, and sadness for the unenlightened and the indifferent.

I don't believe there is any power on earth that could influence me to turn back to the days before I knew the power and security and freedom of Health Independence, and joys of Foods for Pleasure and Health.

THE TREE OF TOXEMIA

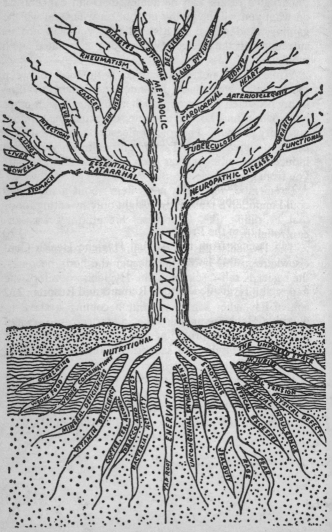

A GRAPHIC ILLUSTRATION OF THE THEORY OF TOXEMIA AS
FORMULATED BY J. H. TILDEN, M.D., WHICH SHOWS HOW
DISEASE IS BUILT BY UNNATURAL LIVING HABITS.

ADDENDUM

ADDENDUM

Section 1.

LAWS OF HUMAN LIFE
(Unchanging Natural Laws)

A. *Life's Great Law or Law of Homeostasis*

Every living cell is endowed with an instinct of self-preservation, sustained by a force inherent in the organism, the success of whose work is directly proportioned to the amount of the force and inversely to the degree of its activity. (If you provide the right conditions for living things, they will automatically proceed in the direction of good health.)

B. *Law of Action*

Whenever action occurs in the living organism as the result of extraneous influences, the action must be ascribed to the living thing which has the power of action and not to the lifeless thing whose leading characteristic is inertia. (If you give living things the wrong conditions, you will produce disease, as the result of the instinctive efforts of the cells to defend themselves.)

C. *Law of Power*

The power employed, and consequently expended, in any vital or medicinal action, is vital power; that is, power from within and not from without. (It is the living thing that acts, it is vital power that produces the action.)

D. *Law of Selective Elimination*

All injurious substances which by any means gain admittance into the living organism are counteracted, neutralized and expelled by such means and through

166

such channels as will produce the least amount of wear and tear to the living structure. (Different drugs have a chemical affinity with certain tissues or parts of the body, which will react to get rid of the drug. Digitalis has a tendency to combine with the heart muscle, and the heart's action responds to this as a defensive action, resulting in eventual destruction of the tissues.)

E. *Law of Dual Effect*

All substances which are taken into the body, or which come in contact with it from without, occasion a twofold and contrary action—the secondary action being the opposite of the primary one, and the more lasting. (If the primary action is stimulation, the secondary effect is depression. When we use a hot pack for swelling, the primary effect is to draw blood to the area; the secondary effect is to deprive other parts of the body of blood, causing exhaustion and stasis, and impairing circulation. A cold shower subsequently make you feel warmer. It is a shock to the body, exhausting, and a good example of secondary effect.)

F. *Law of Special Economy*

The vital organism, under favorable conditions, stores up all excess of vital funds, above the current expenditure, as a reserve fund to be employed in a time of special need. (Power in reserve is the surest guarantee against disease.)

G. *Law of Vital Accommodation* (Nature's Balance Wheel)

The response of the vital organism to external stimuli is an instinctive one, based upon a self-preservative instinct which adapts itself to whatever influence it cannot destroy or control.

H. *Law of Vital Distribution*

If a particular organ needs more energy, the body will draw energy from a part of the body needing less energy, and distribute it where most needed. (Don't eat before or during activity—rest after a meal—the blood is needed by the digestional viscera. During rest and sleep, activity is greatly increased in certain areas of the body and the blood is withdrawn from peripheral areas, and cramps in legs may result in people with impared circulation.)

I. *Law of the Minimum*

The development of living beings is regulated by the supply of whichever element is least bountifully provided. (Long known in plant life.) (Using supplements, by creating an over-abundance of some elements, creates an artificial shortage of other elements, known and unknown, and the element in shortest supply determines the development.)

J. *Law of Quality Selection*

When the quality of the food coming into the body is of higher quality than the body tissues, the body discards the lower-grade materials to make room for the superior materials, which it uses to make new and healthier tissue.

K. *Law of the Gut*

Whenever a peristaltic action occurs, there is a reciprocal contraction which occurs. (There is a wave of relaxation running right before the contraction, and more or less continued relaxation while eating. The habit of chain eating disturbs the normal tone of the stomach and the peristaltic action will not be great enough.)

L. *Law of Development*

The development of any part of the body is in direct proportion to the vital currents (nervous and nutritive) which by exercise are brought to bear upon it. (Intense use produces great development; moderate use, moderate development; no use at all, atrophy.

Energy is for use, and when we cease to use it, we cease to have it.)

M. *Law of Limitation*

Whenever and wherever the expenditure of vital power has advanced so far that a fatal exhaustion is imminent, a check is put upon the unnecessary expenditure of power, and the organism rebels against the further use of even an accustomed "stimulant". (In some cases, at the end of an *extremely* long fast e.g. over 100 days, there may be a diminishing of the capacities of the body, or complete suspension of functions, until prostration and coma may result, and checking of reflexes may find a complete loss of reactions.) Amazing results can be secured through such a fast, but it is a two-edged sword. If reserves are exhausted, the patient needs careful watching, as the coma may be considered a last final effort of the body towards survival. It requires great skill and knowledge to determine the needs of an organism in such a condition.

ADDENDUM

Section 2.

PEARLS FROM THE PROS
(Gleanings from the Annual Hygiene Health
Conferences and Elsewhere)

A. *Mini-Pearls (Mix or Match)*

"To many the words 'Natural Hygiene' may be new and strange. Perhaps a more clarifying designation for this system would be 'Normal Living'—Jack Dunn Trop, "You Don't Have To Be Sick".

"Nature is the expression of a definite order with which nothing interferes successfully, and the chief business of man is to learn the requirements of this order."—R. J. Cheatham, February 1974 Seminar, St. Petersburg, Florida.

"The secret of life is living in the present. Be happy now."—Dr. Alec Burton, D.O., D.C., N.D., July 1971 Annual Hygiene Health Conference.

"Man has a mind which gives him dominion over everything on and in the earth. He has opened many doors and unlocked many mysteries with his mind, but, at the same time, he unfortunately knows more about everything on earth than he does about himself or about self-control. The results of this ignorance and lack of self-control are sickness, pain and premature death. All the collateral sequences, such as crime, perversity, war, and a decaying society are the by-products of this ignorance. Unless man learns to know himself, he will destroy himself."—Dr. William L. Esser, D.C., N.D., "Natural Hygiene, the Real Road to Health".

(Relative to Food Combining): "Simplicity seems to be the name of the game, with sufficient variety over the long range to get all the nutrients."—Dr. John M.

Brosious, B.S., D.C., N.D., 1973 Annual Hygiene Health Conference.

"Darkness is necessary for life. Your cells are active when it's light. You can make chickens lay eggs all night by leaving the light on. Plants will grow when the light is on. But of course they wear out sooner."—Dr. Virginia Vetrano, B.S., D.C., July 1973 Annual Hygiene Health Conference.

"When plants are exposed to light, their cellular activities increase and chemical changes take place."—Dr. David J. Scott, D.C., N.D., July 1973 Annual Hygiene Health Conference.

"During the day, plants take in carbon dioxide, and give off oxygen. This process is reversed at night, when they take in oxygen and give off carbon dioxide. However, you would still get more oxygen sleeping out-of-doors than indoors."—Dr. John M. Brosious, B.S., D.C., N.D., July 1974 Annual Hygiene Health Conference.

"The word 'Health' means 'Whole' and 'Holy'."—Dr. Keki R. Sidhwa, N.D., D.O., July 1969 Annual Hygiene Health Conference.

"We are gradually running down, but we can accelerate it a little by doing stupid things."—Dr. Alec Burton, July 1970 Annual Hygiene Health Conference.

"During a fast, the body gleefully goes about getting rid of the toxins and wastes that have accumulated for years."—Dr. William L. Esser, July 1969 Annual Hygiene Health Conference.

"There is no such thing as moderation in poison."—Jack Dunn Trop, July 1970 Annual Hygiene Health Conference.

"Hygienists are 'out of style' by not being sick all the time."—Dr. John M. Brosious, July 1969 Annual Hygiene Health Conference.

"There are some 300,000 trillion cells in the body. 3,000,000 die every second of our lives and have to be replaced; this is protein synthesis."—Dr. Alec Burton, July 1970 Annual Hygiene Health Conference.

"A tired cell is shrunken and the granules of protoplasm can't be seen under the microscope. After resting, the cell becomes plump and the granules are clearly seen."—Dr. John M. Brosious, B.S., D.C., N.D., July 1974 Annual Hygiene Health Conference.

"Write a card and carry it in your wallet, reading: 'Sensitive to antibiotics, tetanus injections, all drugs. I might die if given any drugs, and you accept full responsibility. If I am given any drugs against my request, I'll see you in Court.' "—Dr. William L. Esser, July 1968 Annual Hygiene Health Conference.

"The prostate gland exhibits the same pattern as the other glands. When the body is overloaded, or when the function of the prostate gland is overworked, it must act as an excretory organ as well as a secretory organ, and it enlarges and swells to the point where the urine is cut off."—Dr. David J. Scott, July 1970 Annual Hygiene Health Conference.

"If you knew how intricate the kidney function is, and how much work it performs for you every day, you wouldn't eat anything that would hurt it."—Dr. Virginia Vetrano, July 1971 Annual Hygiene Health Conference.

"The usual time of each heartbeat is 7/10 second— 3/10 dilation, 3/10 contraction, and 1/10 rest. The heart is about 95% muscle."—Dr. John M. Brosious, July 1974 Annual Hygiene Health Conference.

"Take hold of yourself. Get a firm grip on your way of living. If you do not, no one else can do it for you. Don't feel sorry for yourself. You have a lot going for you, if you will make the best of your life. Develop a positive, constructive set of values. Learn the natural hygienic and vegan living ways, and follow them faithfully. It is your life, and it is well worth the living. Start living it as it should be lived."—H. J. Dinshah, " Overweight and Underweight"

"Hygiene is based upon sound physiological principles and a knowledge of these principles is absolutely necessary in order to intelligently carry out a Hygienic way of life. There is not a day that goes by in the Hygienist's life that he does not have to make a decision regarding some material, factor or facet of living. He will often find himself saying, 'Is this Hygienic, or isn't it?' The answer will be forthcoming if he knows his principles."—Dr. Virginia Vetrano, January 1973 Natural Hygienews

"Natural Hygiene teaches that the laws of life and the laws of Nature cannot be violated with impunity. Can you violate the law of gravitation, by walking off a cliff, without getting shattered? Neither can you violate the laws of your body structure with impunity. Every violation is registered in your body tissues. Your body is like an IBM machine which records every disobedience, adds them up and punishes you as a scofflaw, with the penalty of acute disease; and if you become a recurrent violater, the body punishes you with chronic disease, which is life imprisonment for gross incorrigibility—a lifetime of pain and suffering."
—Irving Davidson, March 1974 Natural Hygienews

"Since I've been interested in human organization primarily, my inclination in Natural Hygiene has been more in the direction of the human organization involved. Think about this. Instead of saying: 'I'm a Hygienist. I've learned what they teach; I've read the books; now I'm going home and I'm going to eat and sleep and exercise according; I've done my job'; why not consider that with all the foment in the world, all the change, at an ever accelerating rate, the more people that get into organized Natural Hygiene and put their shoulders to the wheel, the more they're going to play tremendous roles in the future ahead, because it's a peculiar thing that so many organizations that have very enlightened viewpoints regarding the future of society—the future political and economic society—have got the most stupid viewpoints regarding human life and human health."—Oscar H. Floyd, July 1972 Annual Hygiene Health Conference.

Prayer: "Lord, when I am wrong, make me willing

to change, and when I am right make me easy to live with."—Dr. Keki R. Sidhwa, July 1969 Annual Hygiene Health Conference.

"We synthesize some Vitamin B 12 and are capable of securing enough from a vegetarian diet. When there is a deficiency of Vitamin B 12 (pernicious anemia), it is a complicated situation, and due to impaired digestion and other factors."—Dr. Alec Burton, July 1970 Annual Hygiene Health Conference.

"Health is being able to function without even knowing that we have a body. Health Independence is being our own man." —R. J. Cheatham, February 1974 Seminar, St. Petersburg, Fla.

"You have a new body every seven years—all tissue has been replaced within that period of time. Certain complex tissues, when destroyed, are very difficult to replace. The nerves may take years to regenerate one millimeter. The skin will regenerate quickly."—Dr. Keki R. Sidhwa, July 1969 Annual Hygiene Health Conference.

"Babies should have milk. If mother's milk is not available, they should have the milk of another animal, because they must have galactose, which is found in combination with glucose in milk sugar, and it does not exist in the plant kingdom. Mother's milk is best. It is cleaner, fresher, the cat can't get at it, and it comes in such cute containers."—Dr. Alec Burton, July 1968 Annual Hygiene Health Conference.

"You can avoid or refuse to be vaccinated to go overseas (per a United Nations ruling) except for a few injections, like those for yellow fever."—Dr. William L. Esser, July 1968 Annual Hygiene Health Conference.

"Don't depend on doing wrong and then going on a fast to try to undo the bad effects; it is very difficult to turn back the clock. Fasting will often restore health when other measures fail. There is precious little that Natural Hygiene will not improve. But it is best to live naturally every day for optimal health."—Dr.

John M. Brosious, July 1969 Annual Hygiene Health Conference.

"Vegetarianism is much more economical of the world's resources. The shorter the food chain, the more energy there is to go around. To domesticate animals to provide food is extremely uneconomical. For every 100 calories of energy, supplied by the sun, and stored in plants, 10 calories get to the tissues of the herbivore, one calory of the first level carnivore (the one who eats the plant-eating animal), and one calory to the second level carnivore (the one who eats the flesh-eater). It takes twenty to twenty-five pounds of grass to produce one pound of cow. It takes ten pounds of cow to produce one pound of man."—Dr. Alec Burton, July 1971 Annual Hygiene Health Conference.

"In hypertension, the walls of the arteries are constricted. In arteriosclerosis, the walls are hardened. The causes are:

Nervousness and tension
Toxemia and enervation
Tobacco, coffee and tea
Sexual excesses
Rich diet, fatty food
Salt, Condiments"

—Dr. William L. Esser, July 1969 Annual Hygiene Health Conference.

"Our world is hungry for knowledge. Our restless youth are being pressured by many surrounding demands, confusing circumstances, uncontrollable dilemmas, and are driven by many needs to conform. Fortunate indeed is the young person who has been literally 'spoonfed' the principles engendered in Natural Hygiene —fortunate, because he must, of necessity be a thinking person, one who has to face truth at an earlier age, one who must be accepted for higher values, one who has great reverence for life, and one who can appreciate the wonders of the most miraculous invention called the human body."—Irving Davidson, November 1973 Natural Hygienews

"Some people continue to smoke, using the excuse that it keeps them from becoming more overweight. Smoking may well be deranging profoundly the normal bodily processes . . . hardly a welcome result of this foolhardy practice. In addition, smoking blunts the sense of taste and that of smell, so the smoker does not enjoy his food so much. Upon quitting, he MAY eat more if he is of the type that is prone to excesses anyway, with no exercise of normal will-power and self-discipline. This lack of self-control is often perceived in both the smoker and the glutton. Smoking to curb appetite is a quack drug-pusher's way of symptom-shooting, at best. And when the time comes—as come it must some day—to 'pay the piper', the victim is still a fat person, but now he is a fat person who also has emphysema, gangrenous Buerger's Disease with accompanying loss of extremities, weakened heart; lip, mouth, throat, and/or lung cancer, or any of the other host of serious diseases directly related to the smoke habit. Again, the only sane answer lies in getting back to the right living patterns, controlling false appetites through right thinking and positive acting in life, and maintaining a well-balanced life-view."—H. Jay Dinshah, "Overweight and Underweight"

"Every year in the United States one thousand people die of insecticide poisoning."—Dr. Keki R. Sidhwa, July 1973 Annual Hygiene Health Conference.

"The types of toxins in the blood are:

1. Metabolic (uric acid and other products of digestive functions)
2. Environmental (DDT, smoke, etc.)
3. Disease (i.e. cancer)
4. Incomplete utilization of food.
   This is a big trouble maker. When one is upset emotionally, the food is turned into debris, which is generally removed by the mucous membranes. The liver and kidneys are overworked and slow down, and this produces the 'itis' diseases."

—Dr. David J. Scott, July 1970 Annual Hygiene Health Conference.

"A positive Wasserman test does not usually indicate syphilis, contrary to medical contentions. Mercurial poisoning will bring on symptoms of syphilis."—Dr. Alec Burton, July 1968 Annual Hygiene Health Conference.

(Author's Note: Read "Syphilis, Werewolf of Medicine" by Dr. Herbert M. Shelton)

"The white fluid under a scab is blood plasma."—Dr. John M. Brosious, July 1971 Annual Hygiene Health Conference.

"In cases of athlete's foot, absolute cleanliness is essential, even to washing the feet (and drying carefully) several times a day. Go barefoot and get as much sunlight as possible on the feet."—Dr. William L. Esser, July 1969 Annual Hygiene Health Conference.

"Improper oxygenation can cause a headache, especially if you are somewhat toxic. Heat, lack of ventilation and carbon dioxide contribute to this type of headache. Go out in the fresh air and take a brisk walk, even if for only five minutes."—Dr. Keki R. Sidhwa, July 1969 Annual Hygiene Health Conference.

"What do acupuncture needles do? What is their mystic quality that has endowed them with such a halo of hope for humanity? The answer: They destroy mechanically what drugs destroy chemically! They have no creative or reparative powers. In puncturing the human body they injure and destroy a myriad number of cells. They interfere with nerve function and immobilize whole nerve centers. . . . All such destruction is detrimental to the organism in greater or lesser degree. There are cases that surgeons can correct . . . and the rendering of a part of the body insensitive may be a small price to pay for the benefits of mechanical correction (in a minute percentage of cases). This is an (acceptable) anesthetic tool to be carefully employed in rare surgical cases." From Volume 1, No. 1, The Healthway Advisor.

"The best time to start inculcating better health practices is from birth. Young mothers need access to information. They are being pummeled from all sides with wrong guidance, commercials, and advertisements." Irving Davidson, November 1973 Natural Hygienews.

"It should be noted, that many overeat because the foods they eat are nutritionally inferior. Refined food may fill a person up, yet leave the nutritional needs unsatisfied, leading to snacking to satisfy some vague sense of hidden hunger for what is missing from the lop-sided and ill-planned meals."—H. Jay Dinshah, "Overweight and Underweight"

"Natural Hygiene is rapidly becoming a necessity for the whole human race, and the future presents newer and greater challenges for Natural Hygiene. The challenging conditions in the economic world are making more and more people aware of the harmful effects of medicines and drugs, of the necessity for a better health program to meet all the needs of the individual, and a greater necessity for better methods of caring for the sick and preventing disease."—Irving Davidson, September 1973 Natural Hygienews

"You can as a rule (there are exceptions), measure the status of your health at any given time by determining the workload of your internal transportation system. The workload of your bloodstream can be determined by counting your pulse. As a rule, the more toxic your system, the greater the body's workload. . . . Keep in mind that the faster your heart beats, as a rule, the more toxic is your system. When we run or indulge in vigorous exercise, the increased carbon dioxide of the blood accelerates heart function to pass off the waste through the lungs. Faster blood circulation that results from exercise also increases the supply of oxygen and blood sugar to cells that have expended their supplies. After exercise your pulse shoots up, and, usually, within a few minutes, it returns to normal, the toxic load created by the exercise having been reduced, and the depleted cell supplies having been replenishd. In a state of rest the healthier you are the lower your pulse will be. . . . Your editor regards as reflective of a relatively good state of health the following pulse rates:

IN A STATE OF REST
Adult Male   40 to 50 pulse beats per minute
Adult Female 46 to 56 pulse beats per minute
Child, Male   50 to 60 pulse beats per minute
Child, Female 56 to 66 pulse beats per minute

IN A NORMAL ACTIVE STATE
Adult Male   50 to 60 pulse beats per minute
Adult Female 56 to 66 pulse beats per minute
Child, Male   60 to 70 pulse beats per minute
Child, Female 66 to 76 pulse beats per minute

Higher pulse beats are to be expected after vigorous exercise, or after meals when the blood stream is heavily involved in digestion. Also the pulse may increase normally during the early part of our daily cycle when the body is in a predominantly eliminative phase. This is usually from about 3:00 A.M. to about 7:00 A.M. or even later. . . . Cooked foods and unwholesome foods will cause a pathologically high pulse beat, and this is primarily responsible for the abnormally high pulse beat regarded as normal by physicians. A low pulse is not always an indicator of good health, but a non-ceasing rapid pulse is invariably an indicator of a pathological organism. . . ." From Volume 1, No. 2, Healthway Advisor.

"There is a difference between sleep and narcosis. Movement during sleep is normal and necessary for circulation. When taking drugs, this necessary movement during sleep is inhibited. You are not unconscious when you are asleep. Any unusual noise should awaken you, if you are healthy, and you remember your dreams. If you take drugs, you will be unconscious. Sleep is a sensory depression, when the body metabolizes its energy for the next day. The rhythm of sleep lasts 60 to 90 minutes. Infants become restless every 60 to 90 minutes—they may awake and go to sleep again. There are four stages of sleep:

Stage 1—Eyes under closed lids are extremely active. People dream during this stage, and sometimes don't remember these dreams.

Stage 2—During this stage, there is still a certain amount of activity

Stage 3—During this stage, there are certain cardiac changes, and an increase in the blood supply to certain areas of the brain.

Stage 4—The motor functions have been depressed to the limit during this stage.

Depriving a person of any of the stages of sleep (as by taking drugs) will cause neurotic symptoms. Stages 1 and 4 seem to be the most essential. Animals sleep crouching or on the side. It is better that we rest and sleep on the side than on the back."—Dr. Alec Burton, July 1969, Annual Hygiene Health Conference.

Excerpts from "The Time Factor in Recovery" by Herbert M. Shelton, Ph.D.: "One of the most trying problems of the Hygienist, in dealing with the sick, and this is particularly true of chronic sufferers, is the demand for speedy results. . . . Why do we expect to get well in a hurry of a condition that requires a lifetime for its development? . . . This man has given the methods of "cure" a full fifteen years of time in which to restore health, but if he turns to Hygiene, he wants to get well over night. Not only is he in a hurry, but he wants to achieve his recovery with as little disturbance of his accustomed routine and as little change in his habits of living as possible. . . . Certainly the man whose condition has required a life time for its evolution will require the employment of all of the means of Hygiene to reorganize and re-constitute his organism. . . . It is essential that we recognize the fact that recovery of health is an evolution in reverse and that it requires time to be completed . . . the road back . . . is a slow and gradual one. . . . A stage is reached sooner or later, from which there is no turning back. . . . A cure is the application of something exotic (a drug or a treatment) which, by virtue of its own power, restores the sick man to health. There is no such thing. Recovery is the restoration of health by means of the operation of forces intrinsic to the organism. This is the only force known that is capable of restoring health. . . . We can, with patience and determination, launch overselves into a way of life out of which good health evolves and stick to it until we have achieved the desired results and then stick to it to the end that we may maintain our gains."

(*Author's Note:* Dr. Shelton is the most experienced Professional Hygienist, and has fasted about 40,000 people.)

More Mini-Pearls from a Panel Discussion by:
    Dr. Alec Burton
    Dr. William L. Esser
    Dr. Virginia Vetrano

"The differences and limitations of individuals are due to pathological factors—otherwise all men have the same needs."
    "Man's native home is in the tropics."
    "Sun lamps are dangerous, irritating and harmful."
    "Air conditioning kept at 75 degrees and bringing in fresh air from outside is not harmful."

B. *Allergies*
    "Protein poisoning is called 'allergy'. Undigested proteins are toxic and the cells try to set up a defensive action to sweep them out of the body. How your body handles the food is more important than the

food itself. I became a Hygienist because of 'allergies' to the point where practically all proteins caused reaction and poisoning."—Dr. David J. Scott, July 1973 Annual Hygiene Health Conference.

C. *Altitude*

"Atmospheric pressure forces air into the lung cavity,—fifteen pounds per square inch at sea level. At higher altitudes, the pressure is less, and people must have more red blood cells to be able to breathe. (Insufficiency of red blood cells is anemia.) The body has the ability to compensate for a change in altitude. You are forced to breathe deeper and faster at a higher altitude. If the body is healthy, the accommodation is rapid (hours or days). A diet of salad greens and fruit helps to make the adaptation. The "Haversion System" —the blood producing system—is chiefly designed to produce the blood cells of the body. This has a reservoir of red blood cells to be released faster when needed under change of altitude or stress. Some are released, even though not fully matured, to compensate for need. If no longer needed when you go down to a lower altitude where there is more oxygen, the spleen will take over and handle the wornout blood cells." —Dr. Gerald Benesh, D.C., July 1971 Annual Hygiene Health Conference.

D. *Birth Control and Menstruation*
Birth Control (Free Time Theory)

"The menstrual cycle is usually 28 to 30 days (sometimes 45 days). When does actual ovulation take place? The theory is the egg is released on exactly the 15th day preceding the next menstrual period. Some women claim they know somehow when ovulation occurs. One must determine her own cycle by keeping exact notes for fully one year to utilize this free time theory. If this is done, without errors or miscalculations, it will work. If it is a 28 to 30 day period, and the egg is released 15 days prior to menstruation, she is likely to become pregnant on the 11th to 17th days. Those who advocate this system claim there are no failures where there are no miscalculations."—Dr. John M. Brosious, July 1969 Annual Hygiene Health Conference.

"Menstruation ceases when optimal health is attained. The membrane can be sloughed without bleeding."—Dr. Virginia Vetrano, July 1969 Annual Hygiene Health Conference.

"After a fast, the menstruation might cease for several months because menstruation might not be desirable at that time."—Dr. David J. Scott, July 1973 Annual Hygiene Health Conference.

E. *Cancer*

"In cancer and leukemia, the cells in the body are abnormal and unable to supply the host with normal nutrition, and unable to dispose of the toxins. Toxemia in the host has made the body incapable of producing normal cells. Adjustment of the environment may be successful in reversing this situation."—Dr. Alec Burton, July 1968 Annual Hygiene Health Conference.

"The Six Stages of Cancer, from Perfect Health to Death, are:

1. Enervation
2. Toxemia or Toxicosis or Irritation
3. Inflammation
4. Ulceration
5. Fibrosis
6. Cancer

Enervation: Having used up more energy than you are able to replace, the nervous system has become lessened in efficiency in maintaining the functions of life. The various systems become impaired, especially the elimination systems. This leads to the second stage, Toxemia or Toxicosis, when there are toxins in the blood, fluids and cells, poisoning the organism. The third stage is Inflammation, when vicarious elimination is set up in the body for self-preservation. Then Ulceration occurs, followed by Fibrosis, (i. e. Cirrhosis, Hardening of the Arteries, Arteriosclerosis, and Tumors). The last stage before death is Cancer."—Dr. David J. Scott, July 1970 Annual Hygiene Health Conference.

"I am not in favor of any drugs in the treatment of cancer."—Dr. Alec Burton, July 1969 Annual Hygiene Health Conference.

"I know of 25 or 30 cases of people with malignant tumors, who are still alive after two to five years. However, they *must* stick to a *raw* food diet; no cooked foods, no dairy products, no animal products; fruits, vegetables and nuts only.

"Honey contains irritating acids. A quiescent cancer case (he was rather thin) added honey to his diet at the urging of relatives, who wanted him to try to gain weight, and he died shortly thereafter. I am not saying that honey causes cancer, but the irritating acids were enough to tip the scales.

"I have cared for terminal cancer patients who expired without the usual agony. I fasted them to get rid of the drugs (according to their capacity) and then kept them on an all raw Hygienic diet. (The key is elimination of the *drugs*.)—Dr. Alec Burton, July 1969 Annual Hygiene Health Conference.

"A virus may be present in cancer, but that doesn't prove this is the cause. It is like saying 'flies cause dirty garbage cans'."—Dr. David J. Scott, July 1973 Annual Hygiene Health Conference.

F. *Case Histories*

"A woman who had terminal muscle disease (myasthenia) took three fasts (17 days, 21 days, and one long fast) and ended up well, and could again walk and drive a car."—Dr. Virginia Vetrano, July 1973 Annual Hygiene Health Conference.

"I fasted an asthma patient 26 days, from 72 pounds down to 56 pounds. She had had asthma drugs every day for twenty years, and couldn't absorb nutrition. She recovered, and now weighs 120 pounds."—Dr. Alec Burton, July 1969 Annual Hygiene Health Conference.

"I had a case with part of the colon removed. The patient had been given a six months life expectancy, but after taking a 21 day fast, is still alive twenty years later."—Dr. William L. Esser, July 1973 Annual Hygiene Health Conference.

"I had a patient—a man of 104—he fasted seven days, and is now 115 years old. He has some very good stock behind him, but also has some very good health habits."—Dr. William L. Esser, July 1968 Annual Hygiene Health Conference.

"I fasted a man with carcinoma of the lung, for 103 days. After 75 days, there was a slight movement of the lung. After 90 days, the lung inflated. It is now healed, and the man is back at work."—Dr. Alec Burton, July 1969 Annual Hygiene Health Conference.

"Between the 21st and 33rd day of the fast of one of my patients who had a breast tumor, the tumor was reduced to a small piece of palpating tissue. Now there is nothing to palpate—the tumor never returned."— Dr. Alec Burton, July 1969 Annual Hygiene Health Conference.

"A lady who had gallstones was fasting at my Health Ranch. Her gallstones began breaking down on the 28th day. They began to pass through the duct, to scratch and get caught and cause pain. We eased her pain by hot baths and applications of heat. It took four days, then all symptoms suddenly disappeared. She had had a subnormal temperature for fifteen years. She left for home with a normal temperature. She returned to the physician who had recommended the surgery, and when no gall stones showed in the x-ray, she had to bare her abdomen to prove she had no incision."—Dr. William L. Esser, July 1969 Annual Hygiene Health Conference.

"I had a child patient who was 90% deaf, and would be completely deaf in a few years. After a fast, the deafness had been reduced to only 20%. Many cases of deafness don't respond to fasting at all."—Dr. William L. Esser, July 1969 Annual Hygiene Health Conference.

"I had a lady with a tumor the size of a melon. After a 56 day fast, the tumor was reduced to the size of a walnut, and has remained that way for two years." —Dr. Alec Burton, July 1969 Annual Hygiene Health Conference.

"A twelve year old boy fasted at the Health School for acute appendicitis, and grew up to become an athlete, and is thinking of becoming a Hygienic Practitioner."—Dr. Virginia Vetrano, July 1973 Annual Hygiene Health Conference.

Author's Note: R. J. Cheatham's case history (and his Shangri-La Natural Hygiene Health Institute) are well known in Hygienic circles, and his story really should be included here—with his permission, of course.

Excerpts from "Health and The Shangri-La" by R. J. Cheatham:

"I recovered from cancer and I should like to tell you how it happened:—

April 14, 1948—a day I will always remember . . . I had gone to a hospital for an examination of what I had considered to be a minor problem. It was a lump on my right chest which had developed into an open running sore. After an extensive examination, X-rays, and a biopsy, the physicians came forth with a diagnosis of malignant melanoma or cancer on the right chest area. The physicians recommended an immediate operation.

"The operation was performed at the Hines Veterans Administration Hospital in Hines, Illinois, a suburb of Chicago. I was in the operating room for over five hours and the surgeons removed the entire surface of the right side of my chest, leaving the bones covered with only a little skin and a scar seventeen inches long. The next three months I spent in the hospital recuperating from the operation and trying to regain my health by following the orthodox procedures.

"It was while recuperating in the hospital that I found time to think about my cancer condition and its causes. I began to question the physicians, surgeons, nurses, and the other patients. After considerable questioning, I found that mine had been a very serious condition, the chances of recovering from the operation about fifty-fifty and further, that the maximum life expectancy after such an operation was only about five years.

"During the next two years I ran the gamut of practically all the so-called 'healing professions.' I took their prescribed medicines, pills, shots, drugs, and accepted their treatments of massage, adjustments, vibrations, X-rays, colonics, and a host of other 'cures'. In spite of being continually 'cured' by all this medical science, my condition did not actually seem to improve. To the contrary, on returning to the hospital for routine examinations the surgeons found more lumps and began to operate again to remove sections for biopsy or examining purposes. Hearing of the third death among my cancer-ridden hospital room mates did not improve my mental outlook. To make matters worse, one insurance company cancelled my life insurance and other companies flatly refused to provide me with any insurance at any price.

"One evening I noticed an advertisement in the newspaper about a lecturer who was going to speak on the subject of how to improve health through Natural Hygiene.

"I had been through the mill and by this time was a true skeptic. But the principles of Natural Hygiene, or the laws of Nature, with their simplicity, logic, and common sense impressed me. By the time the lecture was over I felt sure that here was the answer to health and disease, to living or dying.

"Having found what promised to be the answer. I purchased book after book and attended many lectures on the subject. Later I was privileged to attend one of the Annual International Conventions of the American Natural Hygiene Society. After attending the many classes and lectures given by the leading professional and lay hygienists on the many facets of Natural Hygiene, after listening to and participating in the question-and-answer periods and after talking with many people who had followed this way of life, any doubts or reservations I might have had were completely eliminated.

"After giving my body a chance to rehabilitate itself through fasting, working out a daily exercise program, arranging my time so that I could get plenty of rest and sleep, planning for regular sun and air baths, and correcting my diet by eliminating dead substances such as meat, fish, fowl, white bread, white sugar, salt, coffee, soda pops, chewing gum, spices condiments etc. and substituting plenty of live foods such as fresh succulent salads, fresh vegetables, fresh fruits and fresh nuts; I found which I was able to eliminate the eye glasses which I had worn for about ten years. When I took the test for renewing my driver's license, the examiner passed me without question. An insurance company examination found me qualified for a larger policy. My physical examinations have revealed no further lumps or problems.

"Mrs. Cheatham and I have had four additional children since the operation. These children have been brought up from birth in this better way of life. They are all lovely children . . . all pictures of health . . . and without the 'benefit' of any medications, shots or treatments of any kind. Incidentally, our last three children were born at home with myself in attendance for the delivery.

"Perhaps most important, over twenty-five years have passed since my cancer operation. Those who were with me, in the same hospital, with similar conditions and orthodox care, have long since passed away. Not only am I alive, in spite of the operation, but I now feel better than I can ever remember feeling, and I look forward to many more healthy, wonderful years."

Many Hygienists know the astounding case history

of Dr. Jack Goldstein, Detroit podiatrist, which he has related from the podium all over the country. He is a handsome, hale and hearty man in his forties, and it is difficult to imagine how he must have looked ten years ago, when he was literally snatched from Death's door.

In 1958, at age 28, he developed a mild ulcerative colitis, which, by six years later, under the drugging treatments of three consecutive physicians—two years each—the last two years on cortisone—had progressed to a state pronounced hopeless. During the last year of treatment, he had surgery for gangrenous hemorrhoids, and his former weight of 170 (which had jumped to 190 under the cortisone treatment—with the characteristic cortisone elephant hump and moon face) went down to 140 pounds, and the increasing diarrhea, bleeding and debility made it impossible for him to work or have a social or family life. He had recurring thoughts of suicide during the six years of agonizing treatment.

Finally, in 1964, the last specialist told him he had two choices, either he would die, or he might prolong his life by having a total colectomy (removal of the colon and rectum, with a bag on the outside for elimination).

Having previously resisted his wife's suggestions to investigate Natural Hygiene, the verdict of death or mutilation resulted in a decision to obtain some Hygiene literature, which he found convincing. He took an initial fast of six weeks, followed by subsequent annual fasts of between 30 and 40 days each. The first fast restored his functional abilities to the extent that he was able to eat the Hygienic diet of raw fruits, vegetables and nuts, and each subsequent fast raised the level of his health, until today one would never believe he ever suffered through those horrible six years.

Dr. Goldstein has written an in-depth book about his fasting experience and the marvelous benefits he derived from his fast; but as of this writing, it is in the hands of the publisher and does not yet have a title.

Author's Note: On July 13, 1974, I met an attractive, interesting young couple, Leslie Lee Churulich and his wife, Kathy, formerly of Detroit, at the Shangri-La Natural Hygiene Institute, and, with their permission, decided to add Lee's case history to this book.

Lee (as he prefers to be called), now age 23, was on a swimming team seven years ago, and experienced a severely wrenched back in a diving accident. It became progressively worse, and movement was difficult, almost impossible.

The following month, in July, 1967, he entered Spears Chiropractic Hospital in Denver, Colorado, where he remained for a period of about two months. His condition was diagnosed as osteomyelitis of the lumbosacral spine, and x-rays revealed a severe degeneration of the discs in his back, which were starting to fuse. He was treated by chiropractic adjustments, but experienced no improvement. It was during this period that he began to realize that nutritional errors might be playing a part in perpetuating his condition.

In September, 1967 he entered Metropolitan Hospital in Detroit. I quote from a letter from the Metropolitan Hospital, signed by Glaucos Theodoulou, M.D., and dated September 18, 1968 (a year later) giving a report of Lee's condition when he entered the hospital on September 25, 1967:

"Leslie Churulich was admitted on September 25, 1967, with a diagnosis of osteomyelitis of the lumbosacral spine. Needle biopsy showed that the causative organism proved to be Staphylococcus aureus and coagulase positive. He responded to the antibiotic therapy and the back was immobilized in a plaster jacket and later on with hyperextension brace . . . x-ray reports showing changes . . . at the first and second lumbar vertebrae . . . deformity and lateral widening of the second and third lumbar vertebral bodies. Lateral spur formations are present, as well as depression of the lateral superior cribiform plate of L3. . . . Marked narrowing of disc space between L2-3, with indistinct margins of the cribiform plate and the adjacent bony margins. . . . The destruction of the disc space and the marked irregularity of the vertebral bodies are more compatible with an inflammatory process than post-traumatic . . . which is very characteristic of tuberculosis of the bone."

Lee wore the plaster jacket from November, 1967 until January, 1968, and the brace until June, 1968. He was treated with penicillin and streptomycin until January, 1968, and thought he was improving, but started to experience severe drug reactions, culminating in a large boil on his upper arm. He showed me the large ugly scar it left (about three inches in diameter).

Thoroughly disillusioned with the results of the treatment he had been receiving, he turned to Natural Hygiene. During the next six months, from January to July, 1968, he tried to learn as much as he could about Hygienic principles, and implement them to the best of his ability. He took several short fasts, during periods when he felt sick and didn't want food, followed by short periods during which he lived mostly on juices. Subsequently, he followed a Hygienic dietary program.

After a few months of Hygienic living, he noted marked improvement. The boil gradually cleared up and disappeared in July, 1968, shortly after he was able to discard the brace in June.

In April of 1969, the Clinic Director of the Palmer College of Chiropractic, Donald P. Kern, D.C., Ph.C., wrote a letter (attested by a Notary Public, for the draft board), stating that Lee at that time had a chronic bone condition in his lumbar spine, which might be seriously aggravated by any extensive physical exertion, and that this was a partial permanent disability, which could become total and permanent.

In spite of this diagnosis, Lee persisted in following a Hygienic mode of living, including strict adherence to the Hygienic diet, and, as time went on, continued to note a dramatic remission of all symptoms. An x-ray taken late in 1969 by a chiropractor in Showlow, Arizona, revealed almost total reversal and restoration of the discs that had been degenerating and had started to fuse.

Notwithstanding the prognosis in April, 1969 of permanent disability, and the prediction of the dire results of any extensive physical exertion, Lee has been totally free of any symptoms since 1970, and his physical activity has been free of all restrictions.

Lee and Kathy were married in November, 1973. Kathy is also now a practicing Hygienist, and they live and work at the Shangri-La. Lee climbs trees to trim them, engages in carpentry, masonry, landscaping and logging operations, and is an excellent swimmer.

He has had a year of Chiropractic training, and hopes to become a Professional Hygienist.

From a circular by R. J. Cheatham, Director of Shangri-La Natural Hygiene Institute, concerning a book "A Gift of Love" written by Jack Dunn Trop, and published in Australia:

"This book presents MEDICALLY DOCUMENTED PROOF that the 86 children who were raised by L. O. Bailey and Madge Cockburn, in Australia, had a very high standard of health and the BEST TEETH IN THE WORLD. The children were the offspring of American soldiers and Australian mothers. They were raised as vegetarians on a NATURAL diet, with plenty of exercise, rest, fresh air and sunshine. They were never given any drugs or medicines. They were regularly examined and tested, especially as to the condition of their teeth, and these records were printed in six issues of the AUSTRALIAN MEDICAL JOURNAL and the AUSTRALIAN DENTAL JOURNAL.

"A transcript of a goodly portion of these records is reproduced in this book. The objective and scientific evidence, which duly attests that 'the high standard of health and the almost perfect teeth of these Hopewood children is truly remarkable, and the basic reasons for these wonderful results must be their natural diet', and proves conclusively, once and for all that there is only one way to maintain good health and that is by living in accord with Nature's laws."

Jack Dunn Trop says that the book contains a lengthy chapter in which the results of the practical application of these ideas for over twenty years are approved by MEDICAL AND DENTAL AUTHORITIES.

A highlight of the 1974 Annual Hygiene Health Conference was the floor show we enjoyed when a former patient of Dr. Vetrano's demonstrated his recovery from a crippling disability resulting from a childhood accident, by carrying Dr. Vetrano up the stairs to the stage on his shoulders.

At the age of five, a wagon ran over this patient, crushing his lower spine. To quote Dr. Vetrano: "His family was not around, and nothing was actually done for him at that time, until later on." After that accident, he was never able to run. As he grew older, he had increasing pain and a very bad limp—he could barely walk. As an adult, he tried all the cures, with no help. Dr. Vetrano said: "He went to osteopaths, naturopaths, M.D.'s, chiropractors and bonesetters. There was nothing they could do, but they all took his money."

At the age of 32, he came to the Health School, and followed all instructions to the letter. He fasted 52 days. He rested as he should, and maintained emotional poise, and after his fast he was able to walk, and a few days later was able to run. He still has a slight limp, but is strong and healthy, and can run and lift heavy weights, as per the entertaining and heartwarming demonstration.

G. *Colds*

"For a cold, which is vicarious elimination for a crisis in toxemia, the best thing to do (the first choice) would be to fast. A 48 hour fast would be indicated, on water only, followed by 24 hours on juice, and then 24 hours on fruit only, followed by 48 hours on fruits and salads, and then resume a regular Hygienic diet.

"The second choice would be a diet of freshly squeezed juice, one glass three times a day, together with ample rest. The third choice would be an all fruit diet, with ample rest.

The symptoms disappear when they have no food on which to live"—Dr. John M. Brosious, July 1969 Annual Hygiene Health Conference.

H. *Digestion*

"Think of the digestive system as a tube from mouth to anus. The foods pass from one department to another. Changes, absorption and assimilation take place, and the part that the body doesn't want passes out. Emotional upsets during the process of digestion stops digestion for hours or a whole day, and the food in the digestive system poisons the individual. We usually eat about three times as much as we should. We eat one part for our nourishment and two parts to keep the doctor well nourished."—Dr. William L. Esser, D.C., N.D., July 1968 Annual Hygiene Health Conference.

"Raw fruits and vegetables will create sufficient friendly bacteria without cultures (yoghurt)."—Dr. Virginia Vetrano, July 1971 Annual Hygiene Health Conference.

"We have only a dim understanding of the importance of bacteria and flora in the digestive tract."—Dr. Alec Burton, July 1971 Annual Hygiene Health Conference.

"Amino acids are linked together in long chains to form protein. As each cavity (mouth, stomach, duodenum, etc.) performs its function, the chains are broken in half, quarters, eighths, and so on. 95% of the proteins become amino acids, when properly combined, and not overeaten."—Dr. Virginia Vetrano, July 1971 Annual Hygiene Health Conference.

"A hiatus hernia develops through a high degree of fermentation in the stomach. Incomplete digestion causes great distress each time a meal is eaten. This is a difficult condition to correct. Avoid roughage temporarily until digestion has been reestablished. Temporarily, foods may have to be blended or juiced."—Dr. William L. Esser, July 1968 Annual Hygiene Health Conference.

I. *Drugs*

"The body is a fantastically complicated mechanism that we are just beginning to understand. Just imagine the stupidity of introducing drug poisons to interfere with the body chemistry, which can only result in the body's destruction. The body utilizes tremendous amounts of energy to try to break down and expel tea, coffee, alcohol or drugs, for which we get nothing in return except exhausion."—Dr. Alec Burton, July 1968 Annual Hygiene Health Conference.

"The liver is a very complex, marvelous organ, with numerous functions, wth astonishing regenerative powers. If 80% of the liver cells are damaged in an accident, it is possible for the liver to recover completely. Many people have enlarged livers, some are serious conditions, some are not. Drugs add insult to injury, because the liver takes all the abuse. Steroids and cortisones are the most difficult to eliminate, and break down the liver."—Dr. William L. Esser, July 1969 Annual Hygiene Health Conference.

"Some drugs are eliminated with such difficulty that they are hidden around in various areas in the body to get them out of the bloodstream,—Strontium 90 in the bones, DDT in the fatty tissue."—Dr. Virginia Vetrano, July 1968 Annual Hygiene Health Conference.

"Don't take diuretics for fluid accumulation. Diuretics tend to combine chemically with kidney tissue, and the damaged kidney causes high blood pressure."—Dr.

Alec Burton, July 1970 Annual Hygiene Health Conference.

"Diabetics eat frequently—why are they hungry if they are sick? It is not hunger—they are so irritated, they suffer withdrawal symptoms. Also they have to eat regularly to utilize the insulin."—Dr. Alec Burton, July 1969 Annual Hygiene Health Conference.

"There are 6,000,000 drugs in the Pharmacopoeia, but only about a half dozen that have come down as of any value whatsoever, by admission of the medical profession, among which are aspirin, penicillin, morphine and digitalis. Digitalis has a low quotient of beneficial qualities, compared to the danger, as it works havoc with the kidneys."—Dr. John M. Brosious, July 1971 Annual Hygiene Health Conference.

"Drugs always occasion the perpetuation of the very symptoms for which they are taken" (See Law of Dual Effect—Addendum—Section 1). A drug is given to stimulate the tired heart (to whip it into action), which will have to be followed by depression. This applies to the liver, the pancreas, the stomach. If forced into excessive action, the secondary and lasting effect will be depression. The same applies to drinking coffee, cokes, etc. You lose vital power, become enervated and disease begins to evolve. Tranquilizers in the end produce less tranquility. Drugs for pain will only produce more and worse pain later, and will eventually destroy vital organs."—Dr. Virginia Vetrano, July 1968 Annual Hygiene Health Conference.

"Movement during sleep is normal and necessary for circulation. When taking drugs this necessary movement during sleep is inhibited. There is a big difference between sleep and narcosis."—Dr. Alec Burton, July 1969 Annual Hygiene Health Conference.

"If you receive the hormone drugs cortisone or adrenalin by injection (substitution therapy), the organism atrophies and won't function."—Dr. David J. Scott, July 1970 Annual Hygiene Health Conference.

"The taking of any hormone drug will upset all the

other hormones in the body, and will interfere, emphasize or decrease the secretions of all the other glands. When you take cortisone or insulin, tremendous damage occurs to the body, the nervous system, and the glands; the whole pattern is thrown off balance, and this can cause degeneration of the retina of the eyes, or gangrene of the toes. We must deal with fundamental causes, instead of taking hormones."—Dr. Alec Burton, July 1970, Annual Hygiene Health Conference.

J. *Emotions*

"Apprehension, anger, fear, worry, build up in your body. Humility and self-effacement help to eliminate those waves of anger, and helps other people to not do things to hurt us. We are most critical of our families, and it should be the other way around. Be patient. Don't strike back. Apologize, even if it is not your fault. Don't let things engulf you. Control your emotions, don't suppress them and turn them inward. Put problems in proper perspective. All types of meditation are very constructive. Taking time to be alone and look within ourselves can accomplish much."—Dr. William L. Esser, July 1973 Annual Hygiene Health Conference.

"Stress or excitement, anger or frustration, can throw the adrenals into abnormal activity. It is far better for a person who is angry or frustrated, or in the grip of emotion, to run around the block to use up this energy."—Dr. Keki R. Sidhwa, July 1973 Annual Hygiene Health Conference.

"Emotions are among the most enervating factors in life. People under continued emotional stress are more likely to develop tumors."—Dr. Alec Burton, July 1969 Annual Hygiene Health Conference.

K. *Exercise*

"Rest must follow exertion, and activity must follow repose. Form your exercise program to exercise those muscles that you use the least. Growth, development and the strength of your mind are acquired by exercise. You must build strength for the health of the body. If you do heavy work, your muscles will build themselves up to the size necessary for the work you force them to do. Also exercise for endurance, for general health. Oxygen is absolutely necessary when exercising."— Dr. Virginia Vetrano, July 1968 Annual Hygiene Health Conference.

"Lymph bathes every cell of your being. To encourage the circulation of the lymphatic system, man has to use his muscles. Exercise is vitally important."— Dr. Gerald Benesch, July 1971 Annual Hygiene Health Conference.

"If you can run two miles in 12 minutes, that is very good. To run the two miles in 20 minutes is pretty good."—Dr. Alec Burton, July 1970 Annual Hygiene Health Conference.

L. *Fasting*

"Fasting is the closest thing to a panacea that one can find. It is applicable to all ages, from infancy to the very old. It is the quickest assist to the efforts of the body to overcome acute disease, pain and discomfort. It was used in ancient times and is used now, and we should spread this great knowledge that can be had by all."—Dr. William L. Esser, July 1968 Annual Hygiene Health Conference.

"The five basic functions of life, all maintained when fasting, are:

1. Respiration
2. Nutrition
3. Excretion
4. Reproduction
   (of cells or organism)
5. Repair"

—Dr. David J. Scott, July 1970 Annual Hygiene Health Conference.

"We agree that all fasting should be supervised by qualified professionals. Strangely, we have a high percentage of people coming to the Pawling Health Manor for weight reduction, who are referred by their physicians. Most have come because of the inability of the highest medical authorities to bring about results. And interestingly enough, several physicians, including medical school professors, have come and do come here to fast, to observe, and to learn the basic principles of fasting."—Dr. Robert R. Gross, Ph.D., May 1974 Natural Hygienews. (Dr. Gross earned his Ph.D. in physiological chemistry by doing his thesis on "Fasting and Realimentation," and has successfully fasted approximately 15,000 people for varying periods of time.)

"Crises in fasting are created because of stored by-products of metabolism being released into the bloodstream, causing temporary irritation in various parts of the body."—Dr. Alex Burton, July 1969 Annual Hygiene Health Conference.

"You lose all desire to eat when you fast. Hunger is a mouth and throat sensation, it is not an uncomfortable feeling. It is not abdominal, not an all gone feeling, or dizziness or weakness. All these symptoms will subside if you refrain from eating, and the coated tongue, bad breath and bad taste will gradually improve and clear up. Your original symptoms will also disappear. Don't take vitamins while fasting—you will be poisoning the body, and inviting gout and other bad problems. Your continual sufferings when chronically ill are much worse than the ephemeral symptoms and crises of a fast. The more severe your reactions are, the greater is your need·for a fast. Orthopathic means correct suffering. The symptoms during the fast are there for a purpose, and always end in better and better health. One last big meal before a fast can be your undoing. The last supper can be *your last supper*."—Dr. Virginia Vetrano, July 1973 Annual Hygiene Health Conference.

"When an animal is sick, it refuses food until it is well again. We had a Pomeranian who was hit by a car, and refused water for ten days and food for 25 days, and recovered."—Dr. William L. Esser, July 1969 Annual Hygiene Health Conference.

"Fasting will autolyze adhesions. Fatty tumors take a long time to absorb—this may take several fasts. They usually absorb more slowly than fibroids. During fasting, don't overdrink and overwork the kidneys. This actually interferes with the elimination of toxic material. After accidents, tissues will heal much more rapidly while fasting. You usually sleep no more than three or four hours every twenty-four hours during a fast, because you are not forcing the organism to work metabolizing food. You do require darkness and rest from 9:00 P.M. to 7:00 A.M."—Dr. Virginia Vetrano, July 1973 Annual Hygiene Health Conference.

"My mother fasted one day a week until she was 95."—Dr. William L. Esser, July 1969 Annual Hygiene Health Conference.

"In a fast, we can observe the body gleefully going about getting rid of the toxins and wastes accumulated for years, with the greatest capability and intelligence, all on its own. Examinations and tests are not necessary in the majority of cases, but they help in understanding the problem. The body uses the least important stored materials; the heart, nervous system, lungs, and other vital parts remain intact, and calcium is not robbed from teeth, bone and nails."—Dr. William L. Esser, July 1969 Annual Hygiene Health Conference.

"Instructions for breaking a fast:
  3 day fast—1 day of juice
10 day fast—1½ days of juice,
              2 days fruit monotrophic diet,
              1 day leafy greens,
              then regular Hygienic diet."
—Dr. John M. Brosious, July 1971 Annual Hygiene Health Conference.

"For breaking a fast, figure on one day of juice for every week of the fast: three or four ounces every two hours the first day, six to eight ounces at a time the second day, but farther apart."—Dr. William L. Esser, July 1969 Annual Hygiene Health Conference.

New Theory on Breaking Fasts:

". . . I observed that some people have to wait for over a week sometimes for their first bowel movement after a fast. Having studied physiology in detail and the movements of the gastrointestinal tract, this set me thinking. Movement or peristalsis is occasioned by the presence of bulk in the stomach. When a person takes a juice there is no bulk or very little bulk. So peristalsis is not occasioned or started up half as well as when you break the fast on solid food as a fast would be broken in Nature. So I asked, 'Why not break the fast on solid food? They did in the past before they had juicers.' I talked it over with Dr. Shelton, and he said, 'Go ahead and try it if you want to.' . . . The guests actually loved it. . . . Since then I have been observing the average time for their first bowel movement and it comes most of the time on the first or second day . . . and digestion is better this way. On the whole I am very much pleased with the new way of breaking fasts that I instituted."—Dr. Virginia Vetrano, Hygienic Review, June 1974.

M. *Fevers and Temperature*

"Heavy eaters complain of heat. Normal temperature may really be a few degrees lower than 98.6 degrees. In acute disease, temperature and pulse rise together. In chronic disease or in fasting, pulse may fall and temperature remain normal—lower than 98.6 —around 97. Temperature will rise from the sun bath and stay up a couple of hours. Don't fear a fever. Secretions are suspended during a fever, and food cannot be digested. Don't suppress the fever, which is a defensive process. It will come down automatically when the process is completed. The body will not destroy its own living cells. Chronic low temperature or chronic high temperature will change to normal after a fast."—Dr. Virginia Vetrano, July 1973 Annual Hygiene Health Conference.

N. *Food*

"Man is the only animal that must have as many as thirty foods at one sitting."—Dr. John M. Brosious, July 1973 Annual Hygiene Health Conference.

"Relative to the Acid-Alkaline Balance: Vegetables tend to keep you in the right area. Exercise helps some. Fruits tend to swing you into the alkaline side; proteins swing you to acid. Bananas are neutral if you are in good health, otherwise they are slightly alkaline. When you are toxic, all foods throw you off balance. Fasting restores the function—even skipping a meal or two, or fasting for 24 or 36 hours will help. If you eat right, and conserve your energy, your acid-alkaline balance will correct itself."—Dr. David J. Scott, July 1970 Annual Hygiene Health Conference.

"What are the characteristics of substance to be classified as a food?

1. Capable of liberating energy when oxidized.
2. Capable of being utilized for growth, maintenance and repair.
3. Capable of being stored within the body.
4. No toxic effects in nutritionally significant quantities should be observed."

—Dr. Alec Burton, July 1968 Annual Hygiene Health Conference.

"Phytic acid in cereals blocks the absorption of calcium. Fruit acids maintain the calcium of the diet in soluble form."—Dr. Virginia Vetrano, July 1971 Annual Hygiene Health Conference.

O. *Genetic Damage*

"In the fertilized cell is all the information necessary to produce a human being, contained in a single molecule of heredity, the DNA. (DNA = deoxyribonucleic acid = containing chromosomes containing genes.)"

Author's Note: A definition of DNA and RNA, for

clarification, from "Ask Andy", Indianapolis News, September 4, 1970: "The life processes of most cells are governed by two complex acids called DNA and RNA. The DNA molecules in the nucleus carry the blueprint of these activities. Their orders are carried out by RNA—ribonucleic acid—molecules that direct and organize the operations."

"There are fearful results from genetic damage—thalidomide interfered with the information transfer. This genetic material is in the ovaries and testes. In impaired health, genetic information transmission is not accurate and can cause birth defects."—Dr. Alec Burton, July 1970 Annual Hygiene Health Conference.

Author's Note: At this point, it may be appropriate to include a quotation from an article in the St. Petersburg Independent, May 22, 1974, regarding genetic damage produced by smoking marijuana: "Dr. Gabriel Nahas, professor at Columbia University Medical School and consultant to the United Nations on marijuana, and Dr. Edward Domino, director of the neuropsychopharmacology research program at the University of Michigan, recently have reported that there is an active component of marijuana—delta 9-tetrahydrocannabinol (THC) which affects cellular reproduction in both animals and humans. THC is not water soluble and is stored in the fatty tissue of the body, with high concentrations found in the spleen. There is a possibility that the impairment of the immune system in man, found in marijuana smokers, is related to an effect of the THC on the synthesis of DNA. Inhibition of the synthesis of DNA would decrease cell reproduction, or produce cells with faulty DNA—thus, abnormal cells. . . . Such cells are called mutagenic . . . and are responsible for some of the abnormalities found in newborn humans as well as animals. . . . Dr. Nahas feels it may take generations for present mutations to show up."

From a Panel Discussion—Drs. Burton, Esser &

Vetrano, July 1968 Annual Hygiene Health Conference:
"X-Rays, nuclear fallout, fluorescent lights, television sets, and luminous dials give off damaging radiation, and produce genetic damage."

(A new fluorescent bulb was mentioned, put out by a Dr. Ott,—the spectrum of this bulb is said to be the same as natural sunlight.)

P. Germ Theory and Pasteurization

"No one will deny the existence of microbes, or that they are intimately associated with certain diseases. They may be secondary or tertiary factors, but they are not the primary and fundamental causes of disease. They are intimately associated with, and necessary to the evolution of some diseases. The condition of the host is the primary factor. Bacteria are so important to life that we cannot survive without them. They take on certain characteristics, depending on the environment in which they find themselves. Germs don't cause disease—disease creates an environment favorable to the proliferation of germs. Germ warfare is largely fear. Botulism is of the same family as tetanus. It is as poisonous as cyanide and occurs from eating food poisoned with Botulin—usually in canned fish or meat. An epidemic of botulism cannot occur—it cannot be circulated in the atmosphere.

"Immunity? Vaccination is supposed to create artificial immunity. When vaccination in England was compulsory, virtually 100% were vaccinated, and they had their worst smallpox epidemic—42,000 died. Now 2/3 of the children under 5 are not vaccinated, and only four of the unvaccinated died of smallpox. Of the 1/3 who were vaccinated, 86 died. There are the same type of statistics for diphtheria and polio. Vaccination is a commercial enterprise, and will continue as long as people believe and accept it. Viruses are somewhat different from bacteria, but they are still dependent on the state of the host. A susceptible host will contract a disease. "Contagion" is related to the conditions under which individuals are living. Polio was already declining when the Salk vaccine was introduced. Various diseases have come and gone throughout man's history."—Dr. Alec Burton, July 1968 Annual Hygiene Health Conference.

Excerpts from an article by Dr. Robert R. Gross, in Volume 1, No. 2, The Healthway Advisor:

"Fear is the most dreadful of all diseases. . . . To teach people that they live in an atmosphere loaded with disease-provoking germs, ready to attack at any time, no matter how one lives, creates fear and apprehension. . . . The picture is of germs chasing people and of doctors chasing germs. The germs catch up with the people. And the doctors catch up with the germs and the patients.

"Germs do not cause disease! Nature never surrounded her children with enemies. It is the individual himself who makes disease possible in his own body because of poor living habits. . . . Do mosquitoes make the water stagnant, or does stagnant water attract the mosquitoes? We should all be taught that germs are friends and scavengers attracted by disease, rather than enemies causing disease. . . . As the internal environment is, so will be the attraction for any specific micro-organism. . . . The germ theory and vaccination are kept going by commercialism. The evidence is incontrovertible to prove that vaccines and serums have never prevented or lessened disease.

"Rudolph Virchow, a great German scientist, repudiated the germ theory of disease. He said that disease brought on germs rather than that germs caused disease. Claude Bernard, Bechamp and Tissot—great French scientists all—disproved the germ theory of disease. In Dr. Hans Selye's book "Stress of Life" (Page 205), an account is recorded that Louis Pasteur, inventor of the germ theory of disease, admitted he was wrong. Sanitation is the only factor that has reduced the spread of the old-time scourages. The results of combined so-called epidemics are extremely revealing. In those treated hygienically, less than one-seventeenth of one per cent died, while 17% died when treated by "orthodox" methods. . . .

"If the germ theory were founded on facts, there would be no living being to read what is herein written, for germs are ubiquitous—they exist everywhere. In many diseases supposedly caused by a specific germ, that germ is not present. Contrariwise, specific germs said to cause a specific disease are present in huge proportions without the specific disease manifesting itself."

Excerpts from Dr. Herbert M. Shelton's "Evils of Pasteurization":

"The Wisconsin College of Agriculture announced in 1935 that their investigations had shown that raw milk is more nutritive than pasteurized milk. It had been known for many years that infants fed exclusively on pasteurized milk developed scurvy, and that calves fed pasteurized milk die after about 12 weeks. Bircher-Benner of Switzerland wrote several years ago that, according to Dr. Gerber, heat changes the following constituents of milk: the fat (change in power of cream-formation); the lecithin (destroyed through splitting up of phosphoric acid); the casein (changes its reaction to acid and to rennet); the lactose (becomes caramelized); the citric acid (destroyed); the soluble calcium salts (transferred to an insoluble state); the carbonic acid (destroyed); the enzymes and vitamins (also destroyed). All this applies chiefly to the sterilizing of milk, but holds good in a lesser degree for pasteurization.

"It has also been noted that bacteria multiply more rapidly in heat-treated milk than in raw milk. The people are frenzied by fear of typhoid, diphtheria, undulant fever, etc. Orthodox channels of education on infant and child feeding are dedicated to upholding commercial interests, and none of them dares to tell the truth about pasteurization, but seek to convince mothers that pasteurized milk is a wholesome food, and that unpasteurized milk is freighted with dangers galore. In time, people will learn that the fear of unpasteurized milk has grown out of the extension of the same bacteriophobia that warns us against the use of other raw foods." (See previous article from Dr. Gross, on the Germ Theory. "Pasteur, inventor of the germ theory of disease, admitted he was wrong."—Author's Note.)

Q. *Greece: Natural Hygiene Triumphant*

From an editorial by Dr. Herbert M. Shelton, in the February, 1974 Hygienic Review:

"Shortly after New Year's, a card arrived from Greece, addressed to both Dr. Vetrano and Dr. Shelton, saying: "Dear Dr. Shelton and Dr. Vetrano, My best wishes to you for a happy and prosperous New Year. Natural Hygiene is advancing in Greece. In one month from now, my first large book (over 900 pages) on Hygiene will be out of press. This book is mostly based on Dr. Shelton's writings. I have a lot of successes in my Hygienic practice. The future looks promising. Hygienically yours, P. Coumentakis.'

Peter Coumentakis, N.D., came to the Health School a few years ago, after graduating in Naturopathy, and spent a few months with us preparing himself to take Natural Hygiene back home with him to Greece. It was in Greece, about 2400 to 2500 years ago, that mankind took the first misstep away from the system of primitive Hygiene, that had served so long and so well, into the drugging system. It has been a long dark journey, but Hygiene has finally found its way back into the land from which it was first purged."

R. *Hygienic Principles*

"Hygiene is a logical system, which may be supported by empirical facts, but not dependent on them. 'Empirical' refers to experience with experimental techniques. Empiricism needs to be founded on some logical approach. The Hygienic system is based on the fact that the body is self-constructing, self-defending and self-repairing. The body has certain fundamental needs for its survival. It must have a proper and suitable environment to supply materials for growth, defense, development and repair, such as pure water, nutritious food, fresh air, sunshine, exercise, rest, sleep, and so forth. The Hygienic system is designed to understand how we can influence the self-construction, the self-defense and the self-repair, and how we can understand the limitations of the organism in relation to these functions, and how we can modify and enhance these functions by supplying the materials and the influences which are necessary for these processes to take place.

"There are also factors supplied by the internal environment, mental and emotional state, and so forth. Of course the internal environment is influenced very much by the external environment. That is why, in dealing with psychological factors, we must also pay very acute attention to physiological or biological factors.

"Each individual is a law unto himself, but he is not outside the laws of life. There are individual interpretations, considerations, limitations and capacities. In healthy individuals, the individual variations may be very narrow. Where pathology exists, the variations may be very broad."—Dr. Alec Burton, July 1974 Annual Hygiene Health Conference.

Condensed from an Editorial by Dr. Herbert M. Shelton, Ph.D., in the January, 1974 Hygienic Review: "A valid system of mind-body care must not be a fabricated system, but must be the elemental factors of life itself, with roots deep in the early life of plants and animals, and an essential part of the life of the world. It must be easily understood, and must be truth itself, and must meet all of the conditions of existence. It must have met all the basic needs of life, in sickness and in health, from the beginning of life on this earth, and be identical for every human being.

"The modern Hygienic movement that had its beginning in the early part of the last century is not a new creation, but a revival; it is a return to man's primeval way of life, to that way of life that was effective in maintaining his pristine soundness and vigor when the race was young. It is a new enthusiasm for man's normal way of life, despite the powerful commercial forces that are arrayed against it. In its immense span of usefulness, its utter simplicity, its naturalness and its wholesomeness, lie its greatness."

"We must always keep an open mind in Hygiene and not feel that the last word has been spoken. As we learn more, we get a more complete picture."—Dr. Alec Burton, July 1968 Annual Hygiene Health Conference.

"Although at present Hygienists represent a small minority group in our country and in the world, we are the only group with a program that represents the genuine welfare of the people."—Dr. Herbert M. Shelton, "Natural Hygiene, Man's Pristine Way of Life".

"Twenty-one years have taught us the necessity of total dedication and integrity regarding our principles. There can be no compromises, no gimmicks, no backing down under pressure, and no expediencies. This has meant the development of a structure wherein self-aggrandizement or economic profit by membership or association would be impossible. We feel this state has been reached."—Oscar Floyd, from Convention keynote to 22nd Annual Hygiene Health Conference, July, 1970.

"Strong, naked, honest facts are what the public wants, to satisfy them of the virtues of Natural Hygiene. It is not enough to enunciate principles—we must explain their practical operations and show the results of their applications. We must not only show how the sick ought to get well, but how they do get well. One young woman restored, and taught how she may keep the roses blooming in her cheeks, and how to preserve the sparkling luster of her eyes, should be sufficient to reconcile the whole neighborhood to the new way of life."—Dr. Herbert M. Shelton, "Natural Hygiene, Man's Pristine Way of Life".

"Natural Hygiene has four advantages:
1. True enduring principles
2. Constructive means compatible with the needs of life.
3. Comprehensible principles
4. Habit control."
—Dr. Herbert M. Shelton, "Natural Hygiene, Man's Pristine Way of Life".

S. *Living Longer*

"Man is living longer only as a statistic. One baby in four used to die, now only one in sixteen dies. This makes a big difference in statistics. Also, cholera epidemics, etc., have been wiped out. In the past few decades, a man of fifty has much less chance of reaching seventy than he did fifty or sixty years ago.—Dr. Alec Burton, July 1968 Annual Hygiene Health Conference.

"Living Longer Youthfully: Youth is not a time of life, it is a state of mind. Tangled emotions, jealousies, fears and frustrations, tension, boredom, noise, are all aging. Dynamic thoughts are important. Keep on dreaming. People grow old by giving up their enthusiasm and ideals. Learn to be creative. Right thinking, stillness and repose, peace, meditation, will budget our resources. Think of others, do not shut your eyes to cruelty and suffering. Share with someone. Lonely and selfish people grow old."—Dr. Keki R. Sidhwa, July 1969 Annual Hygiene Health Conference.

T. *Nader Committee*

Condensed from a Report by Dr. Alec Burton, July 1971 Annual Hygiene Health Conference:

"I made a report on Natural Hygiene before the Nader Committee and am to send them a systematic presentation. I answered questions concerning the Biological Needs of Man, the Foundation for Social and Cultural Needs, Problems of Sickness and Disease, Hygiene vs. Medicine, Hygiene as a Movement, Biological Base, History of Hygiene, History of Medicine, Departure from Original Aims, Drug Poisons Used, Illness Inevitable Consequences of Departure, Hygienic Way of Life Compared to Conventional, Hygienic Way Simpler and Less Expensive, Education, Political Implications, Repercussions and Persecution of Practitioners, Denial of Media to Hygienic Practitioners, Lack of Opportunity for Hygienic Education, General Role of Hygiene.

"We discussed Cancer in the very cursory sense, and I promised to send more material. The Committee seemed genuinely interested, and if we can supply the right answers to the right questions, I believe they will take some action on it. They knew what questions to ask, and were very knowledgeable and willing to hear our story, and take action if convinced it should be done."

U. *Organic Limitations*

"Patients come with parts missing. If the *thyroid* has been removed" (Author's Note: Or is not functioning because radioactive iodine has been used?) "the patient must continue to take thyroxin while fasting, and it is impossible to control an accurate dose.

"*Diabetics* who have been on insulin for a long time have no chance of secreting insulin. We may improve their health, but cannot necessarily get them away from insulin permanently. Temporary withdrawal of insulin is sometimes possible, when no glucose is being taken in."—Dr. Alec Burton, July 1970 Annual Hygiene Health Conference.

"*Skin Cancers:* Health can be recovered through

fasting and Natural Hygiene. *Multiple Sclerosis* is irreversible. If in the early period, and some tissues have not yet sclerosed, much improvement can be made. You can stop the pathology from increasing by taking a fast, and following Natural Hygiene. *Parkinson's Disease:* In latter stages, lesions prevent rest, and cannot be remedied. However, even where there is extreme degeneration of tissue, improvement can occur, even if full health cannot be achieved. Sometimes the living organism fools us (laboratory tests are not accurate), and even though we think it is irreversible, it may prove to be capable of healing. A *broken bone* that has been set improperly will straighten out if you exercise properly."—Dr. Virginia Vetrano, July 1973 Annual Hygiene Health Conference.

"Many patients with *emphysema* can work full time again after fasting."—Dr. David J. Scott, July 1973 Annual Hygiene Health Conference.

V. *Mental Hygiene Psychiatric Examination from July 1970 Annual Hygiene Health Conference:*

a. Are you happy?

Happiness is a by-product of effective life adjustment. Happiness is like a butterfly. If you chase it, it will always elude you. But if you sit down quietly, it will come in and sit on your shoulder.

b. Do you have zest for living? to love, play, live more, at any age?

A man 35 years old wished he had gone to college. When asked why he didn't go now, he said it would take ten years to complete a course at night. "If I go now, I will be 45 years old in ten years," he said. The next question was, "How old will you be in ten years if you don't go?"

c. Are you socially adjusted? Do you like being with others, sharing with others?

Loss of interest is one of the worst forms of creeping mental illness.

d. Do you have unity and balance?

If you do something, don't worry. If you worry,

don't do it. Don't wrap your life around any one thing—your mate, your job—

e. Can you live with each problem in your life as it arises?
"I'm an old man who has had many troubles, most of which never happened."

f. Do you have insight into your own conduct?
No psychiatrist in the world can ever cure anyone—he may be able to help you help yourself.

g. Do you have a confidential relationship with some other person?
Some people need this so badly they even get married to get it.

h. Do you have a sense of the ridiculous?
Can you laugh loud and long at what the world does to you? Most of all, can you laugh at yourself? The most important chemical law in the Universe: The human body can never sprout an ulcer or get angry while laughing.

i. Are you engaged in satisfying work?
You break down from tension and worry, not work. You go home tired, but you won't break down.

j. Do you know how to worry effectively?
Do something active about it.

W. *Surgery* (Is This Rip Necessary?)

"Constructive Surgery: There are times when surgery, though undesirable, may be necessary. Surgery and post-surgical care involves mutilating, shocking and poisoning the body. There is no clearcut line as to whether or not surgery is necessary. Don't let the surgeon make the decision—let a Professional Hygienist make the decision. A Hygienic program before undergoing surgery is advisable, so that the body will be in better condition.

"Generally, in Cancer, avoid surgery. The patient will live longer, and with less pain, without it. Surgery and anesthetic increase the probability of recurrence.

"Most Tonsils, Appendices and Gall Bladders are unnecessarily removed. Very rarely should a gall blad-

der be removed, and gallstones need not be removed."
(Author's Note: Dr. Burton tells of overcoming his
own case of Acute Appendicitis, years ago, the Hygienic
way, and he still has his appendix.)

"A Caesarian section is sometimes necessary, but,
if repeatedly required, avoid pregnancy. A tumor can
be reduced by fasting, but if it has reached such proportions that there is obstruction or pressure on nerves and
organs, causing serious problems, surgery may be
necessary.

"A cataract may be capable of being broken down
by the body, especially in young people, during a fast.
Removal of hardened calcified lens may restore vision.
Sometimes the surgeon uses an enzyme to release the
lens—this is not advisable, as it could cause a detach-
ment of the retina later. The knife is preferable.
Mechanical techniques are necessary to provide favor-
able conditions for healing fractures and dislocations."
—Dr. Alec Burton, July 1970 Annual Hygiene Health
Conference.

"Additional Constructive Surgery":
  1. Concealed Strangulated Hernia in Infant
  2. Repair of Congenital Defects
  3. Repair after Accidents
  4. Extensive Damage to Joints, and Cartilage prob-
     lems may require surgical intervention.
  5. Do not remove an organ,—except perhaps a
     hysterectomy where a large tumor has reached a
     stage where it is blocking the body processes."

————Dr. Alec Burton,
         July 1974 Annual Hygiene Health Conference
"Fasting will autolyze adhesions—surgery for adhesions is not necessary."—Dr. Virginia Vetrano, July
1973 Annual Hygiene Health Conference.

"It is very rare that the body requires surgical interference, but sometimes it is necessary. I had a case
where a peptic ulcer of years' duration had eaten
through the wall of the stomach, and surgery was neces-

sary to close this opening."—Dr. William L. Esser, July 1969 Annual Hygiene Health Conference.

"A tubal pregnancy requires surgery."—Dr. John M. Brosious, July 1969 Annual Hygiene Health Conference.

"A twelve year old boy fasted at the Health School for acute appendicitis, and grew up to become an athlete, and is thinking of becoming a Hygienic Practitioner."—Dr. Virginia Vetrano, July 1973 Annual Hygiene Health Conference.

"Certain cystic tumors (capsulated) are virtually sealed, and not susceptible to autolytic enzymes. These are not affected by fasts. If located where they can obstruct or impair functions, I would recommend surgery."—Dr. Alec Burton, July 1969 Annual Hygiene Health Conference.

"Tampering with nasal passages by surgery is a great crime."—Dr. Keki R. Sidhwa, July 1969 Annual Hygiene Health Conference.

"Some good teachers of Natural Hygiene have come from the 'cure' schools. For example, William Howard Hay, M.D., who expresses a rational attitude towards surgery in his book, 'Some Human Ailments'."—Jack Dunn Trop, "You Don't Have To Be Sick" (See "You Don't Have To Be Sick", Pages 89, 90, 91 and 92, quoting Dr. Hay as saying that 26 cases of ruptured appendix under his observation recovered without any attempt at surgery. Dr. Hay also quoted Dr. Charles Mayo as telling the American College of Surgeons that nine-tenths of the internal operations performed today should never have occurred, and Dr. Hay said he thought it should be 99%—Author's Note)

"Natural recovery from hernia is possible in the early phases. Some hernias must be surgically corrected."—Dr. Alec Burton, July 1969 Annual Hygiene Health Conference.

"In the case of umbilical hernia, and other types of hernia in relatively young patients, the temporary wearing of a truss, while exercising to develop the abdominal muscles, and going on a Hygienic program, can accomplish recovery in six or eight months."—Dr. Alec Burton, July 1970 Annual Hygiene Health Conference.

"Transplants: Where gross degeneration of the body has taken place, a transplant is not of much value. It is futile—a waste of time and money. If one organ has degenerated beyond the point of repair, then the other organs won't last long either. The person must take anti-rejection drugs for the rest of his life, and will ultimately reach the saturation point. Once we attempt to inhibit the body's defense mechanism, we cripple the powers of life. Transplants are only worth while in extreme cases, where a person is in the prime of life and has had an accident which destroyed an organ, and may survive for a number of years after a transplant, but would die almost immediately without the transplant. Or eye transplants may be worth while, but the person must understand that to restore his sight, he must suffer the consequences of the drugging."—Dr. Alec Burton, July 1973 Annual Hygiene Health Conference.

Some of the professionals at the 1974 Annual Hygiene Health Conference told of patients who came to them with perforated ulcers (they were vomiting blood)—and, of course, they were rushed to the hospital, as immediate surgery was necessary.

X. *Unity of Disease*

"One organ will not be diseased by itself and the rest of the body remain healthy. Treating affected organs or tissues as entities is short-sighted, and not based on sound science. There is unity of the body, as there is unity of the Universe. Remove all disease by removing or correcting the primary factors. Specialization in medicine is nothing but a form of tinkering or patchwork."—Dr. Virginia Vetrano, July 1968 Annual Hygiene Health Conference.

Y. *Weight*

"The bathroom scale is not the sole indicator of true health. . . . Many people cannot understand how a truly natural diet will serve to both slim a "fatty" and build up a "string-bean". . . . You can forget about only exercising to "burn the fat off" without a drastic overhauling of other habits also. It would take a 30 to 50 mile hike to shed a single pound of fat, or climbing to the top of the Washington Monument (898 steps 40 times.) . . . Exercise can help to keep you in trim AS the pounds come off, but it will not do the job alone. . . . Fasting, under competent Hygienic supervision, can be the easiest and best way to lose poundage. It *may* not be required for the mildly overweight, but is very often indicated in the grossly obese. Of course, maintaining the full Hygienic regimen AFTER the fast is of the utmost importance, avoiding a return to the old methods of living that brought the problem in the first place.

"Fasting can also be of great value to the underweight, if the problem is due to an inability to digest or assimilate the food. The best explanation of this practice is given by Dr. Shelton in his book 'Fasting Can Save Your Life' in the chapter on Fasting to Gain Weight. By permitting the body to rest and recuperate, the fast enables the digestive system to return to its tasks with renewed vigor and capabilities, and the weight loss of such a fast can usually be regained and even surpassed in a reasonably short time. . . .

"A good regular program of vigorous exercise may be of even greater importance to the underweight than to the overweight person. . . . Emotional problems that turn one to snacking and overeating must also be faced squarely and rooted out. Only when all causative factors have been set right, and the person returned to a properly balanced and well-adjusted way of living, can any real hope be held out for permanent normalizing of the situation."—H. J. Dinshah, "Overweight and Underweight"

Z. *A Few Interesting Definitions*
Atom and Molecule:

"An atom is the smallest particle of normal matter. A molecule is a group of atoms behaving as a unit (the same substances, or different ones)."—Dr. Alec Burton, July 1968 Annual Hygiene Health Conference.

Autolysis

"Autolysis is disintegration of tissues by the body's own enzymes."—Dr. John M. Brosious, July 1974 Annual Hygiene Health Conference.

"Autolysis (self-dissolving or self-digestion of tissue) is a normal part of physiology, but is speeded up and enhanced by fasting."—Dr. Virginia Vetrano, July 1970 Annual Hygiene Health Conference.

Chemistry and Biochemistry

"Chemistry deals with substances that react to each other. Biochemistry (closely related to physiology) deals with changes that take place in the living organism (preferably normally functioning)."—Dr. Alec Burton, July 1970 Annual Hygiene Health Conference.

"Electrolytes are the minerals in the diet. They will dissolve in water."—Dr. Virginia Vetrano, July 1971 Annual Hygiene Health Conference.

Enzymes

"An enzyme is a protein substance which is an organic catalyst, occasioning a chemical reaction (in the process of digestion), to break down complex substances into simple substances, without itself being used up in the process."—Dr. Virginia Vetrano, July 1971 Annual Hygiene Health Conference.

"Enzymes in the body can be used over and over again, but eventually need to be replaced. They are not the same as enzymes in food."—Dr. Alec Burton, July 1970 Annual Hygiene Health Conference.

Glands and Hormonal System

"The *Pitutary Gland* in the brain is the master gland, and controls the endocrine activity of all the other glands. The *Thyroid Gland* controls calcium metabolism. It also regulates the mechanism of converting molecules into energy and storing them; and the process of converting glucose into glycogen, and storing it in the liver. The hormone insulin facilitates the use of glucose. The *Adrenal Gland* determines the rate of oxidation and speeds up detoxification in the muscles and liver and kidneys. Adrenal cortisone is always present, and can be increased or decreased. Adrenalin is an instantaneous, defensive, short action hormone (fight or flight). Fear and anxiety cause an increase in adrenalin, with harmful effects on the sympathetic nervous system. If you receive cortisone or adrenalin by injection (substitution therapy), the gland atrophies and won't function. The *Pancreas (Isle of Langerhans)* secretes insulin. The *Gonads (Ovaries and Testes)* secrete gonadaltrophic hormone; and lactogenic hormone in a mother after the birth of a child.

"These are all ductless glands and empty directly into the blood. The Liver and Pancreatic secretion of the Pancreas (not the insulin) empty into ducts."—(Also see *Lymph Gland* below) Condensed from Lectures at the July 1970 Annual Hygiene Health Conference by Dr. David J. Scott, and Dr. Alec Burton.

"Hydrolysis is the breakdown of food substances in water added by the body processes, facilitated by enzymes."—Dr. Alec Burton, July 1970 Annual Hygiene Health Conference.

Lymph, Lymph Gland, Lymph Node

"Lymph is the colorless fluid of the body. Lymph is equal to blood minus cells minus colloids. Lymph percolates between the cells. The cell receives nutrition from the lymph and excretes into the lymph. Most of the toxins accumulate into the lymph and cells, very few accumulate in the blood. Fluid is drained into the lymph system and some must percolate through the *Lymph Gland (Filter)* to detoxify the material. The Lymph Node contains defense cells and scavengers. The lymph system is a defense system—so is the blood system. The Lymph Gland becomes swollen because of increased activity, due to an abnormal toxic situation, against which it is attempting to defend the organism."—Dr. David J. Scott, July 1970 Annual Hygiene Health Conference.

Metabolism

"Metabolism is the sum total of all processes involved in transforming the raw material (food) into structure and function, including the processes of digestion, assimilation and utilization, and including the removal of waste products, excretion and the process involved in producing heat and energy for the preservation of life. Normal rate of heat production (oxidation) is basal metabolism. The thyroid gland determines the rate of oxidation."—Dr. David J. Scott, July 1970 Annual Hygiene Health Conference.

"Metabolism is changing foodstuffs into energy and tissue."—Dr. Alec Burton, July 1973 Annual Hygiene Health Conference.

Osmosis

"Osmosis is the diffusion through a membrane of one fluid of greater pressure to another of lesser pressure." —Dr. Alec Burton, July 1968 Annual Hygiene Health Conference.

Oxidation

"Oxidation can be 1. Combination of a substance with oxygen, 2. Removal of hydrogen from the body, 3. Change in the body from ferrous iron to ferric iron.

In vigorous physical activity, 2. and 3. are employed temporarily until enough 1. (oxygen) can come in."—Dr. Alec Burton, July 1968 Annual Hygiene Health Conference. (Author's Note: Ferric iron has a greater capacity than ferrous iron to interact with other elements in the body.)

Toxemia

"When nerve energy is dissipated from physical or mental excitement or bad habits, the body becomes enervated, and elimination is checked, causing a retention of toxins in the blood, or Toxemia. All so-called diseases are crises of Toxemia."—J. H. Tilden, M.D., "Toxemia Explained".

Vitamins

"Vitamins were originally considered to be "vital

minerals", hence the name. A Vitamin is a factor which is involved in regulating the body processes. It is a complex chemical."——Dr. Alec Burton, July 1970 Annual Hygiene Health Conference.

HYGIENIC DOCTORS
(Alphabetically)

Dr. Stanley S. Bass,
   N.D., D.C.
3119 Coney Island Avenue
Corner Oceanview Avenue
Brooklyn, New York 11235
Tel. 212/648-1500

Dr. Gerald Benesh, D.C.
105 S. Twin Oaks Valley Rd.
San Marcos, Calif. 92069
Tel. 714/744-0118

Dr. John M. Brosious,
   B.S., D.C., N.D.
18207-09 Gulf Boulevard
Redington Shores
St. Petersburg, Fla. 33708
Tel. 813/392-8326

Dr. Alec Burton,
   D.O., D.C., N.D.
"Kawana"
Cobah Road
Arcadia, 2159, Australia

Dr. Peter Coumentakis
Greece
address available from
Dr. Shelton's Health School

Dr. William L. Esser,
   D.C., N.D.
P.O. Box 161
Lake Worth, Florida
Tel. 395/965-4360

Dr. Robert R. Gross, Ph.D.
Route 9, Staatsburg
Hyde Park, N. Y. 12538
Tel. 914/889-4141

Dr. David J. Scott,
   D.C., N.D.
Box 8919
Cleveland, Ohio 44136
Tel. 216/238-6930

Dr. Herbert M. Shelton,
   Ph.D.
P.O. Box 1277, Bulverde
San Antonio, Texas 78295
Tel. 512/438-2454

Dr. Keki R. Sidhwa,
   N.D., D.O.
First Ave. Frinton-On-Sea
Essex, England

Dr. Virginia Vetrano,
   B.S., D.C.
Rt. 10, Box 174E
San Antonio, Texas 78216
Tel. 512/497-3613

HYGIENIC FASTING RETREATS
(Alphabetically)

Bay 'N' Gulf Health Resort
18207-09 Gulf Boulevard
Redington Shores
St. Petersburg, Florida 33708
Tel. 813/392-8326

Dr. Shelton's Health School
P.O. Box 1277, Bulverde
San Antonio, Texas 78295
Tel. 512/438-2454

Esser's Hygienic Rest Ranch
P.O. Box 161
Lake Worth, Florida
Tel. 395/965-4360

"Kawana"
Cobah Road
Arcadia, 2159, Australia

Pawling Health Manor
Route 9, Staatsburg
Hyde Park, New York 12538
Tel. 914/889-4141

Scott's Natural Health Institute
Box 8919
Cleveland, Ohio 44136
Tel. 216/238-6930

Shalimar Health Home
First Ave. Frinton-On-Sea
Essex, England

Shangri-La Natural Hygiene Institute
Bonita Springs, Florida 33923-R
Tel. 813/992-3811

OTHER HYGIENIC EDUCATORS,
COMMUNITIES, RESORTS
(Alphabetically)

R. J. Cheatham, Director
Shangri-La Natural Hygiene Institute
Bonita Springs, Florida 33923-R
Tel. 813/992-3811

H. J. Dinshah
Sun Crest Educreational Resort
Box H, 501 Old Harding Highway
Malaga, New Jersey 08328
Tel. 609/694-2887

Mr. and Mrs. Frank P. Peterson
Orange Grove Health Ranch, Inc.
Hygienic Community
Route 4, Box 316
Arcadia, Florida 32821
Tel. 813/494-4844

Mr. David Stry
Villa Vegetariana Health Resort
Box 1228
Cuernavaca, Morelos, Mexico

Bibliography

Andrews, Arthur D., Jr., "Fit Food for Man"   1970
Bass, Stanley S., D.C., "What Symptoms to Expect
      When You Improve Your Diet"   1973
Burton, Alec, D.O., D.C., N.D., "Proteins in Your Diet"   1971
    "The Genesis of Disease"   1973
Corbett, Margaret Darst, "Help Yourself to Better Sight" 1949
Esser, William L., "Dictionary of Man's Foods"   1972
    "Natural Hygiene The Real Road to Health"
Graham, Sylvester; Russell L. Trall, M.D., Herbert M.
      Shelton, Ph.D., and others, "The Greatest
      Health Discovery"   1972
Heritage, Ford, "Composition & Facts About Foods"   1968
Kimmel, Melvin, B.A., Juris Doctor, "Toward Solution
      of America's Pressing Problems"   1970
Parrette, Owen S., M.D., "Why I Don't Eat Meat"   1972
Selye, Dr. Hans, "Stress Without Distress"   1974
Shelton, Herbert M., Ph.D.
    "The Hygienic System, Vol. 1, Orthobionomics"   1934
    "The Hygienic System, Vol. 2, Orthotrophy,
      The Natural Diet of Man"   1935
    "The Hygienic System, Vol. 3, Fasting and
      Sunbathing"   1934
    "Food Combining Made Easy"   1951
    "Fasting Can Save Your Life"   1964
    "Natural Hygiene—Man's Pristine Way of Life"   1968
    "Exercise"   1971
Dr. Shelton's Hygienic Review:
    December 1970
    January 1973
    September 1973
    December 1973
    January 1974
    February 1974
    March 1974
    April 1974
    and many others
Tilden, J. H., M.D., "Toxemia Explained"   1955
Sprouting:
    Cheatham, R. J., "Sprouting Seeds Simply"
    Dinshah, H. Jay, December 1973 Hygienic Review
    Elwood, Catharyn, "Feel Like a Million"
    St. Louis Chapter, A.N.H.S., "Sprouting Seed for Food"
    Vetrano, Virginia, Dr., D.C., B.S., September 1973
      Hygienic Review

INDEX

226

HOW TO COOPERATE
WITH THE SELF-HEALING POWER
OF THE BODY

(Transcript of a Lecture by Hannah Allen
February 1976 and April 1976)

If a mirror is cracked or broken, it does not repair itself. A broken stick remains broken; the parts can not reunite and reinforce themselves. Injuries sustained by inanimate objects, governed entirely by physical laws, are followed by no remedial processes.

Under organic law, on the other hand, a definite remedial process follows each injury, unless it is severe enough to result in immediate death. This self-healing capacity is one which man shares with both plants and animals. Once we have grasped this concept, many seemingly contradictory facts fall into place in a consistent manner. What has appeared to be mysterious becomes understandable.

If a tree is blown over so that most of its roots are torn out of the ground, every root that remains in the ground increases its efforts to supply nutrition and thus preserve life. The tree may even continue to live and to grow and to produce fruit in this position, but it is more likely to succumb to such difficult conditions. Or, some intelligent first aid treatment may restore it to its original position, after which it will resume its normal growth.

One of our papaya trees which was planted too close to the house became so heavy with fruit on the side away from the house that it fell over, almost completely exposing the roots. When we discovered what had happened, we hastily restored its more-or-less upright position, packed the roots with more earth, added another layer of mulch, and tied the tree to a strong stake. It recovered fully, and has been supplying us with excellent fruit. We supplied the needed first-aid treatment, gave the tree optimal conditions for recovery, and its own biological processes continued.

Another one of our papaya trees, also planted too close to the house, and heavy with fruit on the side away from the house, was broken in half by the combined stress of the weight of the fruit and a strong wind. In that instance, we assumed the tree was lost, and intended to remove it as soon as time permitted. To our amazement, within a week or so the torn trunk started to put out green leaves, and in about two weeks the upper part of the trunk was covered with leaves. The roots remained in the ground and the tree made a valiant effort to survive and bear fruit—in this case, with no first aid treatment and no assistance of any kind. The bodies of men and animals are subject to the same organic laws—healing is a biological process.

232

No one denies however, that there are instances where mechanical intervention is indicated and advisable. Intelligent first aid treatment, suturing, reduction of bone dislocation, removal of foreign bodies, corrections, repairs, and other constructive surgery all have an important role, and are discussed in detail in the chapter on applying Hygienic principles in emergency situations, both in accidents and disease.

Healing is a continuous process, initiated as soon as necessary, and continuing until recovery or death. The many little scratches, cuts, bruises, twists and tears which we experience almost daily are quickly healed, sometimes overnight. The healing of more serious injuries is accomplished by the same powers and processes through which these minor injuries are healed, the chief difference being that it takes more time. If the surgeon were not aware of this remarkable and dependable self-healing power of the body, he would not dare to use the scalpel to cut into your flesh or remove your organs. This remarkable power of the body to heal severed flesh and knit broken bones is evident and admitted by all. But it is often difficult for an individual to grasp the basic principles that apply in all circumstances of disease. It is not understood that the disease is actually brought about by the body's efforts to maintain health and life in spite of damaging influences.

It is easy to demonstrate and explain how a cut or broken bone is healed. We know precisely how a callus is formed to knit broken ends of a bone, and the parts played by bone cells, the bone-covering membrane, the cells producing fibrous tissue, and the blood vessels.

When a bone is broken, a bone-ring support is formed around the fractured section, extending in each direction from the point of fracture. After the bone is reunited and knitting or healing is completed, and the circulatory channels are reestablished, the bone-ring support is softened and absorbed—except for about a quarter of an inch around the point of fracture.

We know a cut heals by the production of fibrous tissue by the cells and granulation tissue by the blood vessels to connect the split skin layers.

We know that these wonderful mechanisms of healing are effected by our innate vital force. But most people find it difficult to realize that this same wonderful healing power also plays its part in the eradication of so-called disease.

In terms of Natural Hygiene, acute disease is a normal procedure to eject poisons from the body. The individual is not stricken, but actually blessed because he possesses sufficient vitality for instituting the cleansing processes which create purer and cleaner states in his tissues. For well over a hundred years, Hygienists have maintained that disease is remedial action.

The body is adequately and completely endowed with equipment and power for neutralizing dangerous agents. When foreign material gains access through the skin or other portals of entry, the body reacts with a plan-using wisdom, purposefulness and intelligent direction—with redness, swelling, heat and pain. These four cardinal actions are performed with exactness, skill and precision by the human machine, and could not be duplicated by any man-made machine.

In acute diseases, the dangerous state results from accumulated poisons, toxins and wastes, most of which are by-products of incompletely broken down metabolic substances not oxidized to completion. Acute diseases are efforts of the body to eliminate the toxins accumulated in the tissues, lymph and blood stream. These manifestations are healing crises, instituted by its inherent vital forces, for protection of the organism.

Colds, skin rashes, fever, diarrhea, vomiting, headaches and sickness in general are all remedial processes designed to maintain the integrity of the body. They are self-cleansing actions—processes of vicarious elimination of toxins which the body is not able to dispose of through the regular channels of elimination. If these beneficent processes were correctly interpreted and understood, drugs, infections and serums would not be administered, Nature would not be tampered with, and debilitating chronic diseases would not be thus created.

When symptoms are masked and suppressed by drugs, this is fraught with great incipient harm to the patient. Although symptoms may be relieved, the cause of the sickness still remains and grows greater in scope and insidious in nature. Ultimately, a state of chronic disease is produced, accompanied by organic changes in the tissues. If drugs, herbs and treatments are *not* used, the individual recovers actual health, his blood stream and tissues are not subjected to poisons, and the danger of developing chronic diseases is reduced or eliminated.

Acute diseases are self-limiting conditions. They run a natural course of elimination of poisons and then the process ceases. The person tends to recover regardless of methods and treatment employed—and in spite of them. After an acute disease runs its self-limiting course, the last remedy used usually receives the credit for the "cure." If the patient should happen to die, the treatment is seldom blamed.

All systems and methods of healing ride to glory on the self-healing power of the body. We hear testimony of recoveries under both allopathic and homeopathic care, as well as under osteopathy, naturopathy, neuropathy, chiropractic, hydrotherapy, electrotherapy, psychotherapy, Christian Science, faith healing, occult healing, metaphysics, acupuncture, and the systems of curing and healing go on and on. Many of the sick do get well while under all these various forms of treatment. The body performs the healing, the treater takes the credit and the fees. The body's capacity to heal itself is the unacknowledged common denominator of all the cures.

The healing power resides within the body. Healing is an essential function of the body, just as are respiration, circulation, digestion, assimilation, excretion, and all bodily processes. All the functions of life which enable the ogranism to live and survive are part of the healing process. What we see in sickness is a more or less dramatic exaggeration or diminishing of the normal processes of life.

When we fully understand the significance and application of these facts, and that healing power is intrinsic to the living organism, that restoration of health is a biological process, we know that there can be no healing art and no healing agents. All recovery from injury and illnesses is accomplished by the lawful and orderly processes of life.

The greatest discovery ever made, so far as healing is concerned, has not been the alleged "remedial" properties of plants and drugs, but that the remedial power is in the living organism. The processes of life proceed within the living organism independent of man's will and consciousness, by processes beyond his control, which he can neither imitate nor duplicate.

In a thousand ways, he may throw monkey wrenches into the vital machinery, but he can not control its operations. He can not guide the nutritive materials into the cells, he can not assist in the appropriation and transformation of this material into cell substances, and he can not control the processes of healing.

The living body possesses latent powers of repair far in excess of what will probably ever be needed or called upon. The existence of such preparations for possible future contingencies is almost awesome to contemplate, and, when fully understood, emphasizes the foolhardiness of interference with Nature's processes.

No one denies that there are conditions that can not be remedied by the body, but the swallowing of poison drugs will not render these conditions remediable. If the condition can be remedied, no drugs are required in order to recover health, and no healing is instituted and carried out by the toxic materials introduced into the sick body.

The dramatic modifications of the normal processes of living that are seen in disease are not disorderly and chaotic, but Nature's orderly, lawful modifications which serve a purpose. Coughing and sneezing dislodge and expel from the air passages obstructive and irritating substances. Vomiting rids the stomach of unwanted food or a poison. Diarrhea frees the bowels of unwanted food or a drug or other obnoxious substance. Diuresis, an exaggeration of normal urinary function, expels noxious materials from the blood.

Fever is a means of enabling the body to speed up certain of its activities. For example, the body's production of interferon (a cellular protein which blocks viral infection) is most efficient in the presence of fever; and temperatures of 104 degrees will actually kill the deadly polio virus.

Pain warns us of danger, or that something is wrong. All of the processes of disease are a means to an end. They are remedial efforts by the body.

There is no need for the disease to be "cured," because the disease itself is the process of recovery. To reduce the fever, check the cough, suppress the diarrhea, stop the vomiting, end the diuresis, is to lock up in the body of the sick person the very noxious materials that these processes are trying to eliminate. Pain may be smothered with an anodyne, but not without reducing the body's self-healing efforts. A person who is bleeding into the lungs, and whose lungs are being kept open by coughing, may drown in his own blood if the cough is suppressed. More deaths result from treating disease than from any other cause.

The living organism has power of action and it acts in its own best interests. While life continues it will struggle for survival. It knits its broken bones and heals its wounds by processes that the surgeon can neither duplicate nor imitate. It excretes poisons by means of its own excretory powers; it struggles against every impairing and hurtful substance and influence.

This struggle, which we call disease, or the process of healing, is known to us only by its symptoms. But it is not an attack upon the body by malignant germs, any more than it can be considered an attack by evil spirits. The Hygienic concept of the essential nature of disease is so contrary to the traditional and prevailing view as to its nature that it is very difficult for most people to entertain and grasp the idea, so that they may understand and accept this fundamental truth.

They have been taught that disease is an attack upon the citadel of life by some foreign foe, usually identified as a malevolent microbe, and must be resisted, overpowered and destroyed, and that this destruction constitutes the cure in all cases where the organism is not destroyed as well. If the organism is enfeebled, weakened or destroyed by the same means which destroys the attacking enemy, it is considered sad, but unavoidable. Our assertion that disease is remedial action which restores health, that the only action to be taken in states of disease is cooperation with the living organism, seems, to the average person, too preposterous for rational beings to seriously consider.

They, of course, have never learned that modern textbooks of pathology contain full recognition of the remedial character of most pathological phenomena (diseases). Who has ever brought this to their attention? Certainly not the average medical man, who, for all practical considerations, totally ignores this fact, and rarely attempts to persuade his patient not to insist upon an immediate palliative.

The appearance of symptoms is the signal for the immediate rush to the physician and the pharmacist for the weapon of choice to alleviate the symptoms and foil the villainous microbe. What these misguided people are actually doing is foiling the action of the living organism, and interrupting its defensive, expulsive, remedial and reparative processes. These are, for the most part, only exaggerations of the regular processes of life.

Diarrhea is a dramatic exaggeration of bowel activity. Inflammation is a local modification of circulation. Digestion and secretion may be temporarily suspended, but the most basic processes of nutrition must continue or the cells would perish for lack of sustenance.

Air is needed—so is water. Rest and sleep are required—activity may have to be temporarily suspended. The kidneys continue to excrete waste, the lungs give off carbon dioxide, the heart pulsates and the blood circulates. These processes and functions must continue during the healing crisis, some at a slower rate, and some at an accelerated rate. The body continues to maintain its temperature, which is sometimes accelerated, as in fever, but if the body should discontinue heat production, it would freeze.

The living organism is not static; it is always in action, and it is constantly adjusting its actions to its needs. Even in the highest state of health and under the most ideal conditions conceivable, adjustments will be continuous. When conditions are not ideal, the need for adjustments is greater. In low states of health, the ease with which adjustments may be made is impaired.

Most adjustments are easy and below the levels of conscious awareness; some are painful and register in consciousness. Changes in heart action, breathing, sweating, kidney action, are familiar symptoms of abnormal conditions. Inflammation is uncomfortable and painful, but is not to be regarded as an attack upon the body by some outside foe.

No pathologist today doubts the essentially constructive character of inflammation, although at the time that Jennings and Trall (in the 1800's) first announced the discovery of the remedial character of inflammation, the idea was denounced by the pathologists.

The reaction of the organism to the administration of a drug is also defensive action. Thus when we use drugs to palliate symptoms, we are forcing the body to turn its attention away from its action against the disease, and to deal with the new and more immediate threat of the poison drug.

The skill and power which restores health to the sick belong to the organic and not the intellectual system. It is the work of instinct, not of mind.

The real strength of the body is its integrity and wholeness. The physiological means of maintaining this integrity and wholeness are derived from our environment. Sun, air, water, exercise, and all the other circumstances and means of life are important, but the food you eat plays the greatest part in determining the condition of your body.

If your diet consists principally of raw green leafy vegetables, fresh ripe raw fruits, raw and unsalted nuts and seeds, sprouted grains and

236

seeds, properly combined, your nutritional needs will be adequately provided. Attention to the other essentials of good health—fresh air, pure water, sunshine, adequate rest and exercise, and emotional control, will improve your level of good health.

Avoidance of damaging influences, such as overeating, overworking, and all excesses; as well as drug habits, like coffee, tea, chocolate, carbonated beverages, vitamins, medicines, tobacco, and alcohol, will help to produce optimal health.

Failure to adhere to these principles of Natural Hygiene will produce varying states of enervation and toxemia. The basic cause of all disease is Toxemia, which results when elimination is impaired and toxins accumulate in the body. The pattern of the evolution of disease can be traced through the seven stages of Toxemia, and is reversible in all but the last stage, e.g. cancer.

The first stage is Enervation, or a reduction in nerve energy, and may be brought about by incorrect eating or overeating, overworking, overplaying, inadequate rest or exercise, or other deficiencies or excesses, or poor living habits. Enervation, if continued, begets a toxemic condition, which causes a state of irritation. Continued irritation becomes inflammation (a massive healing effort of the body). If the cause of these problems is not eliminated, the next stages are ulceration, and then induration or fibrosis, and these can evolve into an irreversible condition, such as cancer.

When you are in a debilitated condition, when you are in any of these stages of toxemia, even if you are in a pre-cancerous condition, Hygienic care can help you to return to a state of health consistent with whatever irreversible damage has already occured. The food and other needs of life must be adjusted to the needs of the enfeebled organism—in serious degenerative conditions all food must be withdrawn, and a fast, on water only, must be instituted.

Under a Hygienic regimen, acceleration of poison ejection occurs, resulting in forceful, rapid internal cleansing of the cells throughout the entire body. The chemical and physical equilibrium of the blood and lymph streams is rapidly changed. This state is sometimes manifested by crises, such as colds, pain, fever, headaches, etc.

These symptoms are positive signs that the procedure is effective and elimination is progressing satisfactorily; and they should be welcomed as a barometer of the vitality within the body. The fine line between failure and success in achieving health under Hygienic care depends principally upon patience and persistence. Nature works slowly and progressively—but surely. There is no failure or defeat except in no longer trying.

Health can be regained, providing the agents producing health are utilized rationally—fresh air, sunshine, exercise, diet, fasting and emotional control. Your health will be the result of what you want it to be. You can become as sick as your uncontrolled desires can make you, or as healthy as the potential of your dominant aspirations.

But you cannot provide your body with the means of healing. All you can do is to provide ideal conditions for the body to exercise its own self-healing powers. These ideal conditions exist during a fast—when the body is in a state of mental, sensory, emotional, physical and physiological rest.

If our excesses and deficiencies have produced disease, fasting provides the only rational approach to its reversal, and may be the only hope for restoration of health in chronic degenerative conditions.

During a fast, it is even more important not to subject the body to drugs or vitamins or any substances other than pure water, preferably distilled. Some of the medical people who are experimenting with fasting recommend the use of supplements, or the use of stimulants during the fast, such as caffeine-containing beverages, or so-called "diet" carbonated beverages containing chemical sweeteners. This is a particularly pernicious way to throw a monkey wrench into the delicate machinery of your body, because the destructive effect of these substances is even greater during the fast.

There has been an interesting development on the subject of food supplements (vitamins and minerals, etc.). "Chelated" minerals are now being offered to the public, as a more certain method for adequate absorption by the body, which is a tacit admission that the minerals taken for years by gullible people may have been unavailable to the body. Of course Hygienists have been saying for years that minerals in an inorganic form (pills) are difficult to absorb, and, even if they are absorbed, they are not useable by the cell. A chelated mineral may be described as one that consists of a metal ion attached to two or more nonmetal ions in the same molecule. Most of us will not fully understand this technical definition, nor is it necessary that we do.

What is of great importance is the following quotation from Dr. Vetrano (January 1976 Hygienic Review): "Feeding minerals in chelated form is likely to produce greater harm than the former mineral preparations did. Unfortunately they are in a form that gets past the gastrointestinal membrane into the system where they will upset the mineral balance of the body. . . . Selling chelated minerals is a good way to extract minerals from your pocketbook."

Give the self-healing power of your own body a chance to help you. This power of healing springs instantly and automatically into operation when the need arises and continues until recovery or death. There is nothing else to supplant it. It is your only road to good health.

238

NATURAL HYGIENE PRESS
BOOK ORDER FORM "P"

☐	A—FASTING CAN SAVE YOUR LIFE	$1.75
☐	B—YOU DON'T HAVE TO BE SICK!	$1.45
☐	C—HEALTH FOR THE MILLIONS	$1.45
☐	D—HYGIENIC CARE OF CHILDREN	$1.95
☐	E—EXERCISE!	$1.95
☐	F—THE GREATEST HEALTH DISCOVERY	$1.75
☐	G—DICTIONARY OF MAN'S FOOD	$2.25
☐	H—TOXEMIA	$1.50
☐	I—PROGRAM FOR DYNAMIC HEALTH	$1.00
☐	J—FASTING FOR RENEWAL OF LIFE	$2.25
☐	K—DON'T GET STUCK—VIA VACCINATIONS AND INJECTIONS	$2.00
☐	L—SUPERIOR FOODS, DIET PRINCIPLES AND PRACTICES, ETC.	$1.50
☐	M—THE HAPPY TRUTH ABOUT PROTEIN	$1.00
☐	N—DIAGNOSIS CANCER—ESCAPE FEAR VIA NATURAL HYGIENE	$1.00
☐	O—PLEASE DON'T SMOKE IN OUR HOUSE	$1.50
☐	P—FOODS FOR PLEASURE & HEALTH; HANDBOOK FOR HYGIENIC LIVING	$2.50
☐	Q—FOOD COMBINING MADE EASY	$1.50
☐	R—SUPERIOR NUTRITION	$2.75
☐	T—FIT FOOD FOR MAN	.50
☐	JA—THE HYGIENIC SYSTEM, VOL. I	$5.00
☐	JB—SYPHILIS: THE WEREWOLF OF MEDICINE	$4.50
☐	JC—LIVING LIFE TO LIVE IT LONGER	$3.00
☐	JD—FASTING FOR HEALTH AND LONG LIFE	$3.00
☐	JE—AN INTRODUCTION TO NATURAL HYGIENE	$2.00
☐	JF—THERAPEUTIC FASTING	$2.50
☐	XA—THE HYGIENIC SYSTEM, VOL. II—COMPLETE GUIDE TO FOOD AND FEEDING	$7.50
☐	XB—THE HYGIENIC SYSTEM, VOL. III—FASTING AND SUN BATHING (TO BE REPRINTED)	
☐	XC—NATURAL HYGIENE: MAN'S PRISTINE WAY OF LIFE	$7.50
☐	XD—HUMAN BEAUTY: ITS CULTURE AND HYGIENE	$12.50
☐	XF—CORRECT FOOD COMBINING PLACE MAT (PLUS 45¢ P&H)	$1.50
☐	XH—A GIFT OF LOVE	$7.50
☐	DR. SHELTON'S HYGIENIC REVIEW ($8/YR. Canada, Foreign)	$7.50/YR.

● ADD 25¢ TO EACH BOOK FOR POSTAGE AND HANDLING CHARGES.

● SEE NEXT PAGE FOR ORDER BLANK

TOTAL $_____

NOTICE TO THE READER

If after reading this book, you feel the vital knowledge which it contains deserves to be made widely known, you are urged to become a member of the American Natural Hygiene Society and help to contribute to this worthy cause for the benefit of mankind. (Contributions, wills, bequests are tax exempt.)

As a membership bonus we will send this book or any other N.H.P. publication in value up to $1.95 to anyone of your choice. Fill out the application below and mail your remittance of $11.00 for your membership and the bonus book. Outside U.S.A.—$12.00.

☐—Please enroll me as a member of your worthy cause. Enclosed find $11.00 *payable in U. S. $ to A.N.H.S.* for the annual *membership and bonus book.*

☐—BOOK ORDER—Enclosed find $_____for books indicated on order form "P" Payable in U. S. $ to NATURAL HYGIENE PRESS.

Name_____
(please print)

Address_____

City, State, Zip_____

Phone No._____Age_____

SEND BONUS BOOK TITLED_____

_____

To_____
(please print)

Address_____

City, State, Zip_____

AMERICAN NATURAL HYGIENE SOCIETY, Dept. P.
1920 IRVING PARK ROAD, CHICAGO, ILL. 60613

P

HIISTORICAL BACKGROUND

Natural Hygiene Press, the publisher of this book, is a division of the American Natural Hygiene Society. The Society is a non-profit, tax exempt membership organization founded in 1949 for the primary purpose of public education in *Natural Hygiene,* which is a system, based on biology and physiology, for preserving and recovering health through natural living habits.

Natural Hygiene came on the American scene as an educational movement in 1830 through the lectures of Sylvester Graham in New York, Rochester, Providence, Buffalo and other eastern cities. Modern dietary science is said to have had its beginning with Graham, who stressed the value of fresh fruits and vegetables as the best foods for man. He wrote books and articles on healthful living for 21 years and his greatest work is the *Science of Human Life,* published in 1839.

Graham pioneered in this country in advocating the teaching of physiology in the public schools and in expounding the value of regular physical exercise, fresh air and well ventilated homes, rest and sleep, sunbathing, emotional control and clothing reform for women from the tight waists, corsets and high heeled pointed toed shoes of the day.

Graham was joined in his work of health education by prominent medical people of the time such as Isaac Jennings, M.D., William Alcott, M.D., Russell Thacker Trall, M.D., Thomas Low Nichols, M.D., Susanna Dodds, M.D., James Caleb Jackson, M.D., George H. Taylor, M.D., and later by Robert Walker, M.D., John H. Tilden, M.D.

Many of these pioneers of the *Natural Hygiene* System had suffered serious illness during their early years which became a strong motivating force in seeking the solution to the disease problem. They came to see in wrong living the true cause of disease and sought to induce mankind to return to a normal way of life by adopting good living habits. They wrote prodigiously in books and magazines and some founded colleges to train students in caring for people through hygienic means, rather than drugs and medicines. Many graduates of *Hygienic* Colleges served as doctors in the Civil War and helped their patients recover more quickly by their hygienic methods.

The American Natural Hygiene Society now carries on the educational work of the movement through distribution of books published by its press and other publishers, pamphlets, annual public conventions and seminars and a chapter structure which functions in many large cities through the membership, dispensing *Natural Hygiene* education to the local people. Future goals of the Society are the establishment of colleges to train practitioners in the Hygienic System of health maintenance, institutes to care for the sick the hygienic way, and community centers for family living on an educational, social and recreational basis along *Natural Hygienic* lines.

A—FASTING CAN SAVE YOUR LIFE $1.75
H. M. Shelton. 191 pages. Part I: The basics and benefits of fasting. Tells how, when and where to fast for health restoration and weight reduction. Nine basic steps to a successful fast. Part II: Recovery through fasting from acute or chronic diseases such as asthma, arthritis, ulcers, migraine, high blood pressure, colitis, etc. An excellent introductory book on fasting.

B—YOU DON'T HAVE TO BE SICK! $1.45
J. D. Trop. 231 pages. A step-by-step routine for putting a healthful living program into action. Sample menus and party foods. A primer of Natural Hygiene.

C—HEALTH FOR THE MILLIONS $1.45
H. M. Shelton. 321 pages. 41 chapters on how the body functions, what it needs and what is harmful.

D—HYGIENIC CARE OF CHILDREN $1.95
H. M. Shelton. Over 400 pages. Paperback edition of a hardcover book long out of print. This is the parent's comprehensive guide to the rearing of healthy children and healthy pregnancy. Discusses harmful effects of inoculations.

E—EXERCISE! $1.95
H. M. Shelton. Paperback. A rare, comprehensive book on three levels: the history and role of formal exercise in maintaining good body functioning; how exercise aids in existing impairments by correcting weakened structural faults and muscles; profuse illustrations show how exercises are done. Reprinted from Volume 4 of The Hygienic System.

F—THE GREATEST HEALTH DISCOVERY $1.75
Natural Hygiene and its Evolution, Past, Present and Future. From the works of Sylvester Graham, Dr. R. T. Trall, H. M. Shelton and others. 241 pages, paperback. The health care revolution which started in 19th century America and solved the problem of disease and premature death. Contains portraits of the pioneers who were mostly medical doctors; 18 picture pages of the Hygienic way of life through the medium of traditional ANHS Convention; presents a practical plan for bringing unlimited health on a community level.

G—DICTIONARY OF MAN'S FOODS $2.25
William L. Esser. 179 pages, paperback. Descriptive alphabetic guide to fruits and vegetables and how to combine each for good digestion; table of food composition and nutritional values; seed sprouting instructions; food combining chart; list of food classifications; suggested menus for every day of the week. Separate chapters of fruits, vegetables, nuts, conservative cooking, the kitchen on a budget, best storing methods. Special color section shows varieties of breakfasts, lunches and dinners.

H—TOXEMIA: THE BASIC CAUSE OF ALL DISEASE $1.50
John H. Tilden. Reprinted 1974, 125 pages, paperback. An eminent medical doctor and Natural Hygiene pioneer tells how to get well and stay well the drugless way.

I—PROGRAM FOR DYNAMIC HEALTH $1.00
Compiled by T. C. Fry. A New York businessman gives his testimonial and tells how to practice Natural Hygiene.

J—FASTING FOR RENEWAL OF LIFE $2.25
H. M. Shelton. 320 pages, paperback. (1974) In depth details about what happens while the body is fasting and how this remarkable process, used since Biblical times, brings about renewal and healing.

K—DON'T GET STUCK $2.00
Hannah Allen. 110 pages. Legal and practical ways to avoid vaccinations, inoculations and injections in school and while traveling; plus germ theory refutation.

L—SUPERIOR FOODS, DIET PRINCIPLES, AND PRACTICES FOR PERFECT HEALTH $1.50
T. C. Fry. 64 pages. Reveals proper diets for maximum nutrition and good health, plus many other points on efficient digestion.

M—THE HAPPY TRUTH ABOUT PROTEIN $1.00
Hannah Allen. 32 pages. Useful reference book charting amino acids and protein content of common foods; also details, varieties and quantities needed for optimal nutrition.

N—DIAGNOSIS: CANCER $1.00
Hannah Allen. 23 pages. Futility of surgery; hoax of cancer research; prevention through removal of cause.

O—PLEASE DON'T SMOKE IN OUR HOUSE $1.50
J. D. Trop. 128 pages. Undesirable physiological and social effects of the indulgence in the unnatural habit of smoking. Recommends ideal way to quit.

P—HOMEMAKER'S GUIDE TO FOOD & NATURAL HYGIENE $2.50
Hannah Allen. 275 pages. Encyclopedic book about natural foods and Natural Hygiene. Menus, combinations, recipes, etc.

OTHER NATURAL HYGIENE PUBLICATIONS

Q—FOOD COMBINING MADE EASY $1.50
H. M. Shelton. 71 pages. Everything you need to know to avoid the after-meal discomfort of heartburn, bloating, flatulence, acid indigestion, etc., with proper food combining.

R—SUPERIOR NUTRITION $2.75
H. M. Shelton. 197 pages. Condensed version of Volume 2 of The Hygienic System. Includes basic nutritional needs of the body, processed versus natural foods, organic versus inorganic; requirements of starches, proteins, vitamins, minerals, amino acids; proper diet for well-being, fasting, feeding babies naturally, avoiding gluttony, how to plan and eat meals, menus, feeding the sick.

S—RUBIES IN THE SAND: PRECIOUS HEALTH TRUTHS REDISCOVERED (TO BE REPRINTED)
H. M. Shelton. 331 pages. The history of man's change from a natural way of life to the adoption of the poison habits of today; the only history on natural health available.

T—FIT FOOD FOR MAN $.50
Arthur Andrews. 16 pages. Explains why man functions best on a fruit, nut and vegetable diet. Anatomical comparison chart shows how differences in various animal species (including human beings) determine what type of food they are constituted to eat: shows the carnivora, omnivora, herbivora, and frugivora (man).

JA—THE HYGIENIC SYSTEM: VOLUME I $5.00
H. M. Shelton. 352 pages. (Reprint, revised 1972) The laws governing human life; care of the organs of the body; introduction gives brief historical background of the Hygienic Movement.

JB—SYPHILIS: THE WEREWOLF OF MEDICINE $4.50
H. M. Shelton. 150 pages. Gives the true cause of syphilis and shows why disease or cure is a myth. The cure is deadlier than the disease.

JC—LIVING LIFE TO LIVE IT LONGER $3.00
H. M. Shelton. 139 pages. How to live more joyfully and with fulfillment via Natural Hygiene.

JD—FASTING FOR HEALTH AND LONG LIFE $3.00
H. M. Carrington. 151 pages. Facts about fasting in abbreviated form; covers fasting pros and cons, recovery of colds and other ailments; many diets reviewed; effects of fasting on the body, fasting crises, breaking the fast, etc.

JE—AN INTRODUCTION TO NATURAL HYGIENE $2.00
H. M. Shelton. 92 pages. Basic reading for understanding the principles underlying the Natural Hygiene system of health maintenance and recovery; defines health and disease, reveals the healing powers of the body, methods of care, feeding and fasting.

JF–THERAPEUTIC FASTING $2.50

Explains how fasting is employed therapeutically in tens of thousands of cases. Fasting has been found to be extremely efficient as a remedy for many forms of disease and rejuvenation of the body. This process promotes absorption of abnormal growths, increasing toxic elimination and improving the body's assimilative powers to reestablish normal health.

XA–THE HYGIENIC SYSTEM: VOLUME II (FOOD AND FEEDING) $7.50

H. M. Shelton. 591 pages. A complete guide to correct use of natural foods and feeding from infancy on. Starts with food elements, vitamins, calories, minerals, organic foods, proteins, starches, etc.; covers proper food combining for maximum digestion; raw versus cooked foods; menus; infant feeding, etc. Promises a startling awakening for the reader interested in human nutrition.

XB–THE HYGIENIC SYSTEM: VOLUME III (FASTING)
TO BE REPRINTED

H. M. Shelton. 541 pages. Fasting and Sunbathing; the most comprehensive and authoritative book on fasting, with one chapter on sunbathing and its role in health.

XC–NATURAL HYGIENE: MAN'S PRISTINE WAY OF LIFE $7.50

H. M. Shelton. 638 pages. A complete book on the requirements of the body for health maintenance and recovery. Includes historical background of the Hygienic Movement.

XD–HUMAN BEAUTY: ITS CULTURE AND HYGIENE $12.50

H. M. Shelton. 1039 pages. The important relationship between good body functioning and genetic beauty. Over 100 illustrations. Discusses care of the body and gives exercises for neck, shoulders, arms, chest, back muscles, etc.

XF–CORRECT FOOD COMBINING PLACE MAT (45¢ P&H) $1.50

12 x 18 plastic coated. Foods shown in color, indicating good, fair and poor combinations for efficient digestion. Side Two explains combinations and classifies proteins, carbohydrates, starches, fats, etc. with other useful food information.

XH–A GIFT OF LOVE $7.50

J. D. Trop. 320 pages, hardcover. A documented story of 86 Australian World War II orphans who were raised naturally as an experiment and who subsequently set many health records. A True Gift of Love to humanity by L. O. Bailey and Madge Cockburn—pictures.

DR. SHELTON'S HYGIENIC REVIEW
$7.50/Yr. ($8.00/Yr. Canada, Foreign)

A monthly magazine edited and published by H. M. Shelton. Vital articles on the cause of disease, how to maintain health, errors of medical practices.

● ADD 25¢ TO EACH BOOK FOR POSTAGE AND HANDLING CHARGES. Write for special discounts on quantity lots.

● When writing for information of a general nature, please include a stamped, self-addressed envelope and 25¢ to help defray cost of postage and handling. All prices subject to change. Allow 3 to 4 weeks for delivery (overseas up to 90 days).

NATURAL HYGIENE PRESS
BOOK ORDER FORM "P"

- ☐ A–FASTING CAN SAVE YOUR LIFE — $1.75
- ☐ B–YOU DON'T HAVE TO BE SICK! — $1.45
- ☐ C–HEALTH FOR THE MILLIONS — $1.45
- ☐ D–HYGIENIC CARE OF CHILDREN — $1.95
- ☐ E–EXERCISE! — $1.95
- ☐ F–THE GREATEST HEALTH DISCOVERY — $1.75
- ☐ G–DICTIONARY OF MAN'S FOOD — $2.25
- ☐ H–TOXEMIA — $1.50
- ☐ I–PROGRAM FOR DYNAMIC HEALTH — $1.00
- ☐ J–FASTING FOR RENEWAL OF LIFE — $2.25
- ☐ K–DON'T GET STUCK—VIA VACCINATIONS AND INJECTIONS — $2.00
- ☐ L–SUPERIOR FOODS, DIET PRINCIPLES AND PRACTICES, ETC. — $1.50
- ☐ M–THE HAPPY TRUTH ABOUT PROTEIN — $1.00
- ☐ N–DIAGNOSIS CANCER—ESCAPE FEAR VIA NATURAL HYGIENE — $1.00
- ☐ O–PLEASE DON'T SMOKE IN OUR HOUSE — $1.50
- ☐ P–FOODS FOR PLEASURE & HEALTH; HANDBOOK FOR HYGIENIC LIVING — $2.50
- ☐ Q–FOOD COMBINING MADE EASY — $1.50
- ☐ R–SUPERIOR NUTRITION — $2.75
- ☐ T–FIT FOOD FOR MAN — .50
- ☐ JA–THE HYGIENIC SYSTEM, VOL. I — $5.00
- ☐ JB–SYPHILIS: THE WEREWOLF OF MEDICINE — $4.50
- ☐ JC–LIVING LIFE TO LIVE IT LONGER — $3.00
- ☐ JD–FASTING FOR HEALTH AND LONG LIFE — $3.00
- ☐ JE–AN INTRODUCTION TO NATURAL HYGIENE — $2.00
- ☐ JF–THERAPEUTIC FASTING — $2.50
- ☐ XA–THE HYGIENIC SYSTEM, VOL. II—COMPLETE GUIDE TO FOOD AND FEEDING — $7.50
- ☐ XB–THE HYGIENIC SYSTEM, VOL. III—FASTING AND SUN BATHING (TO BE REPRINTED)
- ☐ XC–NATURAL HYGIENE: MAN'S PRISTINE WAY OF LIFE — $7.50
- ☐ XD–HUMAN BEAUTY: ITS CULTURE AND HYGIENE — $12.50
- ☐ XF–CORRECT FOOD COMBINING PLACE MAT (PLUS 45¢ P&H) — $1.50
- ☐ XH–A GIFT OF LOVE — $7.50
- ☐ DR. SHELTON'S HYGIENIC REVIEW — $7.50/YR. ($8/YR. Canada, Foreign)

- ● ADD 25¢ TO EACH BOOK FOR POSTAGE AND HANDLING CHARGES.

- ● SEE NEXT PAGE FOR ORDER BLANK

TOTAL $_____

NOTICE TO THE READER

If after reading this book, you feel the vital knowledge which it contains deserves to be made widely known, you are urged to become a member of the American Natural Hygiene Society and help to contribute to this worthy cause for the benefit of mankind. (Contributions, wills, bequests are tax exempt.)

As a membership bonus we will send this book or any other N.H.P. publication in value up to $1.95 to anyone of your choice. Fill out the application below and mail your remittance of $11.00 for your membership and the bonus book. Outside U.S.A.—$12.00.

☐—Please enroll me as a member of your worthy cause. Enclosed find $11.00 *payable in U. S. $ to A.N.H.S.* for the annual *membership and bonus book.*

☐—BOOK ORDER—Enclosed find $_____for books indicated on order form "P" Payable in U. S. $ to NATURAL HYGIENE PRESS.

Name_____
(please print)

Address_____

City, State, Zip_____

Phone No._____Age_____

SEND BONUS BOOK TITLED_____

_____

To_____
(please print)

Address_____

City, State, Zip_____

AMERICAN NATURAL HYGIENE SOCIETY, Dept. P.
1920 IRVING PARK ROAD, CHICAGO, ILL. 60613

P